The Young Hitler

By August Kubizek and Eduard Bloch

Ostara Publications

The Young Hitler I Knew

By August Kubizek

First published 1953

And

My Patient, Hitler: A Memoir of Hitler's Jewish Physician

By Dr. Eduard Bloch

First published 1945

This edition 2013

Ostara Publications

www.ostarapublications.com

ISBN 978-1-291-39382-8

Contents

Part I: The Young Hitler I Knew
Introduction: Who Was August Kubizek?..1
Author's foreword...3
Chapter 1: First Meeting...5
Chapter 2: Growth of a Friendship..10
Chapter 3 — Portrait of the Young Hitler..17
Chapter 4 — Portrait of His Mother...25
Chapter 5 — Portrait of His Father...31
Chapter 6 — School...37
Chapter 7 — Stefanie...44
Chapter 8 — The Young Nationalist...54
Chapter 9 — Adolf Rebuilds Linz..62
Chapter 10 — In That Hour It Began..74
Chapter 11 — Adolf Leaves for Vienna...77
Chapter 12 — His Mother's Death..88
Chapter 13 — "Come with me, Gustl!"..110
Chapter 14 — 29 Stumpergasse...118
Chapter 15 — Adolf Rebuilds Vienna...130
Chapter 16 — Solitary Study and Reading...142
Chapter 17 — Nights at the Opera..149
Chapter 18 — Adolf Writes an Opera...155
Chapter 19 — The "Mobile Reichs Orchestra"...................................162
Chapter 20 — Unmilitary Interlude...170
Chapter 21 — Adolf's Attitude to Women...178
Chapter 22 — Political Awakening..188
Chapter 23 — The Lost Friendship...197
Epilogue 208

Part II: My Patient Hitler: A Memoir of Hitler's Jewish Physician
Introduction...231
Part 1..232
Part II...239

List of illustrations

A 1906 watercolor by Hitler given to Kuzibek..................................97
Kubizek at the time of the writing of his book............................98
Kubizek at the time of his friendship with Hitler........................98
A sketch by Hitler of the house he wanted to build for Kubizek.............99
A sketch by Hitler of the interior of house he wanted to build for Kubizek..99
Stefanie, the young Hitler's true love. She was unaware of his devotion..100
Postcards from Hitler to Kubizek from Vienna. The bottom card contains the codeword for Stefanie: "Benkieser." Hitler writes: "Must also see Benkieser again."..101
A postcard from Hitler to Kubizek from Vienna..........................102
A postcard from Hitler to Kubizek from Weitra im Waldviertel, wishing him the best on his "naming day" (a German tradition separate from a birthday)..103
Postcard from Hitler to Kubizek 1906...104
Postcard from Hitler to Kubizek when he was living in Vienna...............105
The first card that Kubizek received from Hitler in Vienna. The text describes the music conservatory and adds that Hitler wants to show his friend the wonderful buildings on the city's Ringstrasse..........................106
Postcard to Kubizek from Hitler, 18 February 1908, in which he asks his friend to come to Vienna..106
Letter from Hitler to Kubizek, written while he was traveling to Linz during the Easter weekend...107
Letter from Hitler to Kubizek telling him that he would come back to visit his parents in Linz during the summer.......................................107
The last letter written by the young Hitler to Kubizek in 1908. After this, Hitler disappeared, plunged into poverty and too ashamed to be seen by his friend again..108
Letter to Kubziek from Hitler after he became Chancellor in 1933, saying that the time they spent together were the "best of our lives."......108
Dr. Eduard Bloch, who was Jewish, treated Hitler as a young man, along with his mother and other members of the Hitler family. This picture of Dr. Bloch in his office in Linz was taken in 1938 on order of Martin Bormann for Hitler's "personal film file." The inscription reads: "The Führer often sat on the chair beside the desk."...........................109
Klara Hitler, Adolf's mother, treated by Dr. Bloch...........................109

Part I: The Young Hitler I Knew
August Kubizek

Introduction: Who Was August Kubizek?

August Kubizek, called Gustl by his friend Adolf Hitler, was born on August 3, 1888, in Linz, Austria.

He met Hitler while they were attending an opera at the State Theater in Linz, in 1904, and soon became close friends. When they both moved to Vienna to try and gain entrance to college, they shared a room in the city until July 1908.

This book deals with this "lost period," 1904–1908, which was little remarked upon, even by Hitler. It was Adolf Hitler who, at the age of eighteen, successfully persuaded Kubizek's father to let his son go to the metropolis to attend the conservatory. This, Kubizek wrote, changed the course of his life for good. He was immediately accepted into the Vienna Conservatory where he quickly made a name for himself.

Kubizek completed his studies in 1912 and was hired as conductor of the orchestra in Marburg on the Drau, Austria. He was later offered a position at the City Theater in Klagenfurt, but this job and his musical career were cut short by the beginning of World War I.

Before leaving for the front he married Anna Funke (October 7, 1887–October 4, 1976), a violinist from Vienna with whom he had three sons: Augustin, Karl Maria, and Rudolf.

From August 1914 until November 1918 Kubizek served as a reservist in Regiment 2 of the Austro–Hungarian Infantry. In the Carpathian winter campaign of 1915, he was wounded at Eperjes in Hungary and later evacuated to Budapest in an ambulance train.

After months of convalescence, he returned to the front and was attached to a mechanized corps in Vienna. After the war Kubizek accepted a position as an official in the municipal council of Eferding, Upper Austria and music became his hobby.

After seeing Hitler on the front page of a newspaper in 1920, Kubizek followed his friend's career and finally contacted him again in 1933 when he sent a letter congratulating him upon becoming Chancellor of Germany.

Hitler replied to this letter in person, and the two old friends were reunited in April 1938, the day before the Austrian people voted 97.5 percent in favor of the country's annexation to Germany.

The two men spent more than an hour together at the Hotel Weinzinger in Linz, and Hitler offered Kubizek the conductorship of an orchestra, which Kubizek politely refused. Upon learning of his friend's three sons Hitler did, however, insist on financing their educations at the Anton Bruckner Conservatory in Linz.

Hitler later invited Kubizek to attend the Bayreuth festival as his guest in 1939 and again in 1940, experiences described by Kubizek as "the happiest hours of my earthly existence."

In 1938, Kubizek was hired by the Nazi party to write two short propaganda booklets called *Reminiscences* about his youth with Hitler. In one episode Kubizek said Hitler had a great love for a girl named «Stefanie» and wrote her many love poems but never sent them.

Kubizek saw Hitler for the last time on July 23, 1940, although as late as 1944 Hitler sent Kubizek's mother a food basket for her 80th birthday. His friend told him: "This war will set us back many years in our building program. It is a tragedy. I did not become Chancellor of the Greater German Reich to fight wars."

Kubizek became a member of the NSDAP in 1942, but due to his age, was never called up to serve in the war. After the end of the war, he remained unnoticed by the Allied victors until December 1945. Aware of the sudden attention, he hid his collection of postcards and letters from Hitler in the basement of his house in Eferding.

Shortly afterward, he was arrested by the US Army Criminal Investigation Command and detained for sixteen months before being released without charge.

In 1951, Kubizek completed his book, titled originally in Germany as *Adolf Hitler, mein Jugendfreund (Adolf Hitler, My Childhood Friend)*. It was finally published in 1953. As he had predicted in the book's foreword, his health had declined during his imprisonment, and he died in October 1956, aged 68. He is buried in Eferding, Upper Austria.

RESOLUTION AND JUSTIFICATION—Author's foreword

It was a hard decision on my part to write down my childhood memories of Adolf Hitler because of the strong danger that it would be misunderstood. But I am not in robust health after spending sixteen months in an American prison—at the age of 56—starting in 1945, so I have decided to use what time is still available to me to produce this book.

During the years 1904–1908, I was the only and exclusive friend of Hitler, first in Linz, and then in Vienna, where we lived together in one room. Although those years of his development are the focus of much interest, little is known about it, and much of what is said about it, is incorrect. Even Hitler did not say much of importance about this period.

So I can presume that my remarks will contribute to clarify and explain this time and the image of Adolf Hitler, no matter from which way one wants to view him.

My main principle in writing these youthful memories is not to conceal or exaggerate anything, but just to say it how it was. In this regard, I wanted to wait until the time was right to publish this book, when the prevailing common literature about him had run its course and it would be possible to read a honest and objective account, aimed at all serious-minded people.

It would be wrong to presume that these shared youthful experiences would have translated into thoughts and ideas later in Hitler's life.

I have reduced the risk of misinterpretation by the use of my scrupulously-kept notes taken at the time, and have reproduced them in exactly the same way as if Adolf Hitler, with whom I was so close and an intimate friend, had remained unknown.

I am aware of the extreme difficulty of my project in recalling all events that occurred more than forty years previously. But friendship with Adolf Hitler was from the outset unusual, and as a result its details were imprinted far more solidly in my mind than with other friendships I might have had.

I also felt a great gratitude to Hitler, because he succeeded in convincing me—where my father was trying to convince me otherwise—that my musical talent belonged not in the workshop, but in the Conservatory. It was this decisive turn in my life that the then eighteen-year-old Hitler was able to prevail against the resistance of my surroundings, which in my

Author's foreword

eyes gave friendship something of a higher consecration. Therefore also, so much of it remained cleared in my memory.

In addition, thank God, I have an excellent memory as a result of my acoustic training. Another great help in the writing of this book has been the surviving letters, postcards, and drawings I received from my friend.

If our people wish to win back their self-confidence, they must be able to overcome this portion of our history without coercion from outside. This cannot come about through one-sided revelations, but only by an objective, fair, and therefore really convincing representation of the real historical facts.

It is to this end that I hope the modest effort of this book may contribute.

August Kubizek

Eferding, August 1953.

Chapter 1: First Meeting

I was born in Linz on the third of August, 1888. Before his marriage my father had been an upholsterer's assistant at a furniture manufacturer's in Linz. He used to have his midday meal in a little café and it was there he met my mother who was working as a waitress. They fell in love, and were married in July, 1887.

At first the young couple lived in the house of my mother's parents. My father's wages were low, the work was hard, and my mother had to give up her job when she was expecting me. Thus I was born in rather miserable circumstances. One year later my sister Maria was born, but died at a tender age. The following year, Therese appeared; she died at the age of four. My third sister, Karoline, fell desperately ill, lingered on for some years, and died when she was eight. My mother's grief was boundless. Throughout her life she suffered from the fear of losing me, too; for I was the only one left to her of her four children. Consequently all my mother's love was concentrated upon me.

Meanwhile, my father had set up on his own and had opened an upholsterer's business at No. 9 Klammstrasse. The old Baernreiterhaus, heavy and ungainly, which still stands there unaltered, became the home of my childhood and youth. The narrow, sombre Klammstrasse looked rather poor in comparison with its continuation, the broad and airy promenade, with its lawns and trees.

Our unhealthy housing conditions had certainly contributed to the early death of my sisters. In the Baernreiterhaus things were different. On the ground floor there was the workshop and, on the first floor our apartment, which consisted of two rooms and a kitchen. But now my father was never free from money troubles. Business was bad. More than once he comtemplated closing down the business and again taking a job with the furniture makers. Yet each time, he managed to overcome his difficulties at the last moment.

I started school, a very unpleasant experience. My mother wept over the bad reports I brought home. Her sorrow was the only thing that could persuade me to work harder. Whereas for my father there was no question but that I should in due course take over his business — why else did he slave from morning till night? — it was my mother's desire that I should study in spite of my bad reports; first I should have four years at

Chapter 1: First Meeting

the Grammar School, then perhaps go to the Teachers' Training College. But I would not hear of it, I was glad when my father put his foot down and, when I was ten, sent me to the Council School. In this way, my father thought, my future was finally decided.

For a long time, however, there had been another influence in my life for which I would have sold my soul: music, This love was given full expression when, at nine years of age, I was given a violin as a Christmas present. I remember distinctly every single detail of that Christmas, and when today in my old age I think back, my conscious life seems to have started with that event.

The eldest son of our neighbour was a young pupil-teacher and he gave me violin lessons. I learned fast and well.

When my first violin teacher took a job in the country I entered the lower grade of the Linz School of Music, but I did not like it there very much, perhaps because I was much more advanced than the other pupils. After the holidays I once more had private lessons, this time with an old Sergeant-Major of the Austro-Hungarian Army Music Corps, who straightway made clear to me that I knew nothing and then began to teach me the elements of violin playing "in the military fashion." It was real barrack-square drill with old Kopetzky. Sometimes when I got fed up with his rough sergeant-major manners he consoled me by assuring me that, with more progress, I should certainly be taken as apprentice-musician into the army, in his opinion the peak of a musician's glory. I gave up my study with Kopetzky and entered the intermediate class of the School of Music where I was taught by Professor Heinrich Dessauer, a gifted, efficient and sensitive teacher. At the same time I studied the trumpet, trombone and musical theory, and played in the students' orchestra.

I was already playing with the idea of making music my life's work when hard reality made itself felt. I had hardly left the Council School when I had to join my father's business as an apprentice.

Formerly, when there was a shortage of labour, I had had to lend a hand in the workshop and so was familiar with the work.

It is a repulsive job to re-upholster old furniture by unravelling and remaking the stuffing. The work goes on in clouds of dust in which the poor apprentice is smothered. What rubbishy old mattresses were brought to our workshop! All the illnesses that had been overcome — and some of them not overcome — left their mark on these old beds. No wonder that upholsterers do not live long. But soon I also learnt the more pleasant aspects of my work: personal taste and a feeling for art are necessary in it, and it is not too far removed from interior decorating. One would visit well-to-do homes, one saw and heard a lot and, above all, in winter there was little or nothing to do. And this leisure, naturally, I devoted to music. When I had successfully passed my journeyman's test, my father wanted to take on jobs in other workshops. I saw his point, but for me the essential thing was, not to improve my craftsmanship, but to advance my musical studies.

Thus, I chose to stay on in my father's workshop, since I could dispose of my time with more freedom there than under another master.

"There are generally too many violins in an orchestra, but never enough violas." To this day I am grateful to Professor Dessauer for having applied this maxim and turned me into a good viola player. Musical life in Linz in those days was on a remarkably high level; August Göllerich was the Director of the Music Society. Being a disciple of Liszt's and a collaborator of Richard Wagner's at Bayreuth, Göllerich was the very man to be the musical leader of Linz, so much maligned as a "peasants' town." Every year the Music Society gave three symphony concerts and one special concert, when usually a choral work was performed, with orchestra. My mother, in spite of her humble origin, loved music, and hardly ever missed one of these performances. While still a small boy, I was taken to concerts. My mother explained everything to me, and, as I came to master several instruments, my appreciation of these concerts grew. My highest aim in life was to play in the orchestra, either on the viola or the trumpet.

But for the time being it was still a matter of remaking dusty old mattresses and papering walls. In those years my father suffered much from the usual occupational diseases of an upholsterer.

When persistent lung trouble once kept him in bed for six months, I had to run the workshop alone. Thus the two things existed side by side in my young life: work, which made calls on my strength and even on my lungs, and music, which was my whole love. I should never have thought that there could be a connection between the two. And yet there was. One of my father's customers was a member of the Provincial Government, which also controlled the theatre. One day there came to us for repair the cushions of a set of rococo furniture. When the work was done my father sent me to deliver them to the theatre. The stage manager directed me to the stage, where I was to replace the cushions in their frames.

A rehearsal was in progress. I don't know which piece was being rehearsed, but it was certainly an opera. What I remember still is the enchantment which came over me as I stood there on the stage, in the midst of the singers. I was transformed as though now, for the first time, I had discovered myself. Theatre! What a world! A man stood there, magnificently attired. He seemed to me like a creature from another planet. He sang so

Chapter 1: First Meeting

gloriously that I could not imagine this man could ever speak in the ordinary way. The orchestra responded to his mighty voice. Here I was on more familiar ground, but in this moment everything that music had hitherto meant to me seemed to be trifling. Only in conjunction with the stage did music seem to reach a higher, more solemn plane, the highest imaginable. But there I stood, a miserable little upholsterer, and fitted the cushions back into their place in the rococo suite.

What a lamentable job! What a wretched existence! Theatre, that was the word that I had searched for. Play and reality became confused in my excited mind. That awkward fellow with ruffled hair, apron and rolled-up shirt sleeves who stood in the wings and fumbled with his cushions as though to justify his presence — was he really only a poor upholsterer? A poor, despised simpleton, pushed from pillar to post and treated by the customer as if he were a stepladder, placed here, placed there according to the moment's need and then, its usefulness over, put aside? It would have been absolutely natural if that little upholsterer with his tools in his hand had stepped forward to the footlights and, at a sign from the conductor, had sung his part only to prove to the audience in the stalls, nay to an attentive world, that in reality he was not that pale, lanky fellow from the upholsterer's shop in the Klammstrasse, but that his place was really on the stage in the theatre! Ever since that moment I have remained under the spell of the theatre. Washing down the walls in a customer's house, slapping on the paste, affixing the undercoat of newspaper and then pasting on the wallpaper, I was all the time dreaming of roaring applause in the theatre, seeing myself as conductor in front of an orchestra. Such dreaming did not really help my work, and at times it would happen that the pieces of wallpaper were sadly out of position. But once back in the workshop, my sick father soon made me realise what responsibilities faced me.

Thus I swayed between dream and reality. At home nobody had any inkling of my state of mind; for rather than utter a word about my secret ambitions, I would have bitten off my tongue. Even from my mother I hid my hopes and plans, but she perhaps guessed what was occupying my thoughts. But should I have added to her many worries? Thus there was no one to whom I could unburden myself. I felt terribly lonely, like an outcast, as lonely as only a young man can be to whom is revealed, for the first time, life's beauty and its danger.

The theatre gave me new courage. I didn't miss a single opera performance. However tired I was after my work, nothing could keep me from the theatre. Naturally, with the small wages that my father paid me, I could only afford a ticket for standing room. Therefore I used to go regularly into the so-called Promenade, from which one had the best view; and moreover, I found, no other place had better acoustics. Just above the promenade was the Royal box supported by two wooden columns. These columns were very popular with the habitués of the Promenade as they were the only places where one could prop oneself up with an undisturbed view of the stage. For if you leaned against the walls, these very columns were always in your field of vision. I was happy to be able to rest my weary back against the smooth pillars, after having spent a hard day on the top of the stepladder! Of course, you had to be there early to be sure to get that place.

Often it is the trivial things which make a lasting impression on one's memory. I can still see myself rushing into the theatre, undecided whether to choose the left — or the right hand pillar.

Often, however, one of the two columns, the right-hand one, was already taken; somebody was even more enthusiastic than I was.

Half annoyed, half surprised, I glanced at my rival. He was a remarkably pale, skinny youth, about my own age, who was following the performance with glistening eyes. I surmised that he came from a better-class home, for he was always dressed with meticulous care and was very reserved.

We took note of each other without exchanging a word. During the interval of a performance some time later we started talking, as apparently neither of us approved of the casting of one of the parts. We discussed it together and rejoiced in cur common adverse criticism. I marvelled at the quick, sure grasp of the other. In this he was undoubtedly my superior. On the other hand, when it came to talking of purely musical matters, I felt my own superiority. I cannot give the exact date of this first meeting; but I am sure it was around All Saints' Day in 1904.

This went on for some time — he revealing nothing of his own affairs, nor did I think it necessary to talk about myself. But all the more intensely did we occupy ourselves with whatever performance there happened to be and sensed that we both had the same enthusiasm for the theatre.

Once, after the performance, I accompanied him home to No. 31 Humboldtstrasse. When we took leave of each other he gave me his name: Adolf Hitler.

Chapter 2: Growth of a Friendship

From now on we saw each other at every Opera performance and also met outside the theatre, and on most evenings we would go for a stroll together along the Landstrasse.

While Linz, in the last decade, has become a modern industrial town and attracted people from all parts of the Danube region, it was then only a country town. In the suburbs there were still the substantial, fortresslike farmhouses, and tenement houses were springing up in the surrounding fields where cattle were still grazing. In the little taverns the people sat drinking the local wine; everywhere you could hear the broad country dialect. There was only horse-drawn traffic in the town and the carriers took care to see that Linz remained "in the country."

The townspeople, though largely themselves of peasant origin and often closely related to the country folk, tended to draw away from the latter the more intimately they were connected with them. Almost all the influential families of the town knew each other; the business world, the civil servants and the military determined the tone of society.

Everybody who was anybody took his evening stroll along the main street of the city, which leads from the railway station to the bridge over the Danube and is called significantly "Landstrasse." As Linz had no university, the young people in every walk of life were all the more eager to imitate the habits of university students. Social life on the Landstrasse could almost compete with that of Vienna's Ringstrasse. At least the Linzers thought so.

Patience did not seem to be one of Adolf's outstanding characteristics; whenever I was late for an appointment, he came at once to the workshop to fetch me, no matter whether I was repairing an old, black horsehair sofa or an oldfashioned fashioned wing chair, or anything else. My work was to him nothing but a tiresome hindrance to our personal relationship. Impatiently he would twirl the small black cane which he always carried. I was surprised that he had so much spare time and asked innocently whether he had a job.

"Of course not," was his gruff reply.

This answer, which I thought very peculiar, he elaborated at some length. He did not consider that any particular work, a "bread-and-butter job" as he called it, was necessary for him. Such an opinion I had never heard from anybody before. It contradicted every principle which had so far governed my life. At first I saw in his talk nothing more than youthful bragging, although Adolf's bearing and his serious and assured manner of speaking did not strike me at all as that of a braggart. In any case, I was very surprised at his opinions but refrained from asking, for the time being at least, any further questions, because he seemed to be very sensitive about questions that did not suit him; that much I had already discovered. So it was more reasonable to talk about *Lohengrin*, the opera which enchanted us more than any other, than about our personal affairs.

Perhaps he was the son of rich parents, I thought, perhaps he had just come into a fortune and could afford to live without a "bread-and-butter job" — in his mouth that expression sounded full of contempt. By no means did I imagine he was work-shy, for there was not even a grain of the superficial, carefree idler in him. When we passed by the Café Baumgartner he would get wildly worked up about the young men who were exhibiting themselves at marble-topped tables behind the big windowpanes and wasting their time in idle gossip, without apparently realising how much this indignation was contradicted by his own way of life. Perhaps some of those who were sitting "in the shop window" already had a good job and a secure income.

Perhaps this Adolf is a student? This had been my first impression. The black ebony cane, topped by an elegant ivory shoe, was essentially a student's attribute. On the other hand it seemed strange that he had chosen as his friend just a simple upholsterer, who was always afraid that people would smell the glue with which he had been working during the day. If Adolf were a student he had to be at school somewhere. Suddenly I brought the conversation round to school.

"School?" This was the first outburst of temper that I had experienced with him. He didn't wish to hear anything about school. School was no longer his concern, he said. He hated the teachers and did not even greet them any more, and he also hated his schoolmates whom, he said, the school was turning into idlers. No, school I was not allowed to mention. I told him how little success I had had at school myself. "Why no success?" he wanted to know. He did not like it at all that I had done so badly at school in spite of all the contempt he expressed for schooling. I was confused by this contradiction. But so much I could gather from our conversation, that he must have been at school until recently, probably a grammar school or perhaps a technical school, and that this presumably had ended in disaster. Otherwise this complete rejection would hardly have been possible. For the rest, he presented me with ever recurring contradictions and riddles. Sometimes he seemed to me almost sinister. One day when we were taking a walk he suddenly stopped, produced from his pocket a little black notebook

Chapter 2: Growth of a Friendship

— I still see it before me and could describe it minutely — and read me a poem he had written.

I do not remember the poem itself any longer; to be precise, I can no longer distinguish it from the other poems which Adolf read to me in later days. But I do remember distinctly how much it impressed me that my friend wrote poetry and carried his poems around with him in the same way that I carried my tools. When Adolf later showed me his drawings and designs which he had sketched — somewhat confused and confusing designs which were really beyond me – when he told me that he had much more and better work in his room and was determined to devote his whole life to art, then it dawned on me what kind of person my friend really was.

He belonged to that particular species of people of which I had dreamed myself in my more expansive moments; an artist, who despised the mere bread-and-butter job and devoted himself to writing poetry, to drawing, painting and to going to the theatre. This impressed me enormously. I was thrilled by the grandeur which I saw here. My ideas of an artist were then still very hazy — probably as hazy as were Hitler's. But that made it all the more alluring.

Adolf spoke but rarely of his family. He used to say that it was advisable not to mix too much with grownups, as these people with their peculiar ideas would only divert one from one's own plans.

For instance, his guardian, a peasant in Leonding called Mayrhofer, had got it into his head that he, Adolf, should learn a craft. His brother-in-law, too, was of this opinion.

I could only conclude that Adolf's relations with his family must have been rather peculiar.

Apparently among all the grownups he accepted only one person, his mother. And yet he was only sixteen years old, nine months younger than I.

However much his ideas differed from bourgeois conceptions it did not worry me at all — on the contrary! It was this very fact, that he was out of the ordinary, that attracted me even more. To devote his life to the arts was, in my opinion, the greatest resolution that a young man could take; for secretly I, too, played with the idea of exchanging the dusty and noisy upholsterer's workshop for the pure and lofty fields of art, to give my life to music. For young people it is by no means insignificant in what surroundings their friendship first begins. It seemed to me a symbol that our friendship had been born in the theatre, in the midst of brilliant scenes and to the mighty sound of great music. In a certain sense our friendship itself existed in this happy atmosphere.

Moreover my own position was not dissimilar to Adolf's. School lay behind me and could give me nothing more. In spite of my love and devotion to my parents, the grownups did not mean very much to me. And, above all, in spite of the many problems that beset me there was nobody in whom I could confide.

Nevertheless, it was at first a difficult friendship because our characters were utterly different.

Whereas I was a quiet, somewhat dreamy youth, very sensitive and adaptable and therefore always willing to yield, so to speak, a "musical character," Adolf was exceedingly violent and high-strung.

Quite trivial things, such as a few thoughtless words, could produce in him outbursts of temper which I thought were quite out of proportion to the significance of the matter. But probably I misunderstood Adolf in this respect. Perhaps the difference between us was that he took things seriously which seemed to me quite unimportant. Yes, this was one of his typical traits; everything aroused his interest and disturbed him — to nothing was he indifferent.

But in spite of all the difficulties arising out of our varying temperaments, our friendship itself was never in serious danger. Nor did we, as so many other youngsters, grow cool and indifferent with time. On the contrary! In everyday matters we took great care not to clash. It seems strange, but he who could stick so obstinately to his point of view could also be so considerate that sometimes he made me feel quite ashamed. So, as time went on we got more and more used to each other.

Soon I came to understand that our friendship endured largely for the reason that I was a patient listener. But I was not dissatisfied with this passive role, for it made me realise how much my friend needed me. He, too, was completely alone. His father had been dead for two years.

However much he loved his mother, she could not help him with his problems. I remember how he used to give me long lectures about things that did not interest me at all, as for example the excise duty levied at the Danube bridge, or a collection in the streets for a charity lottery. He just had to talk and needed somebody who would listen to him. I was often startled when he would make a speech to me, accompanied by vivid gestures, for my benefit alone. He was never worried by the fact that I was the sole audience.

But a young man who, like my friend, was passionately interested in everything he saw and experienced had to find an outlet for his tempestuous feelings. The tension he felt was relieved by his holding forth on these things. These speeches, usually delivered somewhere in the open, seemed to be like a volcano erupting. It was as though something quite apart from

Chapter 2: Growth of a Friendship

him was bursting out of him. Such rapture I had only witnessed so far in the theatre, when an actor had to express some violent emotions, and at first, confronted by such eruptions, I could only stand gaping and passive, forgetting to applaud. But soon I realised that this was not play-acting. No, this was not acting, not exaggeration, this was really felt, and I saw that he was in dead earnest.

Again and again I was filled with astonishment at how fluently he expressed himself, how vividly he managed to convey his feelings, how easily the words flowed from his mouth when he was completely carried away by his own emotions. Not what he said impressed me first, but how he said it. This to me was something new, magnificent. I had never imagined that a man could produce such an effect with mere words. All he wanted from me, however, was one thing — agreement. I soon came to realise this. Nor was it hard for me to agree with him, because I had never given any thought to the many problems which he raised.

Nevertheless, it would be wrong to assume that our friendship confined itself to this unilateral relationship only. This would have been too cheap for Adolf and too little for me. The important thing was that we were complementary to each other. In him, everything brought forth a strong reaction and forced him to take a stand; for his emotional outbursts were only a sign of his passionate interest in everything. I, on the other hand, being of a contemplative nature, accepted unreservedly all his arguments on things that interested him and yielded to them, always excepting musical matters. Of course, I must admit that Adolf's claims on me were boundless and took up all my spare time.

As he himself did not have to keep to a regular timetable I had to be at his beck and call. He demanded everything from me, but was also prepared to do everything for me. In fact I had no alternative. My friendship with him did not leave me any time for cultivating other friends; nor did I feel the need of them, Adolf was as much to me as a dozen other ordinary friends. Only one thing might have separated us — if we had both fallen in love with the same girl; this would have been serious. As I was seventeen at the time this might well have happened. But it was precisely in this respect that fate had a special solution in store for us. Such a unique solution-I describe it later in the chapter called "Stefanie" — that, rather than upsetting our friendship, served to deepen it.

I knew that he, too, had no other friends besides me. I remember in this connection a quite trivial detail. We were strolling along the Landstrasse when it happened. A young man, about our age, came around the corner, a plump, rather dandified young gentleman. He recognised Adolf as a former classmate, stopped, and grinning all over his face, called out, "Hello, Hitler!" He took him familiarly by the arm and asked him quite sincerely how he was getting on. I expected Adolf to respond in the same friendly manner, as he always set great store by correct and courteous behaviour.

But my friend went red with rage. I knew from former experience that this change of expression boded ill. "What the devil is that to do with you?" he threw at him excitedly, and pushed him sharply away. Then he took my arm and went with me on his way without bothering about the young man whose flushed and baffled face I can still see before me. "All future civil servants," said Adolf, still furious, "and with this lot I had to sit in the same class." It was a long time before he calmed down.

Another experience sticks out in my memory. My venerated violin teacher, Heinrich Dessauer, had died. Adolf went to the funeral with me, which rather surprised me as he did not know Professor Dessauer at all. When I expressed my surprise he said, "I can't bear it that you should mix with other young people and talk to them." There was no end to the things, even trivial ones, that could upset him. But he lost his temper most of all when it was suggested that he should become a civil servant.

Whenever he heard the word "civil servant," even without any connection with his own career, he fell into a rage. I discovered that these outbursts of fury were, in a certain sense, still quarrels with his long-dead father, whose greatest desire it had been to turn him into a civil servant. So to speak, a "posthumous defence."

It was an essential part of our friendship at that time, that my opinion of civil servants should be as low as his. Knowing his violent rejection of a career in the civil service, I could now appreciate that he preferred the friendship of a simple upholsterer to that of one of those spoilt darlings who were assured of patronage by their good connections and knew in advance the exact course their life would follow. Hitler was just the opposite. With him everything was uncertain.

There was another positive factor which made me seem, in Adolf's eyes, predestined to be his friend: like him I considered art to be the greatest thing in man's life. Of course, in those days, we were not able to express this sentiment in such hifalutin words. But in practice we conformed to this principle, because in my life music had long since become the decisive factor — I worked in the workshop only to make my living. For my friend art was even more. His intense way of absorbing, scrutinising, rejecting, his terrific seriousness, his ever active mind needed a counterpoise. And only art could provide this. Thus I fulfilled all the requirements he would look for in a friend: I had nothing in common with his former classmate, I had

Chapter 2: Growth of a Friendship

nothing to do with the civil service and I lived entirely for art. In addition I knew a lot about music.

The similarity of our inclinations welded us closely together as did the dissimilarity of our temperaments.

I leave it to others to judge whether people who, like Adolf, find their way with a sleepwalker's sureness, pick up at random the companion that they need for that particular part of their path, or whether fate chooses for them. All I can say is that from our first meeting in the theatre up to his decline into misery in Vienna I was that companion for Adolf Hitler.

Chapter 3 — Portrait of the Young Hitler

Adolf was of middle height and slender, at that time already taller than his mother. His physique was far from sturdy, rather too thin for its height, and he was not at all strong. His health, in fact, was rather poor, which he was the first to regret. He had to take special care of himself during the foggy and damp winters which prevailed in Linz. He was ill from time to time during that period and coughed a lot. In short, he had weak lungs.

His nose was quite straight and well proportioned, but in no way remarkable. His forehead was high and receded a little. I was always sorry that even in those days he had the habit of combing his hair straight down over his forehead. Yet this traditional forehead-nose-mouth description seems rather ridiculous to me. For in this countenance the eyes were so outstanding that one didn't notice anything else. Never in my life have I seen any other person whose appearance — how shall I put it — was so completely dominated by the eyes.

They were the light eyes of his mother, but her somewhat staring, penetrating gaze was even more marked in the son and had even more force and expressiveness. It was uncanny how these eyes could change their expression, especially when Adolf was speaking. To me his sonorous voice meant much less than the expression of his eyes. In fact, Adolf spoke with his eyes, and even when his lips were silent one knew what he wanted to say.

When he first came to our house and I introduced him to my mother, she said to me in the evening, "What eyes your friend has!" And I remember quite distinctly that there was more fear than admiration in her words. If I am asked where one could perceive, in his youth, this man's exceptional qualities, I can only answer, "In the eyes." Naturally his extraordinary eloquence, also, was striking.

But I was then too inexperienced to attach to it any special significance for the future. I, for one, was certain that Hitler some day would be a great artist, a poet I thought at first, then a great painter; until later, in Vienna, he convinced me that his real talent was in the field of architecture. For these artistic ambitions his eloquence was of no use, rather a hindrance. Nevertheless, I always liked to listen to him. His language was very refined. He disliked dialect, in particular Viennese, the soft melodiousness of which was utterly repulsive to him. To be sure, Hitler did not speak Austrian in the true sense. It was rather that in his diction, especially in the rhythm of his

Chapter 3 — Portrait of the Young Hitler

speech, there was something Bavarian. Perhaps this was due to the fact that from his third to his sixth year, the real formative years for speech, he lived in Passau, where his father was then a customs official.

There is no doubt that my friend Adolf had shown a gift for oratory from his earliest youth. And he knew it. He liked to talk, and talked without pause. Sometimes when he soared too high in his fantasies I couldn't help suspecting that all this was nothing but an exercise in oratory.

Then again I thought otherwise. Did I not take everything for gospel that he said? Sometimes Adolf would try out his powers of oratory on me or on others. It always stuck in my memory how, when not yet eighteen, he convinced my father that he should release me from his workshop and send me to Vienna to the Conservatory. In view of the awkward and unforthcoming nature of my father this was a considerable achievement. From the moment I had this proof of his talent — for me so decisive — I considered that there was nothing that Hitler could not achieve by a convincing speech.

He was in the habit of emphasizing his words by measured and studied gestures. Now and then, when he was speaking on one of his favourite subjects, such as the bridge over the Danube, the rebuilding of the Museum or even the subterranean railway station which he had planned for Linz, I would interrupt him and ask him how he imagined he would ever carry out these projects — we were only poor devils. Then he would throw at me a strange and hostile glance as though he had not understood my question at all. I never got an answer; at the most he would shut me up with a wave of his hand. Later I got used to it and ceased to find it ridiculous that the sixteen- or seventeen-year-old boy should develop gigantic projects and expound them to me down to the last detail. If I had listened only to his words the whole thing would have appeared to be either idle fantasy or sheer lunacy; but the eyes convinced me that he was in deadly earnest.

Adolf set great store by good manners and correct behaviour. He observed with painstaking punctiliousness the rules of social conduct, however little he thought of society itself. He always emphasized the position of his father, who as a customs official ranked more or less with a captain in the army. Hearing him speak of his father, one would never have imagined how violently he disliked the idea of being a civil servant. Nevertheless, there was in his bearing something very precise. He would never forget to send regards to my people, and every postcard bore greetings to my "esteemed parents."

When we lodged together in Vienna, I discovered that every evening he would put his trousers carefully under the mattress so that the next morning he could rejoice in a faultless crease. Adolf realised the value of a good appearance, and, in spite of his lack of vanity, knew how to make the best of himself. He made excellent use of his undoubted histrionic talents, which he cleverly combined with his gift for oratory. I used to ask myself why Adolf, in spite of all these pronounced capabilities, did not get on better in Vienna; only later did I realise that professional success was not at all his ambition.

People who knew him in Vienna could not understand the contradiction between his well-groomed appearance, his educated speech and his self-assured bearing on the one hand, and the starveling existence that he led on the other, and judged him either haughty or pretentious. He was neither. He just didn't fit into any bourgeois order.

Adolf had brought starvation to a fine art, though he ate very well when occasion offered. To be sure, in Vienna he generally lacked the money for food. But even if he had it, he would prefer to starve and spend it on a theatre seat. He had no comprehension of enjoyment of life as others knew it. He did not smoke, he did not drink, and in Vienna, for instance, he lived for days on milk and bread only.

With his contempt for everything pertaining to the body, sport, which was then coming into fashion, meant nothing to him. I read somewhere of how audaciously the young Hitler had swum across the Danube. I do not recollect anything of the sort; the most swimming we did was an occasional dip in the Rodel stream. He showed some interest in the bicycle club, mainly because they ran an ice rink in the winter. And this only because the girl he adored used to practise skating there.

Walking was the only exercise that really appealed to Adolf. He walked always and everywhere and, even in my workshop and in my room, he would stride up and down. I recall him always on the go. He could walk for hours without getting tired. We used to explore the surroundings of Linz in all directions. His love of nature was pronounced, but in a very personal way. Unlike other subjects, nature never attracted him as a matter for study; I hardly ever remember seeing him with a book on the subject. Here was the limit of his thirst for knowledge. Details did not interest him, but only nature as a whole. He referred to it as "in the open." This expression sounded as familiar on his lips as the word "home." And, in fact, he did feel at home with nature. As early as in the first years of our friendship I discovered his peculiar preference for nocturnal excursions, or even for staying overnight in some unfamiliar district.

Being in the open had an extraordinary effect upon him. He was then quite a different person from what he was in town. Certain sides of his character revealed themselves nowhere else. He was never so collected and concentrated as when walking along the quiet paths in the beech woods of the Mühlviertel, or at night when we took a quick walk on the Freinberg. To the rhythm of his steps his thoughts would flow more smoothly and to better purpose than elsewhere. For a long time I could not understand one peculiar contradiction in him. When the sun shone brightly in the streets and a fresh, revivifying wind brought the smell of the woods into the town, an irresistible force drove him out of the narrow, stuffy streets into the woods and fields. But hardly had we reached the open country, than he would assure me that it would be impossible for him to live in the country again. It would be terrible for him to have to live in a village. For all his love of nature, he was always glad when we got back to the town.

As I grew to know him better, I also came to understand this apparent contradiction. He needed the town, the variety and abundance of its impressions, experiences and events; he felt there that he had his share in everything; that there was nothing in which his interest was not engaged. He needed people with their contrasting interests, their ambitions, intentions, plans and desires. Only in this problem-laden atmosphere did he feel at home. From this point of view the village was altogether too simple, too insignificant, too unimportant, and did not provide enough scope for his limitless need to take an interest in everything. Besides, for him, a town was interesting in itself as an agglomeration of houses and buildings. It was understandable that he should want to live only in a town.

On the other hand, he needed an effective counterweight to the town, which always troubled and excited him and made constant demands on his interests and his talents. He found this in nature, which even he could not try to change and improve because its eternal laws are beyond the reach of the human will. Here he could once more find his own self, since here he was not obliged, as he was in town, eternally to be taking sides.

My friend had a special way of making nature serve him. He used to seek out a lonely spot outside the town, which he would visit again and again. Every bush and every tree was familiar to him. There was nothing to disturb his contemplative mood. Nature surrounded him like the walls of a quiet, friendly room in which he could cultivate undisturbed his passionate plans and ideas.

For some time, on fine days, he used to frequent a bench on the Turmleitenweg where he established a kind of openair study. There he would read his books, sketch and paint in water colours. Here were born his first poems. Another spot, which later became a favourite, was even more lonely and secluded. We would sit on a high, overhanging rock looking down on the Danube. The sight of the gently flowing river always moved Adolf. How often did my friend tell me of his plans up there! Sometimes he would be overcome by his feelings and give free reign to his imagination. I remember him once describing to me so vividly Kriemhild's journey to the country of the Huns that I imagined I could see the mighty ships of the kings of Burgundy drifting down the river.

Quite different were our far-ranging excursions. Not much preparation was necessary — a strong walking stick was the only requisite. With his everyday clothes Adolf would wear a coloured shirt and, as a sign of his intention to undertake a long trip, would sport instead of the usual tie a silk cord with two tassels hanging down. We wouldn't take any food with us, but somewhere would manage to find a bit of dry bread and a glass of milk. What wonderful, carefree times those were! We despised railways and coaches and went everywhere on foot. Whenever we combined our Sunday trip with an outing for my parents, which for us had the advantage that my father treated us to a good meal in a country inn, we started out early enough to meet them at our destination, to which they had come by train. My father was particularly fond of a little village called Walding, which attracted us because nearby was the Rodel stream in which we liked to bathe on warm summer days.

A little incident stands out in my memory. Adolf and I had left the inn for a bathe. We were both fairly good swimmers, but my mother, nevertheless, was nervous. She followed us and stood on a protruding rock to watch us. The rock sloped down to the water and was covered with moss. My poor mother, while she was anxiously watching us, slipped on the smooth moss and slid into the water. I was too far away to help her at once, but Adolf immediately jumped in after her and dragged her out. He always remained attached to my parents. As late as 1944, on my mother's eightieth birthday, he sent her a food parcel, and I never discovered how he came to know about it.

Adolf was particularly fond of the Mühlviertel. From the Pöstlingberg we would walk across the Holzpoldl and the Elendsimmerl to Gramastetten or wander through the woods round the Lichtenhag Ruins. Adolf measured the walls, though not much of them remained, and entered the measurements in his sketchbook, which he always carried with him. Then with a few strokes he sketched the original castle, drew in the moat and the drawbridge and adorned the walls with fanciful pinnacles and turrets. He exclaimed there once to my surprise, "This is the ideal setting for my sonnet!" But when I wanted to know more about it he said, "I must first see what I make of it." And on our way home he confessed that he was

Chapter 3 — Portrait of the Young Hitler

going to try to extend the material into a play. We would go to St. Georgen on the Gusen to find out what relics of that famous battle in the Peasants' War still remained. When we were unsuccessful Adolf had a strange idea. He was convinced that the people who lived there would have some faint memory of that great battle. The following day he went again alone, after a vain attempt to get my father to give me the day off. He spent two days and two nights there, but I don't remember with what result.

For the sole reason that Adolf wanted, for a change, to see his beloved Linz from the east, I had to make with him the unattractive climb up the Pfennigberg, in which the Linzers, as he complained, didn't show enough interest. I also liked the view of the city, but least of all from this side. Nevertheless, Adolf remained for hours in this uninviting spot, sketching.

On the other hand, St. Florian became for me, too, a place of pilgrimage, for here, where Anton Bruckner had worked and hallowed the surroundings by his memory, we imagined that we actually met "God's musician" and heard his inspired improvisations on the great organ in the magnificent church.

Then we would stand in front of the simple gravestone let into the floor beneath the choir, where the great master had been buried ten years earlier. The wonderful monastery had aroused my friend to the heights of enthusiasm. He had stood in front of the glorious staircase for an hour or more — at any rate much too long for me. And how much did be admire the splendour of the library! But the deepest impression was made on him by the contrast between the overdecorated apartments of the monastery and Bruckner's simple room. When he saw its humble furniture, he was strengthened in his belief that on this earth genius almost always goes hand in hand with poverty.

Such visits were revealing to me, for Adolf was by nature very reserved. There was always a certain element in his personality into which he would allow nobody to penetrate. He had his inscrutable secrets, and in many respects always remained a riddle to me. But there was one key that opened the door to much that would have remained hidden: his enthusiasm for beauty. All that separated us disappeared when we stood in front of such a magnificent work of art as the Monastery of St. Florian. Then, fired by enthusiasm, Adolf would lower all his defences and I felt to the full the joy of our friendship.

I have often been asked, and even by Rudolf Hess, who once invited me to visit him in Linz, whether Adolf, when I knew him, had any sense of humour. One feels the lack of it, people of his entourage said. After all, he was an Austrian and should have had his share of the famous Austrian sense of humour. Certainly one's impression of Hitler, especially after a short and superficial acquaintance, was that of a deeply serious man. This enormous seriousness seemed to overshadow everything else. It was the same when he was young. He approached the problems with which he was concerned with a deadly earnestness which ill suited his sixteen or seventeen years. He was capable of loving and admiring, hating and despising, all with the greatest seriousness.

One thing he could not do was to pass over something with a smile. Even with a subject in which he did not take a personal interest, such as sport, this was, nevertheless, as a phenomenon of modern times, just as important to him as any other. He never came to the end of his problems. His profound earnestness never ceased to attack new problems, and if he did not find any in the present, he would brood at home for hours over his books and burrow into the problems of the past. This extraordinary earnestness was his most striking quality. Many other qualities which are characteristic of youth were lacking in him: a carefree letting go of himself, living only for the day — the happy attitude of "What is to be, will be." Even "going off the rails," in the coarse exuberance of youth, was alien to him. His idea, strange to say, was that these were things that did not become a young man. And because of this, humour was confined to the most intimate sphere as if it were something taboo. His humour was usually aimed at people in his immediate circle, in other words a sphere in which problems no longer existed for him. For this reason his grim and sour humour was often mixed with irony, but always an irony with friendly intent. Thus, he saw me once at a concert where I was playing the trumpet. He got enormous amusement out of imitating me and insisted that with my blown-out cheeks I looked like one of Rubens' angels.

I cannot conclude this chapter without mentioning one of Hitler's qualities which, I freely admit, seems paradoxical to talk about now. Hitler was full of deep understanding and sympathy. He took a most touching interest in me. Without my telling him, he knew exactly how I felt. How often this helped me in difficult times! He always knew what I needed and what I wanted. However intensely he was occupied with himself he would always have time for the affairs of those people in whom he was interested. It was not by chance that he was the one who persuaded my father to let me study music and thereby influenced my life in a decisive way. Rather, this was the outcome of his general attitude of sharing in all the things that were of concern to me. Sometimes I had a feeling that he was living my life as well as his own.

Chapter 3 — Portrait of the Young Hitler

Thus, I have drawn the portrait of the young Hitler as well as I can from memory. But for the question, then unknown and unexpressed, which hung above our friendship, I have not to this day found any answer: "What were God's intentions when he created this man?"

Chapter 4 — Portrait of His Mother

When I first met her, Klara Hitler was already forty-five years old and a widow of two years' standing. Whenever I saw her I had — I don't know why — a feeling of sympathy for her, and felt that I wanted to do something for her. She was glad that Adolf had found a friend whom he liked and trusted, and for this reason Frau Hitler liked me, too. How often did she unburden to me the worries which Adolf caused her. And how fervently did she hope to enlist my help in persuading her son to follow his father's wishes in the choice of a career! I had to disappoint her, yet she did not blame me, for she must have felt that the reasons for Adolf's behaviour were much too deep, far beyond the reach of my influence.

Just as Adolf often enjoyed the hospitality of my parents' home, I went often to see his mother and on taking leave was unfailingly asked by Frau Hitler to come again. I considered myself as part of the family — there was hardly anybody else who visited them.

No. 31 Humboldtstrasse is a three-storied, not unpleasant tenement building. The Hitlers lived on the third floor. I can still visualise the humble apartment.

The small kitchen, with green painted furniture, had only one window, which looked out on to the courtyard. The living room, with the two beds of his mother and little Paula, overlooked the street. On the side wall hung a portrait of his father, with a typical civil servant's face, impressive and dignified, whose rather grim expression was mitigated by the carefully groomed whiskers à la Emperor Franz Joseph. Adolf lived and studied in the closet, off the bedroom.

Paula, Adolf's little sister, was nine when I first met the family. She was a rather pretty girl, quiet and reserved. I never saw her gay. We got on rather well with each other but Adolf was not particularly close to her. This was due perhaps to the difference in age — he always referred to her as "the kid." Paula never married and now lives in Königsee, near Berchtesgaden.

Another acquaintance I made in the Hitler family was a striking-looking young woman of just over twenty, called Angela, whose place in the family puzzled me at first, although she addressed Klara Hitler as "Mother," just as Paula did. Later I learned the solution of the mystery. Angela, born on the twenty-eighth July, 1883, that is to say six years before Adolf, was a child of the father's previous marriage. Her mother, Franziska Matzelsberger, died the year after her birth.

Chapter 4 — Portrait of His Mother

Five months later the father married Klara Pölzl. Angela, who naturally had no recollection of her own mother, looked upon Klara as her mother. In September 1903, a year before I became acquainted with Adolf, Angela had married a revenue official called Raubal. She lived with her husband nearby and often came to visit her stepmother, but never brought him with her; at any rate, I never met Raubal. Angela was quite unlike Frau Hitler, a jolly person who enjoyed life and loved to laugh. She brought some life into the family. She was very handsome with her regular features, and her beautiful hair which was as dark as Adolf's.

From Adolf's description, but also from some hints of his mother's, I gathered that Raubal was a drunkard. Adolf bated him. He saw in him a personification of everything he despised in a man.

He spent his time in the pub, drank and smoked, gambled his money away, and on top of that — he was a civil servant. And as though that were not enough, Raubal thought it was his duty to support his father-in-law's views by urging Adolf to become a civil servant himself. This was enough to antagonise Adolf completely.

When Adolf talked of Raubal his face assumed a truly threatening aspect. Perhaps it was Adolf's pronounced hatred of his half sister's husband that kept Raubal away from the Humboldtstrasse. At the time of Raubal's death, only a few years after his marriage to Angela, the break between him and Adolf was already complete. Angela remarried later, an architect in Dresden, and died in Munich in 1949.

I learned from Adolf that from his father's second marriage there was also a son, Alois, who spent his childhood with the Hitler family but left them while they were living in Lambach. This half brother of Adolf's — born on December 13, 1882, in Braunau — was seven years older than Adolf. While his father was alive he still came to Leonding a couple of times, but as far as I know he never appeared in the Humboldtstrasse. He never played any important part in Hitler's life, nor did he take any interest in Adolf's political career. He turned up once in Paris, then in Vienna, later in Berlin, and today, seventy years old, lives in Hamburg. His first marriage was to a Dutchwoman and they had a son, William Patrick Hitler, who in August 1939 published a pamphlet, *My Uncle Adolf;* a son by his second wife, Heinz Hitler, fell as an officer on the Eastern Front.

Frau Hitler did not like to talk about herself and her worries, yet she found relief in telling me of her doubts about Adolf. Naturally she didn't get much satisfaction from the vague and, for her, meaningless utterances of Adolf about his future as an artist. The preoccupation with the wellbeing of her only surviving son depressed her increasingly. "Our poor father cannot rest in his grave," she used to say to Adolf, "because you will flout his wishes. Obedience is what distinguishes a good son, but you don't know the meaning of the word. That's why you did so badly at school and why you're not getting anywhere now." Gradually I learned to understand the suffering this woman endured. She never complained, but she told me about the hard time she had had in her youth.

So I came to know, partly by experience, partly by what I was told, the circumstances of the Hitler family. Occasionally mention was made of some relations in the Waldviertel, but it was difficult for me to understand whether these were his father's relations or his mother's. In any case, the Hitler family had relations only in the Waldviertel, quite unlike other Austrian civil servants, who had relatives scattered all over the country.

Only later did I come to realise that Hitler's paternal and maternal lineage already merged in the second generation, so that from the grandfather upwards Adolf had only one set of forebears. I remember that Adolf did visit some relatives in the Waldviertel. Once he sent me a picture postcard from Weitra, which is in the part of the Waldviertel nearest to Bohemia. I do not know what had taken him there. He never spoke very willingly about his relations in that part of the country, but preferred to describe the landscape; poor, barren country, a striking contrast to the rich and fertile Danube valley of the Wachau. This raw, hard peasant country was the homeland of both his maternal and paternal ancestors.

Frau Klara Hitler, nee Pölzl, was born on August 12, 1860, in Spital, a poor village in the Waldviertel. Her father, Johann Baptist Pölzl, was a simple peasant. Her mother's maiden name was Johanna Hüttler. The name Hitler is spelt differently in the various documents. There is the spelling Hiedler and Hüttler, while Hitler is used for the first time by Adolf's father.

This Johanna Hüttler, Adolf's maternal grandmother, was, according to the documents, a daughter of Johann Nepomuk Hiedler. Thus Klara Pölzl was directly related to the Hüttler—Hiedler family, for Johann Nepomuk Hiedler was the brother of that Johann Georg Hiedler who appears in the baptismal register of Döllersheim as Adolf's father's father. Klara Pölzl was, therefore, a second cousin of her husband. Alois Hitler always referred to her before their marriage simply as his niece.

Klara Pölzl had a miserable childhood in the poor and wretched home where there were so many children. In 1875, when she was fifteen years old, her relative, the customs official Alois Schicklgruber at Braunau, invited her to come and help his wife in the house. Alois Schicklgruber, who only in the following year assumed the name Hiedler, which he changed into Hitler, was then married to Anna Glasl-Hörer.

Chapter 4 — Portrait of His Mother

This first marriage of Alois Hitler with a woman fourteen years older than himself remained without issue and they finally separated. When his wife died in 1883, Alois Hitler married Franziska Matzelsberger, who was twenty-four years his junior. The children of this marriage were Adolf's half brother Alois and half sister Angela. Klara, who had continued living in the house during the time he was separated from his first wife, left on the second marriage and went to Vienna. As Franziska, the second wife, fell gravely ill after the birth of her second child, Alois Hitler called his niece back to Braunau.

Franziska died on August 1,0, 1884, barely two years after her marriage. (Alois, the first child of this union, had been born out of wedlock and adopted by his father.) On January 7, 1885, six months after the death of his second wife, Alois Hitler married his "niece" Klara, who was already expecting a child by him, the first son, Gustav, who was born on May 17, 1885, that is to say five months after the marriage, and who died on December 9, 1887.

Although Klara Pölzl was only a second cousin, the couple needed an ecclesiastical dispensation for their marriage. The application for this, in the clean, copper-plate handwriting of an Austro-Hungarian civil servant, still exists in the archives of the Episcopate in Linz under the number 6.911/11/2 1884. The documents read as follows:

Application of Alois Hitler and his fiancée, Klara Pölzl, for permission to marry.

Most Reverend Episcopate! Those, in humblest devotion undersigned, have decided to marry. According to the enclosed family tree they are prevented by the canonical impediment of collateral affinity in the third degree touching the second. They therefore humbly request the Reverend Episcopate to graciously procure them dispensation on the following grounds: According to the enclosed death certificate the bridegroom has been a widower since 10th August of this year and is father of two infant children, a boy of two and a half (Alois) and a girl of one year and two months (Angela) for whose care he needs a woman-help as he, being a customs official, is away from his home the whole day and also often at night, and therefore hardly able to supervise the education and upbringing of the children. The bride has looked after the children ever since the death of the mother and they are very fond of her, so that it may be justifiably assumed that the upbringing would be successful and the marriage a happy one. Moreover, the bride is without means and it is therefore unlikely that she will ever have another opportunity of a good marriage.

For these reasons the undersigned repeat their humble petition for the gracious procurement of dispensation from the impediment of affinity.

> *Braunau, 27th October, 1884 ALOIS HITLER, Bridegroom — KLARA PÖLZL, Bride*

The family tree that accompanied the application was as follows: Johann Georg Hiedler —— Johann Nepomuk Hiedler | Alois Hitler Johanna Hiedler (married Pölzl) | Klara Pölzl

The Linz Episcopate declared itself not competent to issue the dispensation and forwarded the application to Rome where it was granted by papal decree.

Alois Hitler's marriage with Klara was described by various acquaintances as very happy, which was presumably due to the submissive and accommodating nature of the wife. Once she said to me in this respect, "What I hoped and dreamed of as a young girl has not been fulfilled in my marriage;" and added resignedly, "But does such a thing ever happen?"

The birth of the children in quick succession was a heavy psychological and physical burden for the frail woman: in 1885 the son Gustav was born, in 1886 a daughter, Ida, who died after two years, in 1887 another son, Otto, who only lived three days, and on April 20, 1889, again a son, Adolf. How much suffering is hidden behind these bare figures! When Adolf was born the three other children were already dead. With what care the sorely tried mother must have looked after this fourth child! She told me once that Adolf was a very weak child and that she always lived in fear of losing him, too.

Perhaps the early death of the three children was due to the fact that the parents were blood relations. I leave it to the experts to give the final verdict. But in this connection I would like to draw attention to one point to which, in my opinion, greatest importance should be attached.

The most outstanding trait in my friend's character was, as I had experienced myself, the unparalleled consistency in everything that he said and did. There was in his nature something firm, inflexible, immovable, obstinately rigid, which manifested itself in his profound seriousness and was at the bottom of all his other characteristics. Adolf simply could not change his mind or his nature. Everything that lay in these rigid precincts of his being remained unaltered for ever.

How often did I experience this! I remember what he said to me when we met again in 1938 after an interval of thirty years. "You haven't changed, Kubizek, you have only grown older." If this was true of me, how much more was it of him! He never changed.

I have tried to find an explanation for this fundamental trait in his character. Influence of surroundings and education can hardly account for

Chapter 4 — Portrait of His Mother

it, but I could imagine — although a complete layman in the field of genetics — that the biological effect of the intermarriage in the family was to fix certain spheres and that those "arrested complexes" have produced that particular type of character. It was just this inflexibility that was responsible for Adolf Hitler's causing such innumerable sorrows to his mother.

Once more the mother's heart was sorely tried by destiny. Five years after Adolf's birth, on March 24, 1894, she gave birth to a fifth child, a son, Edmund, who also died young, on June 29, 1900, in Leonding. Although Adolf had no recollection of the first three children in Braunau, and never spoke of them, he could clearly remember his brother Edmund, at the time of whose death he was already eleven years old. He told me once the Edmund had died of diphtheria. The youngest child, a girl called Paula, born on January 21, 1896, survived.

Thus, an early death had deprived Klara Hitler of four of her six children. Perhaps her mother's heart was broken by these terrible trials. Only one thing remained, the care of the two surviving children, a care which she had to bear alone after the death of her husband. Small comfort that Paula was a quiet, easily led child; all the greater was the anxiety over the only son, an anxiety that only ended with her death.

Adolf really loved his mother. I swear to it before God and man. I remember many occasions when he showed this love for his mother, most deeply and movingly during her last illness; he never spoke of his mother but with deep affection. He was a good son. It was beyond his power to fulfil her most heartfelt wish to see him started on a safe career. When we lived together in Vienna he always carried his mother's portrait with him.

Chapter 5 — Portrait of His Father

Although his father had been dead nearly two years when I first met Adolf he was still "ever present" to his family. The mother perpetuated his personality in every way, for with her malleable nature she had almost entirely lost her own, and what she thought, said and did was all in the spirit of the dead father. But she lacked the strength and energy to put into effect the father's will.

She, who forgave everything, was handicapped in the upbringing of her son by, her boundless love for him. I could imagine how complete and enduring the influence of this man had been on his family, a real partriarchal father-of-the-family, whose authority was unquestioningly respected.

Now his picture hung in the best position in the room. On the kitchen shelves, I still remember, there were carefully arrayed the long pipes which he used to smoke. They were almost a symbol in the family of his absolute power. Many a time, when talking of him, Frau Hitler would emphasise her words by pointing to these pipes as though they should bear witness how faithfully she carried on the father's tradition.

Adolf spoke of his father with great respect. I never heard him say anything against him, in spite of their differences of opinion about his career. In fact he respected him more as time went on.

Adolf did not take it amiss that his father had autocratically decided on his son's future career; for this was considered his right, even his duty. It was quite a different matter when Raubal, his stepsister's husband, this uneducated person, who was himself only a little revenue official, arrogated to himself this right. Adolf would certainly not permit him to interfere in his personal affairs. But the authority of his father still remained, even after his death, the force in the struggle with which Adolf developed his own powers. His father's attitude had provoked him first to secret, then to open rebellion. There were violent scenes, which often ended in the father giving him a good hiding, as Adolf told me himself. But Adolf matched this violence with his own youthful obstinacy, and the antagonism between father and son grew sharper.

The customs official Alois Hitler showed a marked sense of ceremony all his life. Consequently we have good pictures showing him at various stages of his life. Not so much at his weddings, which were always under an unlucky star, but at the various promotions in his career, did he have his picture taken. Most of the pictures show him, with his dignified

Chapter 5 — Portrait of His Father

civil servant's face, in gala uniform of white trousers and dark tunic, on which the double row of highly polished buttons gleamed. The man's face is impressive. A broad, massive head, the most notable feature being the side whiskers, modelled on those of his supreme master, the Emperor. The expression of the eyes is penetrating and incorruptible, the eyes of a man who, as a customs official, is obliged to view everything with suspicion. But in most pictures dignity prevails over the "inquisitiveness" of the gaze. Even the pictures taken at the time when Alois Hitler had already retired show that this man was, in spirit, still on duty. Although he was past sixty he didn't show any of the typical signs of age. One of the pictures, probably the last one, which can also be seen on his grave in Leonding, shows Alois Hitler as a man whose life consisted of service and duty. To be sure there is also an earlier photograph, dating from his Leonding days, which, emphasising his private life, depicts him as a comfortable, well-to-do citizen, fond of good living.

Alois Hitler's rise from being the illegitimate son of a poor servant girl to the position of a respected civil servant is the path from insignificance and inferior status to the highest rank open to him in the service of the State.

His colleagues in the Customs Service describe him as a precise, dutiful official who was very strict and had his "weak spots." As a superior Alois Hitler was not very popular. Out of office he was considered a liberal-minded man who did not conceal his convictions. He was very proud of his rank. Every day he would pay his morning visit to the inn with an official's punctuality. His regular drinking companions found him good company but he could flare up over trifles and become rude, displaying both his inborn violence and the sternness that he had acquired in his job.

His illegitimate birth is conclusively proved by the Church register of the Parish of Strones.

According to this, the forty-two-year-old servant maid Anna Maria Schicklgruber gave birth to a son on July 7, 1837, who was christened Alois. The godfather was her employer, the peasant Johann Trummelschlager, in Strones. As far as is known the child was the first and the only one.

The identity of the father was not revealed by the mother.

Anna Maria Schicklgruber married the mill worker Johann Georg Hiedler in 1842 when the illegitimate child was already five years old. The Church Register of Döllersheim contains the following entry: *The undersigned hereby confirm that Johann Georg Hiedler, who is well known to the undersigned witnesses, has acknowledged paternity of the child Alois of Anna Maria Schicklgruber and requests that his name be entered in the Baptismal Register.*

The entry is signed by the Parish priest and four witnesses.

Johann Georg Hiedler again acknowledged his paternity in an official document concerning some inheritance in 1876 before the Notary in Weitra. He was then eighty-four years old and the child's mother had been dead for over thirty years. Alois Schicklgruber had been a customs official in Braunau for many years.

As the boy was not officially adopted after his mother's wedding, his name remained Schicklgruber. He would have kept this name throughout his life had not Johann Nepomuk Hiedler, Johann Georg's younger brother, made a will and left a modest sum to the illegitimate son of his brother. But he made the condition that Alois should assume the name Hiedler, and on June 4, 1876, the name Alois Schicklgruber in the Church Register of the Parish of Döllersheim was altered to Alois Hiedler; the local government authority in Mistelbach ratifying this alteration on January 6, 1877. From now on Alois Schicklgruber called himself Alois Hitler, a name which meant as little as the other, but which secured him his legacy.

Once when we were talking about his relatives Adolf told me the story of his father's change of names. Nothing his "old man" ever did pleased him as much as this; for Schicklgruber seemed to him so uncouth, so boorish, apart from being so clumsy and unpractical. He found "Hiedler" too boring, too soft; but "Hitler" sounded nice and was easy to remember.

It is typical of his father that instead of accepting the version "Hiedler," as did the rest of his relations, he invented the new spelling, "Hitler." It was in keeping with his mania for ceaseless change. His superiors had nothing to do with this; for in all his forty years of service he was transferred only four times. The towns to which he was posted, Saalfelden, Braunau, Passau and Linz, are so favourably situated that they form the ideal setting for a customs official's career. But hardly had he settled down in one of these places, when he began to move house. During his period of service in Braunau there are recorded twelve changes of address; probably there were more. During the two years in Passau he moved twice. Soon after his retirement he moved from Linz to Hafeld, from there to Lambach — first in the Leingartner Inn, then to a mill, that is to say, two changes in one year — then to Leonding. When I met Adolf he remembered seven removals and had been to five different schools. It would not be true to say that these constant changes were due to bad housing conditions. Surely the Pommer Inn — Alois Hitler was very fond of living in inns — (where Adolf was born) was one of the finest and most presentable buildings in the whole of Braunau. Nevertheless, the father left there soon after Adolf's birth. Actually he often moved from a decent dwelling into a poorer one.

Chapter 5 — Portrait of His Father

The house was not the important thing; rather the moving. How can one explain this strange mania? Perhaps Alois Hitler simply hated to remain in one spot; and as his service forced on him a certain stability, he at least wanted some change in his own sphere. As soon as he had got used to certain surroundings, he grew weary of them. To live meant to change one's conditions, a trait which I experienced in Adolf too.

Three times Alois remodelled his family. It is perhaps true that this was due to outside circumstances. But if so, certainly fate played strangely into his hands. We know that his first wife, Anna, suffered very much from his restlessness, which eventually led to their separation and was partly responsible for her unexpected death. For while his first wife was still alive, Alois Hitler already had a child by the woman who became his second wife. And again when the second wife fell gravely ill and died, Klara, the third, was already expecting a child of his. Just sufficient time elapsed for the child to be born in wedlock. Alois Hitler was not an easy husband. Even more than from Frau Hitler's occasional hints could one gather this from her weary, drawn face. This lack of inner harmony was perhaps partly due to the fact that Alois Hitler never married a woman his own age. Anna was fourteen years older, Franziska twenty-four years younger, and Klara twenty-three years younger.

This strange and unusual habit of the father's, always to change his circumstances, is all the more remarkable as those were peaceful, comfortable times without any justification for such change. I see in the father's character an explanation of the strange behaviour of the son, whose constant restlessness puzzled me for so long. When Adolf and I strolled through the familiar streets of the good, old town — all peace, quiet and harmony — my friend would sometimes be taken by a certain mood and begin to change everything he saw. That house there was in a wrong position; it would have to be demolished. There was an empty plot which could be built up instead. That street needed a correction in order to give a more compact impression. Away with this horrible, completely bungled tenement block! Let's have a free vista to the Castle. Thus he was always rebuilding the town. But it wasn't only a matter of building. A beggar, standing before the church, would be an occasion for him to hold forth on the need for a State scheme for the old, which would do away with begging. A peasant woman coming along with her milk cart drawn by a miserable dog — occasion to criticize the Society for Prevention of Cruelty to Animals for their lack of initiative. Two young lieutenants sauntering through the streets, their sabres proudly clanking — sufficient reason for him to inveigh against the shortcomings of a military service which permitted such idleness. This inclination to be dissatisfied with things as they were, always to change and improve them, was ineradicable in him.

And this was by no means a peculiarity which he had acquired through external influences, by his upbringing at home or at school, but an innate quality that was also apparent in his father's unsettled character. It was a supernatural force, comparable to a motor driving a thousand wheels.

Nevertheless, father and son were affected by this quality in different ways. The father's unruly nature was bridled by one steadying factor — his position. The discipline of his office gave his volatile character purpose and direction. Again and again he was saved from complications by the hard exigencies of his duties.

The uniform of the customs official served as a cover for anything that may have gone on in the stormy sphere of his private life. In particular, being in the service, he unreservedly accepted the authority on which the service was built. Although Alois Hitler was inclined to liberal views — an inclination not uncommon in the Austrian Civil Service — he would never have questioned the authority of the State, epitomized in the person of the Emperor. By fully submitting to this accepted authority, Alois Hitler was able to steer safely through all the dangerous reefs and sandbanks of his life, on which otherwise he might have foundered.

This also throws a different light on his obstinate efforts to make a civil servant of Adolf. It was for him more than a father's usual preoccupation with his son's future. His purpose was rather to direct his son into a position which necessitated submission to authority. It is quite possible that the father did not himself realise the inner reason of his attitude, but his determination in insisting on his point of view shows that he must have felt how much was at stake for his son. So well did he know him.

With equal determination Adolf refused to comply with his father's wishes, although he himself had only very hazy ideas about his future. To become a painter would have been the worst possible insult to his father, for it would have meant just that aimless wandering to which he (the father) was so much opposed.

With his refusal to enter the Civil Service, Adolf Hitler's path diverges sharply from that of his father; it takes a different course, final and irrevocable. It was, indeed, the great decision of his life. The years that followed it I spent at his side. I could observe how earnestly he tried to find the right path for his future, not merely a job that would provide a livelihood, but real tasks for which his talents were fitted.

Alois Hitler died suddenly. On January 3, 1903 — he was sixty-five and still strong and active — he went, as usual, punctually at ten o'clock in

Chapter 5 — Portrait of His Father

the morning to have his drink. Without warning he collapsed in his chair. Before a doctor or a priest could be called, he was dead.

When the fourteen-year-old son saw his dead father he burst out into uncontrollable weeping.

Chapter 6 — School

When I first knew Adolf Hitler he had, as far as he was concerned, already finished with school.

To be sure, he was still attending the technical school in Steyr and frequently came home, usually every Sunday. Only for his mother's sake had he — as he put it — consented to this "last of all attempts." His report from the third form of the technical school in Linz had indeed been so bad that Frau Hitler had been advised to let Adolf continue his studies at another school. To put it bluntly, the difficult pupil had been promoted only on the condition that he left. In this manner the school in the capital of the Province got rid of its less satisfactory pupils by pushing them off into the schools of the smaller towns.

Adolf himself was infuriated by this sly method and from the very start regarded his attempt in the fourth form of the technical school in Steyr as a failure. By this time he knew all that there was to know about schools and had come to the conclusion that in view of his own plans for his future, school was of no more use to him. The knowledge that he lacked he would make up by studying by himself.

Art had long since captured him. To art he dedicated himself with youthful passion, convinced that this was his true vocation. Compared with art, school with its routine appeared grey and monotonous. At long last he wanted to be free and go his own way, and despised those young men who did not think likewise. As he emancipated himself from the hated atmosphere of school, so did our friendship gain in value and importance.

What his old classmates in all their insignificance had not been able to give him he expected from his new friend.

At the elementary school Hitler was always one of the best pupils. He was quick to learn and made progress even without working very hard. His first teacher, Karl Mittermaier, gave him a report, "Full marks in every subject." Mittermaier lived till 1938, when he was naturally asked to tell what he remembered of his former pupil. Although he still remembered the pale and sickly boy, he had little to say about him. The little Adolf had been very docile, his school things always in perfect order.

For the rest there was nothing outstanding about him, either good or bad. Incidentally, when Adolf Hitler was Chancellor in 1939 he visited that school again and seated himself at the same desk at which he had learned to read and write. As usual, he made good use of his visit and

Chapter 6 — School

changed everything possible. He personally bought the old school building and ordered the construction of a fine new school. The teacher who had succeeded old Mittermaier was invited to Obersalzburg, together with her pupils.

But things altered when Adolf Hitler in September 1900 entered the technical school at Linz. He himself writes about those years: *Only one thing was certain, my obvious failure at school. I learned what I liked — in particular, all that which I considered would be useful to me as a painter later. What I thought was unimportant in this respect or what did not attract me, I neglected completely. My marks in this period show extremes, varying according to the subject and my regard for it: there is "Praiseworthy" and "Excellent" but also "Fair" and "Unsatisfactory". By far my best efforts were in geography and even more in history, my favourite subjects, in which I was far ahead of the rest of the class.*

One is apt to get a wrong picture of Adolf's schooldays from his own words. Although Adolf spoke to me of his schooldays with reluctance and always with a curious indignation, nevertheless our friendship was, so to speak, overshadowed by them. In this way I got quite a different impression from the one he conveys in his writings of fifteen years later.

In the first place the eleven-year-old boy found it difficult to adapt himself to the new surroundings. Every day he had to make the long journey from Leonding into the town to school.

He often told me that, nevertheless, this daily walk was one of the nicest things he could remember of those years. At least this hour's journey to school assured him a bit of freedom, which he appreciated all the more as until then he had always lived in the country. Everything in town seemed strange and unfriendly to him. His classmates, mostly from rich homes, did not accept as an equal the queer youngster who came daily to town "from the peasants." His teachers' interest in him was confined to their classes.

All this had been so different at the elementary school, where the easygoing teacher knew all his pupils intimately and used to take his regular drink with their fathers in the evening. At the elementary school the boy had been accustomed to passing up each year without any special effort. At his new school, to start with, he also tried improvisation at which he was a master.

He had to do it all the more as he found little pleasure in learning by heart, so much valued by his teachers. But here the trick did not work. So he started to sulk and let things drift. Nobody took much notice of him in class; he had no friends and did not want any. Sometimes some of his spoiled classmates would make him feel that they did not accept as one of them this village boy — a sufficient reason for him to withdraw even more.

It is significant that not one of his many schoolmates could claim any close relationship or friendship with him.

Thus, after his first year at the technical school, Hitler brought home to his father a report bearing twice "Unsatisfactory" and the verdict that the pupil would not pass up into the next class. Adolf never told me how his father reacted to this, but it can be imagined.

Now he had to start all over again. His form master was now Professor Eduard Huemer, who besides German, also taught French, the only foreign language taught in the lower forms of the technical school and also, to my knowledge, the only foreign language which Adolf Hitler ever studied, or rather was made to study. But in the meantime he had "acclimatised" himself.

His second year in the first form was more successful and he was promoted to the second form. But from there, again, he passed only by the skin of his teeth. Again his father had to acknowledge a report which showed "Unsatisfactory" in mathematics. Obviously this judgment was not due to illwill on the part of the teachers. Hitler hated mathematics because it was too dry and required hard, systematic work. We often talked about it. Later in Vienna Hitler realised that he would need mathematics if he wanted to become an architect. But this made no difference to his violent aversion.

He finished the third form again with two "Unsatisfactory" reports, again in mathematics and in addition in German, although Professor Huemer was one of the teachers whom, he later admitted, he respected. This was the year of his father's death. Professor Huemer explained to his mother that promotion to the fourth form was only possible if he went to another school. It is, therefore, not correct to say that Adolf Hitler was thrown out of the Linz technical school. He was only moved "to the country." If up till now it was by his father's order that he stayed at school, so now it was mother's love which urged him to continue his studies. He did not like his transfer to Steyr.

After reading Dante's *Divine Comedy* he talked to me of the school as "Purgatory." In Steyr Hitler lodged with a court official by the name of Edler von Cichini at No. 19 Grünmarkt, but whenever he had a moment's spare time he would come to Linz. As could be foreseen, the result was bad and remained so when he repeated his examination between September 1 and 15, 1905. As well as the usual "Unsatisfactory" for mathematics, there appeared another "Unsatisfactory" for practical geometry.

When Professor Huemer, who had been Hitler's form master for three years, gave evidence as to his pupil's character at the Treason Trial after the unsuccessful Putsch of November 1923 he said: "Hitler was certainly

Chapter 6 — School

gifted, although only for particular subjects, but he lacked self-control and, to say the least, he was considered argumentative, autocratic, self-opinionated and badtempered, and unable to submit to school discipline. Nor was he industrious; otherwise he would have achieved much better results, gifted as he was." Having passed this rather negative judgment Professor Huemer, in a more sentimental mood, added: "Yet, as experience shows, what happens at school has not much bearing on life, and while model pupils sink from view without leaving a trace, the difficult boys develop only when they have the elbow room they need. My former pupil Hitler seems to belong to this latter species and I hope from the bottom of my heart that he will recover from his recent hardships and upsets and live to see the fulfillment of those ideals which he harbours in his bosom, which do credit to him, as they do to any German."

These words, written in 1924, are certainly not influenced by wisdom after the event. They show remarkable solidarity between teacher and former pupil. In an indirect way, Professor Huemer proclaims that the ideals for which Adolf Hitler was then standing his trial were indeed the ideals of his school. And this, in spite of the fact that in the subject which Dr. Huemer taught, German, Hitler by no means excelled; which is borne out by the many spelling mistakes in the letters and cards which he sent to me.

Among the teachers who, although their subject did not appeal to him, were favourably looked upon by Hitler for their personality was the science master, Professor Theodor Gissinger, who replaced Professor Engstler. Gissinger was very fond of the open air, a hardy walker and mountaineer and enthusiastic about gymnastics. He was the most rabid of all the Nationalist teachers. The political differences of that period were also evident within the teaching body, indeed even more so than in the general public. This atmosphere charged with political tension was more important for the intellectual development of the young Hitler than anything he was taught. As is generally the case, not the subjects taught, but the atmosphere of a school determines its value.

Incidentally, Professor Gissinger too has in later years given his judgment on his former pupil, Hitler. This remarkable document reads: "As far as I was concerned, Hitler left neither a favourable nor an unfavourable impression in Linz. He was by no means a leader of the class. He was lender and erect, his face pallid and very thin, almost like that of a consumptive, his gaze unusually open, his eyes brilliant." The history teacher, Dr. Leopold Pötsch, was the third and last of those teachers who found favour in Hitler's eyes. He is the only one of almost a dozen teachers of whom Hitler, already at that time, approved. However reluctant Hitler was to talk to me of his former teachers, he made an exception of Pötsch.

The words which Hitler dedicated to his former history teacher are well known: *It was perhaps decisive for my whole life that chance gave me a history teacher who understood, as few others did, the paramount importance of this principle in teaching and examining (viz., to retain the essential and to forget the inessential). My teacher, Herr Doktor Leopold Pötsch of the Technical School in Linz, fulfilled this condition in truly ideal manner. An old gentleman, kind but at the same time firm, he was able not only to hold our attention by his brilliant eloquence but to fire us with enthusiasm. I am still touched when I think of the grey-haired man, the fire of whose words sometimes made us forget the present and, as though by magic, transported us into the past, and out of the mists of time transformed the dry historical facts into vivid reality. There we sat, wildly enthusiastic, sometimes moved to tears.*

Undoubtedly this subsequent judgment is exaggerated. This is borne out by the fact that Hitler's last school report in Linz shows only a "Fair" for history, although perhaps the change of school had something to do with it. Nevertheless this teacher's influence on the very sensitive boy should not be underestimated. If it is true to say that the greatest value of the study of history is the enthusiasm which it arouses, then Dr. Pötsch has achieved his end.

Pötsch was a native of the southern border region and before he came to Linz had taught in Marburg and other places near the German language border. He therefore had a vivid experience of the struggle among the nationalities. I believe that the absolute love for everything that was German which Pötsch combined with his aversion to the Hapsburg Monarchy was the decisive revelation for the young Hitler. This fervent devotion to the German people gave him a firm foundation for the rest of his life.

Adolf Hitler remained grateful to his old history teacher throughout his life, indeed his attachment to school and teacher grew with the passing of the years. In 1938 Hitler came to Klagenfurt and met Pötsch again. He spent more than an hour in a room alone with the frail old man, When he left the room he said to those accompanying him, "You cannot imagine how much I owe to that old man." But these subsequent opinions of Hitler's about his teachers should not falsify the real picture of his schooldays anymore than the subsequent opinions of the teachers about their former pupil — not to speak of the very contradictory opinions of his numerous classmates.

The truth is — and I am witness to it — that Adolf left school with a fundamental hatred for it. I would take care not to bring the conversation round to the subject; but he sometimes would be seized by the necessity to

Chapter 6 — School

hold forth against it violently. He never tried to keep in touch with any of the teachers, not even with Pötsch. On the contrary, he avoided them and pretended not to recognise them when he met them in the street.

His quarrel with school was going on at the same time as another conflict, which was much more important to him: his settling of accounts with his mother. This expression should not be misunderstood. Adolf tried to spare his mother as much as he could. But this became impossible when he finally failed at school and so gave up the career which his father had envisaged for him.

Adolf was much more preoccupied with this psychological conflict than with the eternal guerrilla war with the teachers. What did he care about bad reports? But to his mother they meant that Adolf would not reach his goal.

I myself witnessed how Adolf tried to spare his mother during the last school year, and yet he could not spare her because it was impossible to convince her that his future lay elsewhere. Where, he did not yet know himself; and not for many years after his mother's death. So she took this, her greatest worry, the future of her son, with her into the grave.

In those gloomy days of autumn, 1905, Adolf was on the razor's edge. Superficially, the decision the sixteen-year-old had to take was whether to repeat the fourth form in the technical school at Steyr, or leave school forever. But its meaning for him was graver: should he, for his mother's sake, continue on a path which he knew was mistaken and hopeless for him; or should he ignore the grief that he would cause his mother and choose the other way, of which he could only say that it was the path towards art, a word which, one can understand, didn't offer much comfort to his mother? But in view of his nature this was not for Adolf really a decision in the true sense of the word; for in reality there was no dilemma at all. He simply could not do otherwise and, leaving school, he embarked on the second path without looking back. But he knew how upset his mother was by this decision and this, I know, caused him immeasurable grief.

In those months Adolf passed through a grave crisis, the gravest during the years of our friendship. It manifested itself by his falling seriously ill. He describes it in his book as lung trouble. His sister Paula mentions a hemorrhage. Others again assert that it was some gastric trouble brought on by autosuggestion. I visited him almost every day during his illness, because I had to give him regular reports about Stefanie, who even at that time he worshipped. As far as I can remember, his illness was actually some lung trouble. I know that for a long time afterwards he was plagued by coughs and nasty catarrhs, especially on damp, foggy days.

Also, in his mother's eyes, he was released by this illness from continuing school. Thus, it just suited his decision. To what extent this illness was autosuggestion, to what extent it was the natural consequence of his inner crisis, to what extent it was purely constitutional, I cannot say.

When Adolf rose from his sickbed, he had made up his mind. He had definitely finished with school and without the slightest doubt or inhibition he steered his way towards the career of an artist.

The two years of his life that followed were without any visible aim. "In the hollowness of the life of leisure" is the title he gave to this phase when, in compiling *Mein Kampf*, he discovered with some uneasiness this gap in his career. Superficially this title is correct. He did not go to school, he did not bother about any practical training, he lived with his mother and let her keep him.

In reality, this chapter of his life was filled with unceasing activity. He sketched, he painted, he wrote poems and he read. I cannot remember that Adolf was ever idle or felt bored even for a single hour. If by chance he got fed up with something, as for instance a play that we saw, his boredom made him condemn the play so vehemently that, in this way, he roused himself to highest activity. To be sure, he was as yet not very systematic. There was no apparent purpose, no clear goal. He only accumulated with unbounded energy impressions, experience and material. What would ever become of it all remained an open question. He did nothing but search, he searched everywhere and always.

Meanwhile Adolf found a way of proving to his mother how useless any further schooling would have been for him. He proved it — how typical of his way of tackling problems — by convincing his mother of the futility of the whole school system. "One can learn much better by oneself," he told her. He subscribed to the library of the Adult Education. He joined the Museum Society and borrowed books from its library. He also used some lending libraries. From that moment I remember Adolf as always surrounded by books, especially by the volumes of his favourite work, with which he never parted, the German Mythology. How often did he persuade me, when I came from my work, to take with me and study this or that book which he had just read so that he could discuss it with me. Now suddenly he had all the qualities which he had lacked at school; application, interest and pleasure in learning. He had, as he said, beaten the school at its own game.

Chapter 7 — Stefanie

To tell the truth, it is not very agreeable for me to be the only witness — apart from Stefanie herself — who can tell of my friend's youthful love, which lasted four years from the beginning of his sixteenth year. I fear that by giving a picture of the actual facts, I shall disappoint those who are expecting sensational disclosures. Adolf's relations with this girl from a much respected family were confined to those permitted by the prevailing code of morals and were absolutely normal, unless today's conception of sexual morality is so upside-down that one considers it abnormal if two young people have an affair and — to put it briefly — "nothing happens." I must ask to be excused from mentioning this girl's surname as well as her later married name.

Occasionally I have revealed it to persons engaged in research on Hitler's youth, who had satisfied me as to their good faith. Stefanie, who was one, or perhaps, two years older than Adolf, later married a high-ranking officer and now lives, a widow, in Vienna. The reader will therefore understand my discretion.

One evening in the spring of 1905, as we were taking our usual stroll, Adolf gripped my arm and asked me excitedly what I thought of that slim blonde girl walking along the Landstrasse arm-in-arm with her mother. "You must know, I'm in love with her," he added resolutely.

Stefanie was a distinguished-looking girl, tall and slim. She had thick fair hair, which she mostly wore swept back in a bun. Her eyes were very beautiful — bright and expressive. . She was exceptionally well dressed and even her bearing indicated that she came from a good, well-to-do family.

The photograph by Hans Zivny, taken in Urfahr, on her leaving school was somewhat earlier than this meeting and Stefanie could only have been then seventeen, or, at the most, eighteen years old. It shows a young girl with pretty, regular features. The expression of the face is completely natural and open. The abundant hair, still worn in the Gretel fashion, serves to strengthen this impression. A freshness and lack of affectation show in the girl's healthy countenance.

The evening stroll along the Landstrasse was, in those years, a favourite habit with the Linzers.

The ladies looked at the shopwindows and made little purchases. Friends met — and the younger generation amused themselves in innocent ways. There was a lot of flirting and the young army officers were particularly good at it. It seemed to us that Stefanie must live in Urfahr, for she always came from the bridge up the main square, and strolled down the Landstrasse arm-in-arm with her mother. At five o'clock, almost precisely, mother and daughter appeared — we stood waiting at the Schmiedtoreck. It would have been improper to salute Stefanie, as neither of us had been introduced to the young lady. A glance had to take the place of a greeting. From then on, Adolf did not take his eyes off Stefanie. In that moment he was changed, no longer his own self.

I found out that Stefanie's mother was a widow and did, indeed, live in Urfahr, and that a young man who occasionally accompanied them, to Adolf's great irritation, was her brother, a law student in Vienna. This information eased Adolf's mind considerably. But from time to time the, two ladies were to be seen in the company of young officers. Poor, pallid youngsters like Adolf naturally could not hope to compete with these young lieutenants in their smart uniforms. Adolf felt this intensely and gave vent to his feelings with eloquence. His anger, in the end, led him into uncompromising enmity towards the officer class as a whole, and everything military in general.

"Conceited blockheads," he used to call them. It annoyed him immensely that Stefanie mixed with such idlers who, he insisted, wore corsets and used scent.

To be sure, Stefanie had no idea how deeply Adolf was in love with her; she regarded him as a somewhat shy but, nevertheless, remarkably tenacious and faithful admirer, When she responded with a smile to his inquiring glance, he was happy, and his mood became unlike anything I had ever observed in him; everything in the world was good and beautiful and well ordered, and he was content. When Stefanie, as happened just as often, coldly ignored his gaze, he was crushed and ready to destroy himself and the whole world.

Certainly such phenomena are typical of every first great love, and one might perhaps be tempted to dismiss Adolf's feelings for Stefanie as calf love. This may have been true as far as Stefanie's own conception of them was concerned, but for Adolf himself, his relation to Stefanie was more than calf love. The mere fact that it lasted more than four years, and even cast its splendour over the subsequent years of misery in Vienna, shows that Adolf's feelings were deep and true, and real love. Proof of the depth of his feelings is that for Adolf, throughout these years, no other woman but Stefanie existed — how unlike the usual boy's love, which is always changing its object. I cannot remember that Adolf ever gave any thought to another girl. Later, in Vienna, when Lucie Weidt roused his enthusiasm

Chapter 7 — *Stefanie*

in the part of Elsa in *Lohengrin*, the highest praise he could give her was that she reminded him of Stefanie. In appearance, Stefanie was ideally suited for the part of Elsa, and other female roles of Wagner's operas, and we spent much time wondering whether she had the necessary voice and musical talent. Adolf was inclined to take it for granted.

Just her Valkyrie-like appearance never failed to attract him and to fire him with unbounded enthusiasm. He wrote countless love poems to Stefanie. "Hymn to the Beloved" was the title of one of them, which he read to me from his little black notebook. Stefanie, a high-born damsel, in a dark blue, flowing velvet gown, rode on a white steed over the flowering meadows, her loose hair fell in golden waves on her shoulders. A clear spring sky was above. Everything was pure, radiant joy. I can still see Adolf's face glowing with fervent ecstasy and hear his voice reciting these verses. Stefanie filled his thoughts so completely that everything he said, or did, or planned for the future, was centred around her. With his growing estrangement from his home, Stefanie gained more and more influence over my friend, although he never spoke a word to her.

My ideas about these things were much more prosaic, and I remember very well our repeated arguments on the subject — and my recollections of Adolf's relationship to Stefanie are particularly distinct. He used to insist that, once he met Stefanie, everything would become clear without as much as a word being exchanged. For such exceptional human beings as himself and Stefanie, he said, there was no need for the usual communication by word of mouth; extraordinary human beings would understand each other by intuition. Whatever the subject we might discuss at any time, Adolf was always sure that Stefanie not only knew his ideas exactly, but that she shared them enthusiastically. If I dared to comment that he hadn't spoken to Stefanie about them, and to express my doubts as to whether she was at all interested in such things, he became furious and shouted at me: "You simply don't understand, because you can't understand the true meaning of extraordinary love."

In order to quiet him down, I asked him if he could transmit to Stefanie the knowledge of such complicated problems simply by gazing at her. He only replied, "It's possible! These things cannot be explained. What is in me, is in Stefanie too." Of course, I took great care not to push these delicate matters too far. But I was pleased that Adolf trusted me so much, for to nobody else, not even to his mother, had he talked about Stefanie.

He expected Stefanie to reciprocate his love for her to the exclusion of all others. For a long time he put up with the interest she took in other young men, especially the officers, because he regarded it as a sort of deliberate diversion to conceal her own tempestuous feelings for him. But this attitude often gave way to fits of raging jealousy; then Adolf would be desperate when Stefanie ignored the pale youth who was waiting for her, and concentrated her attention instead on the young lieutenant escorting her.

Why, indeed, should a lively young girl have been satisfied with the anxious glances of a secret admirer, while others expressed their admiration so much more gracefully? But I, of course, would never have dared to express such a thought in Adolf's presence.

One day he asked me, "What shall I do?" Never before had he asked for my advice and I was extremely proud that he did; at last, for a change, I could feel superior to him. "It's quite simple," I explained. "You approach the two ladies and, raising your hat, introduce yourself to the mother by giving your name, and ask her permission to address the daughter and to escort them." Adolf looked at me doubtfully and pondered my suggestion for quite a while.

In the end, however, be rejected it. "What am I to say if the mother wants to know my profession? After all, I have to mention my profession straightway; it would be best to add it to my name — 'Adolf Hitler, academic painter,' or something similar. But I am not yet an academic painter, and I can't introduce myself till I am. For the mama, the profession is even more important than the name." I thought for a long time that Adolf was simply too shy to approach Stefanie. And yet it was not shyness that held him back. His conception of the relationship between the sexes was already then so high that the usual way of making the acquaintance of a girl seemed to him undignified.

As he was opposed to flirting in any form, he was convinced that Stefanie had no other desire but to wait until he should come to ask her to marry him. I did not share this conviction at all; but Adolf, as was his habit with all problems that agitated him, had already made an elaborate plan.

And this girl, who was a stranger to him and had never exchanged a word with him, succeeded where his father, the school and even his mother had failed: he drew up an exact program for his future which would enable him, after four years, to ask for Stefanie's hand. We discussed this difficult problem for hours, with the result that Adolf commissioned me to collect further information about Stefanie.

In the Music Society there was a cellist whom I had occasionally seen talking to Stefanie's brother. Through him I learned that Stefanie's father, a higher government official, had died some years earlier. The mother had a comfortable home and was in receipt of a widow's pension,

Chapter 7 — *Stefanie*

which she used to give her two children the best possible education. Stefanie had attended the Girl's High School and had already matriculated. She had a great number of admirers — small wonder, beautiful as she was. She was fond of dancing and, the previous winter, had gone with her mother to all the important dances of the town. As far as he knew, the cellist added, she was not engaged.

Adolf was highly satisfied with the result of my investigations — that she was not engaged he had, anyhow, taken for granted. There was only one point in my report that disturbed him greatly: Stefanie danced, and, according to the cellist's assurance, she danced well, and enjoyed it.

This did not fit at all into Adolf's own image of Stefanie. A Valkyrie who waltzed round the ballroom in the arms of some "blockhead" of a lieutenant, was for him too terrible to be contemplated.

What was the origin of this strange, almost ascetic trait in him which made him reject all the pleasures of youth? Adolf's father, after all, had been a man who enjoyed life and who, as a good-looking custom's official, had certainly turned many a girl's head. Why was Adolf so different? After all, he was a most presentable young man, well built, slender, and his somewhat severe and exaggeratedly serious features were enlivened by his extraordinary eyes, whose peculiar brilliance made one forget the sickly pallor of his face. And yet — dancing was as contrary to his nature as smoking or drinking beer at a pub. These things simply did not exist for him, although nobody, not even his mother, encouraged him in this attitude.

After having been his butt for so long, at last I had a chance of pulling his leg. I proclaimed, with a straight face, "You must take dancing lessons, Adolf." Dancing immediately became one of his problems. I well remember that our lonely perambulations were no longer punctuated by discussions on "The Theatre" or "Reconstruction of the Danube Bridge," but were dominated by one subject — dancing.

As with everything that he couldn't tackle at once, he indulged in generalisations. "Visualise a crowded ballroom," he said once to me, "and imagine that you were deaf. You can't hear the music to which these people are moving, and then take a look at their senseless progress, which leads nowhere. Aren't these people raving mad?" "All this is no good, Adolf," I replied, "Stefanie is fond of dancing. If you want to conquer her, you will have to dance around just as aimlessly and idiotically as the others." That was all that was needed to set him off raving. "No, no, never!" he screamed at me. "I shall never dance! Do you understand! Stefanie only dances because she is forced to by society on which she unfortunately depends. Once she is my wife, she won't have the slightest desire to dance!" Contrary to the rule, this time his own words did not convince him; for he brought up the question of dancing again and again. I rather suspected that, secretly at home, he practised a few cautious steps with his little sister. Frau Hitler had bought a piano for Adolf. Perhaps, I thought, I might soon be asked to play a waltz on it, and then I would chaff Adolf about being deaf while he danced. He did not need music for his movements. I also intended to point out to him the harmony between music and bodily movements, of which he did not seem to have any conception.

But it never got as far as this. Adolf went on brooding for days and weeks trying to find a solution.

In his depressed mood, he hit on a crazy idea: he seriously contemplated kidnaping Stefanie. He expounded his plan to me in all its details and assigned me my role, which was not a very rewarding one; for I had to keep the mother engaged in conversation, while he seized the girl.

"And what are you both going to live on?" I asked prosaically. My question sobered him up a little and the audacious plan was abandoned.

To make matters worse, Stefanie was at that time in an unfriendly mood. She would pass the Schmiedtoreck with her face averted, as though Adolf didn't exist at all. This brought him to the verge of despair. "I can't stand it any longer!" he exclaimed. "I will make an end of it!" It was the first and, as far as I know, the last time that Adolf contemplated suicide seriously. He would jump into the river from the Danube bridge, he told me, and then it would be over and done with. But Stefanie would have to die with him — he insisted on that. Once more a plan was thought up, in all its details. Every single phase of the horrifying tragedy was minutely described, including the part I would have to play; even my conduct as the sole survivor was ordained. This sombre scene was with me, even in my dreams.

Soon the sky was blue again and for Adolf came that happiest of days in June 1906 which I am sure remained in his memory as clearly as it did in mine. Summer was approaching and a flower festival was held in Linz. As usual, Adolf waited for me outside the Carmelite Church, where I used to go every Sunday with my parents; then we took up our stand at the Schmiedtoreck. The position was extremely favourable, as the street there is narrow and the carriages in the parade had to pass quite close to the pavement. The regimental band led the string of flower-decked carriages, from which young girls and ladies waved to the spectators. But Adolf had no eye nor ears for any of this; he waited feverishly for Stefanie to appear.

I was already giving up hope of seeing her when Adolf gripped my arm so violently that it hurt. Seated in a handsome carriage, decorated with flowers, mother and daughter turned into the Schmiedtorstrasse. I still have

Chapter 7 — Stefanie

the picture clearly in my mind. The mother, in a light grey silk dress, holds a red sunshade over her head, through which the rays of the sun seemed to cast, as though by magic, a rosy glow over the countenance of Stefanie, wearing a pretty silk frock. Stefanie has adorned her carriage, not with roses as most of the others, but with simple, wild blossoms — red poppies, white marguerites and blue cornflowers. Stefanie holds a bunch of the same flowers in her hand. The carriage approaches Adolf is floating on air. Never before has he seen Stefanie so enchanting. Now the carriage is quite close to us. A bright glance falls on Adolf. Stefanie sends him a beaming smile and, picking a flower from her bouquet, throws it to him.

Never again did I see Adolf as happy as he was at that moment. When the carriage had passed he dragged me aside and with emotion he gazed at the flower, this visible pledge of her love. I can still hear his voice, trembling with excitement, "She loves me! You have seen! She loves me!" During the following months, when his decision to leave school had caused a conflict with his mother, and he was ill, his love for Stefanie was his only comfort and he always kept her flower in his locket. Adolf was never in greater need of my friendship; for as I was the only person who shared his secret, it was only through me that he could get news about her. I had to go every day to the usual spot at the Schmiedtoreck and to report to him all my observations and tell him, in particular, who had spoken to mother and daughter. That I stood alone at the familiar corner, Adolf felt, would naturally upset Stefanie immeasurably. It did not, but I kept it from him.

Fortunately, it had never occurred to Adolf that I might fall in love with Stefanie, for his slightest suspicion in this respect would have meant the end of our friendship; and as there was no real reason for it, I was able to give my reports to my poor friend wholly disinterestedly.

Adolf's mother had been aware for a long time of the change in her son. One evening — I remember it well because it embarrassed me considerably — she asked me straight out: "What's the matter with Adolf? He's so impatient to see you." I muttered some excuse and hurried into Adolf's room. He was happy when I brought him some new facts concerning Stefanie. "She has a good soprano voice," I told him one day. He jumped up. "How do you know that?" "I followed her very closely for some time and I heard her speak. I know enough music to be able to tell that somebody with such a clear and pure voice must be a good soprano." How happy this made Adolf. And I was pleased that he, languishing in his bed, had a moment of happiness.

Every evening I had to get back to the Humboldtstrasse from the evening stroll by the quickest route. I would often find Adolf sketching a big blueprint. "Now I have made up my mind," he said, in dead earnest, after having heard my report, "I have decided to build the house for Stefanie in Renaissance style." And then I had to give my opinion, especially as to whether I was satisfied with the shape and size of the music room. He had paid special attention to the acoustics of the room, he said, and asked me to say where the piano should go, and so on, and so on. All this in a manner as though there were not the slightest doubt that the plans would be carried out. A timid inquiry about the money brought forth the rude reply, "Oh, to hell with the money!" — an expression which he frequently employed.

We had some arguments as to where this villa would be built; as a musician I was all for Italy.

Adolf insisted that it could only be built in Germany, in the neighbourhood of a big city so that he and Stefanie could go to the opera and concerts.

As soon as he could leave his bed he went down and took up his position at the Schmiedtoreck; he was still very pale and ill. Punctually as usual, Stefanie and her mother appeared. Seeing Adolf, pale-faced and hollow-eyed, she smiled at him. "Did you notice?" he asked me happily.

From that moment on, his health improved rapidly.

In spring 1906, when Adolf left for Vienna, he gave me detailed instructions how I should behave vis-à-vis Stefanie; for he was convinced that she would soon ask me whether my friend, was ill again, as I was there alone. Then I was to answer as follows: "My friend is not ill, but he had to go to Vienna to take up his studies at the Academy of Art. When his studies are finished he will spend a year travelling, abroad, of course." (I insisted on being allowed to say "in Italy." Very well, then, Italy.) "In four years' time he will return and ask for your hand in marriage. In case of an affirmative answer, the preparations for the wedding would be put in hand forthwith."

While Adolf was in Vienna, I naturally had to send him regular written reports about Stefanie. As it was cheaper to send postcards than letters, Adolf gave me a code word for Stefanie before he left. It was Benkieser, the name of a former classmate. A picture postcard which he sent me on May 8 from Vienna shows how much this "Benkieser" was still on his mind in spite of his many new and varied impressions in Vienna.

"I am longing to return to my beloved Linz and Urfahr," it reads. The word Urfahr is underlined, alluding, of course, to Stefanie, who lived there. "I have to see Benkieser again. I wonder what he's doing." A few weeks later Adolf returned from Vienna and I met him at the station. I still remember how we took turns carrying his bag and he urged me to tell him all about Stefanie, at once. We were in a hurry because the evening stroll

Chapter 7 — Stefanie

would begin in an hour's time. Adolf would not believe that Stefanie had not asked after him, for he took it for granted that she was longing for him just as much as he was for her. But at heart he was glad that I had not had the opportunity to tell Stefanie about his grandiose plans for the future, as his prospects at the moment were not very bright. We hardly stopped in the Humboldtstrasse to greet his mother before we hurried off to the Schmiedtoreck. Full of excitement, Adolf waited. Punctually Stefanie and her mother appeared.

She threw him a surprised glance. That was sufficient — he did not want more. But I became impatient. "You can see that she wants you to talk to her," I said to my friend. "Tomorrow," he answered.

But the morrow never came, and weeks, months and years passed without his taking any steps to change this state of affairs which caused him so much unrest. It was natural that Stefanie did nothing beyond that first phase of exchanging glances. The most Adolf could have expected of her was the flower thrown at him with a roguish smile in the carefree atmosphere of the Flower Festival. Besides, any move of hers beyond the rigid limits of convention would have destroyed the picture of her which Adolf kept in his heart.

Perhaps even his strange timidity was prompted by the fear that any closer acquaintance might destroy this ideal. For to him Stefanie was not only the incarnation of all womanly virtues, but also the woman who took the greatest interest in all his wide and varied plans. There was no other person, apart from himself, whom he credited with so much knowledge and so many interests. The slightest divergence from this picture would have filled him with unspeakable disappointment. Of course, I am convinced the first words he exchanged with Stefanie would have caused that very disappointment, because she was fundamentally a young, happy girl, like thousands of others, and certainly had the same kind of interests. Adolf would have sought in vain for those grandiose thoughts and ideas with which he had surrounded her to such an extent as to make her the female image of himself. Only the most rigid separation could preserve his idol.

It is most revealing that the young Hitler, who so thoroughly despised bourgeois society, nevertheless, as far as his love affair was concerned, observed its codes and etiquette more strictly than many a member of the bourgeoisie itself. The rules of bourgeois conduct and etiquette became for him the barricade behind which he built up his relationship to Stefanie. "I have not been introduced to her."

How often have I heard him say these words, although ordinarily he would make light of such obstacles. This strict observance of social customs was part of his whole nature. It was apparent in his neat dress and in his correct behaviour as much as in his natural courtesy, which my mother liked so much about him. I never heard him use an ambiguous expression or tell a doubtful story.

So, in spite of all apparent contradictions, this strange love of Hitler for Stefanie falls into the pattern of his character. Love was a field where the unforeseeable might happen, and which might become dangerous. How many men who had set out with great intentions had been forced off their path by irregular and complicated love affairs. It was imperative to be on one's guard! Instinctively, the young Hitler found the only correct attitude in his love for Stefanie: he possessed a being whom he loved, and at the same time, he did not possess her. He arranged his whole life as though he possessed this beloved creature entirely. But as he himself avoided any personal meeting, this girl, although he could see that she walked the earth, remained nevertheless a creature of his dream world, towards whom he could project his desires, plans and ideas.

And thus he kept himself from deviating from his own path; indeed, this strange relationship, through the power of love, increased his own will. He imagines Stefanie as his wife, builds the house in which they live together, surrounds it with a magnificent garden and arranges his home with Stefanie, just as, in fact, he did later on the Ober-Salzburg, though without her. This mixing of dream and reality is characteristic of the young Hitler. And whenever there is a danger that the beloved would entirely escape into the realm of fantasy, he hurries to the Schmiedtoreck and makes sure that she really walks the earth. Hitler was confirmed in the choice of his path, not by what Stefanie actually was, but by what his imagination made of her. Thus, Stefanie was two things for him, one part reality and one part wish and imagination. Be that as it may, Stefanie was the most beautiful, the most fertile and purest dream of his life.

Chapter 8 — The Young Nationalist

As I begin to describe the young Hitler's political beliefs and ideas, I seem to hear his voice again, saying, "You don't understand it," or, "These are matters I can't discuss with you"; sometimes he was even more scathing, as for instance when listening to some of his political observations, I would nod assent, instead of expressing disgust, as he had expected: "In politics, Gustl, you are nothing but a fool." After all, I had only one interest in life: music. To begin with, Adolf agreed with me about the supremacy of art. But during the years we spent together, his interest in politics gradually became paramount, although he never lost sight of his artistic aspirations. One could put it this way: the years in Linz were dominated by art, the following years in Vienna, by politics. I was fully aware that it was only in artistic matters I counted for him. And the more he became interested in politics, the less our friendship mattered. Not that he showed it to me; for one thing he took our friendship too seriously and, for another, perhaps he didn't even realise it himself.

Politics had always been the critical point in our relationship. Having no political ideas of my own, or where I did have, not feeling strongly enough about them to defend them or to impose them on others, I was an unsatisfactory partner for Adolf in our discussions. He would rather have converted me than convinced me. But in fact, I accepted everything he said readily and uncritically, and even retained something so that I could occasionally throw in a clever remark, But to contradict, as he would have liked, I was not capable. I just was not fertile soil for politics. I was like a deaf-mute in front of an orchestra, who sees that the musicians are playing, but hears nothing. I had simply no political sense.

This reduced Adolf to despair. It seemed inconceivable to him that there should be on earth a specimen so absolutely innocent of politics. He tried all means to prove to me that this was impossible. And he was none too gentle with me. In Vienna he compelled me repeatedly to go with him to Parliament, although I did not like it at all and would have preferred to spend the time at the piano. But Adolf did not yield. I had to go with him, although he knew very well that I was always terribly bored by this Parliament business. But Heaven help me if I had said so.

It is generally believed that politicians come from politically conscious circles. This was certainly not so in the case of my friend. On the contrary! Here again is one of Hitler's innumerable contradictions. The father was rather fond of talking politics and never hid his liberal opinions. But he would not hear a word against the Monarchy: this old, faithful civil servant would never go as far as that. When on the Emperor's birthday on the eighteenth of August, he put on his gala uniform, he was a loyal servant of his Imperial and Royal Majesty. Probably Adolf, when little, never beard much talk of politics from his father, for politics, the father believed, was not a matter to be discussed in the family circle, but in the pub. And I cannot remember that Adolf had ever quoted his father for any one of his political opinions.

Still less was there any sign of it in the quiet home in the Humboldtstrasse. Adolf's mother was a simple, devout woman, far removed from politics. When the father was still alive she might have heard him grumble occasionally about the political situation, but it had not sunk in and certainly she had not passed it on to the children. After his death, they never had visitors who might have introduced politics and I cannot remember ever hearing any political discussion in Frau Hitler's house. Even when some political event was agitating the whole town, nothing of it would penetrate into this quiet household, for even Adolf would not mention such things at home. Their life flowed quietly on. The only change I ever saw in the family was that Frau Klara towards the end of 1906 moved from the Humboldtstrasse to Urfahr. This was by no means an after-effect of the father's restlessness, it was rather the result of purely practical considerations.

In those days Urfahr, which is now a part of Linz, was still a separate parish of mainly rural character, a favourite residence for retired people. As no excise duties were levied there, many things, for instance meat, were cheaper than in town. Frau Klara hoped to be able to manage better with her modest pension of 140 crowns (90 for herself and 25 each for Adolf and Paula). And she was glad to be living among meadows and fields again. The quiet house at No. 9 Blütengasse still stands as it was, and sometimes when I pass by, I think I can see Frau Klara standing on the little balcony. For Adolf it was a special source of satisfaction to live "on the same bank" as Stefanie.

Our nightly journey home was made longer because of the move to Urfahr. But this suited us well, for the problems which we tackled had become more profound and numerous. The way across the bridge was sometimes too short for us, so that if we were particularly concerned with a problem we had to walk to and fro across the Danube until our subject was exhausted. To be exact, Adolf needed the time for talking, and I for listening In studying the political career of such an extraordinary man as Adolf Hitler, one has to distinguish between external influences and the man's own predispositions, for I believe that the latter are much more important than the external events. After all, many other young people had the same teachers as Adolf, experienced the same political incidents, rejoicing or getting angry over them, and yet these very same people have become worthy businessmen, technicians or manufacturers and never rose to political significance.

The spirit of nationalism dominated the Linz Technical School. The class was secretly opposed to all traditional institutions, such as patriotic plays, dynastic manifestations and festivals, to Divine Service in school and to Corpus Christi processions. Adolf Hitler describes in his book this atmosphere which to him was more important than the lessons.

Money was collected for Sudmark and Schulverein, one's sentiments were manifested by wearing cornflowers and black-red-gold colours, we used "Heil" as a greeting and sang "Deutschland über Alles" instead of the Hapsburg Imperial Hymn. All this in spite of warnings and punishment.

The struggle for existence of the German population in the Austro-Hungarian Monarchy agitated the younger generation in those days; understandably, for Austria's German population stood alone in the midst of the Slav, Magyar and Italian nations of Austria-Hungary. Linz, to be sure, was remote from the racial border and was entirely German. But there was always trouble in neighbouring Bohemia. In Prague one street demonstration after another took place. Even in Linz much indignation was caused by the fact that the Imperial and Royal police were not capable of protecting German houses from the Czech mob, so that it was necessary to proclaim a state of siege in Prague in peacetime. Budweis was then still a German town with German administration and a German majority in the Town Council.

Those of Adolf's classmates who came from Prague, Budweis or Prachatitz used to weep with rage when they were jokingly called "Bohemians"; for they wanted to be solely German, like the others. Soon there was even unrest in Linz. A few hundred Czechs lived there, as quiet and modest workmen and artisans, without anybody taking much notice of them. Now a Capucine Monk, a Czech named Jurasek, founded a Sokol Club, preached in St. Martin's Church in Czech, and collected money for the building of a Czech school. This caused a great sensation in the town and some worthy Nationalists already saw in the action of the fanatic monk the preparation of a Czech invasion. Of course that was exaggerated. Nevertheless, just this Czech activity made the indolent Linzers feel that they were threatened, with the result that, almost unanimously, they joined in the Nationalist struggle.

Those teachers of the Technical School, who were nationalists, led the struggle. Dr. Leopold Pötsch, the history teacher, was an active politician. As a member of the Town Council he was one of the leading lights of the Nationalist Party. He hated the Hapsburg multi-racial state (which today — what a change — seems to us to be the very model of a supranational community) and all the enthusiastic young Nationalists took up his watchword.

"Who could remain loyal to a dynasty which again and again vilely betrayed, past and present, the interests of the German people for their own advantage?" Thus Hitler definitely and irrevocably had abandoned his father's ways in favour of a pan-German program. When Adolf, raging on, let himself go on this train of thought, I could hardly keep up with what he was saying, let alone take an active part in the discussion. Yet one word, which regularly cropped up in his discourse, always struck me: the "Reich."

With this word he used to wind up his long outpourings. Whenever he had talked himself into a blind alley and was at a loss how to continue, he would say categorically: "This problem will be solved by the Reich"; if I asked, for instance, who would finance all these gigantic building projects which he sketched on his drawing board, his brief answer was, "The Reich." Even trivialities were left to the care of the "Reich." There was a "Reich's Stage Designer," who would improve the unsatisfactory equipment of provincial theatres. (It is well known that, after 1933, there really was a man who filled that post. I remember that Adolf Hitler coined that term as far back as his Linz days, when he was sixteen or seventeen.) Even the care of the blind, or the protection of animals belonged, in his opinion, to the jurisdiction of the "Reich"! The word "Reich" is used in Austria for the territory of Germany; its inhabitants are called Reich's Germans. But my friend's use of the term, meant more than merely the German State, though he carefully avoided any more exact definition. For to him the word was simply a portmanteau expression, which comprised everything that was politically important for him-and that was a lot.

With the same fanaticism with which he loved the German people, and this "Reich," did he reject everything foreign. He had no desire to know other countries. That longing for distant lands so typical of all open-minded young people was utterly alien to him — even the artist's classical enthusiasm for Italy. There was only one place for his plans and ideas — the Reich.

His violent nationalism, which was unequivocally directed against the Hapsburg Monarchy, showed all the particular predispositions of his character, especially the iron consistency with which he stuck to everything he had once accepted as correct. The Nationalist ideology became his

Chapter 8 — The Young Nationalist

political creed and formed an unalterable element of his nature. No failure or setback would change him. He remained till his death what he had been at sixteen — a Nationalist.

With this end firmly fixed before his eyes, he observed and studied the existing political conditions. Nothing was too unimportant; he gave his attention to even the most trivial things. He took a stand in regard to everything-the less it concerned him, the more heatedly. He made up for the utter insignificance of his own existence by taking an interest in all public affairs, thus giving aim and direction to his urge to change things. With all his all-embracing interests, he had so much against him, and he saw everywhere only obstacles and hostility. And yet, nobody had ever heard of him. Sometimes I was even sorry for him. With his undoubted gifts, what a happy life he could have led; and how difficult he made things for himself! He was always up against something and at odds with the world. Just that healthy, carefree spirit which distinguishes most young people was utterly alien to him. I never saw him take anything lightly; everything had to be thoroughly studied and tested for how it would fit into his great political design. Tradition, in the political sense, meant nothing to him. To sum up — the world had to be radically changed in all its aspects.

Yet it would be wrong to conclude that the young Hitler threw himself heart and soul into the political struggle of the day. A pale, sickly, lanky youth, quite unknown and inexperienced in the ways of the city, shy and reticent rather than pushing, he carried on this intense activity all on his own. Only the most important ideas and solutions, that needed an audience, would he propound in the evening to me, an equally insignificant and lonely figure. The young Hitler's relationship to politics is similar to his attitude to love — if I may be permitted this rather indelicate comparison.

The more intensely he was intellectually occupied with politics, the more did he refrain from taking part in practical, political activity. He did not join any party or organization, did not take part in party manifestations, and took care not to spread his own ideas outside of our friendship. What I noticed then in him in Linz — to stick to my metaphor — may be described as a first ogling with politics, nothing more, as though he had had a presentiment of what politics would come to mean to him.

For the time being, politics remained for him only an exercise in the realm of ideas. This striking reticence shows a trait in his character that seems to contradict his impatience — his ability to wait. Politics remained for him for some years a matter of watching, of criticising social conditions, of study, gathering experience; it remained a matter private to himself, and consequently without any importance for the public life of that day.

It is interesting to note that the young Hitler in those years was strongly opposed to everything military. This seems to be contradicted by a passage in *Mein Kampf*.

While going through my father's library, I came across several books on military subjects, among them a popular edition of the history of the Franco-German War. 1870 1871; two volumes of an illustrated magazine of those years now became my favourite reading, and before long this heroic struggle had become my greatest intellectual experience. From now on, I grew increasingly enthusiastic for everything that had anything to do with war or soldiers.

I suspect that this recollection owes its existence to the circumstances of his imprisonment in Landsberg, where his book was written; for when I knew Adolf Hitler, he was utterly averse to "anything to do with war or soldiers." Of course he was annoyed by the young lieutenants who fluttered around Stefanie. But his aversion was deeper. Even the idea of compulsory military service could infuriate him. No, he would never let himself be forced into being a soldier. If he ever became a soldier he would do it of his own free will, and certainly never in the Austrian army.

Before concluding this chapter on Adolf Hitler's political development, I would like to deal with two questions, which seem to me to be more important than anything else there is to say about politics: the young Hitler's attitude to Jewry and to the church. Adolf Hitler himself writes about his attitude to the Jewish problem during the years in Linz: *It is difficult, if not impossible, for me today to say when the word "Jew" first gave me food for thought. At home, in my father's lifetime, I cannot remember ever having heard the word. I believe that the old gentleman would have thought it a cultural retrogression to give this word any special emphasis. In the course of his life he had acquired some more or less cosmopolitan ideas, which not only coexisted with his strong nationalism, but influenced me too. And at school nothing led me to change this inherited conception.*

It is true that at the Technical School I met a Jewish boy, whom we all handled with care, but only because owing to various experiences, we couldn't rely on him not to give us away. But we didn't give the matter any thought.

Not before I was fourteen or fifteen years old did I occasionally hear the word "Jew," partly in the course of political conversations. I felt a slight resentment against it and the usual unpleasant feeling that overcame me when people quibbled about religious matters in my presence.

That was all I knew about it. There were not many Jews in Linz....

All this sounds very plausible, but it doesn't correspond to my impressions.

To begin with, it seems to me that the character sketch of his father had been touched up to emphasise his liberal ideas. The circle in which

Chapter 8 — The Young Nationalist

he moved in Linz already subscribed to the ideas of Schönerer, and it can therefore be presumed that his father was also against Jews.

In describing the school years, Hitler omits to mention that some of the teachers of the Technical School were openly anti-Semitic and made no bones about acknowledging their hatred of the Jews in front of their pupils; and Hitler, at the Technical School, must certainly have been aware of the political aspects of the Jewish problem. It cannot have been otherwise, for when I met Adolf Hitler first, his anti-Semitism was already pronounced. I remember distinctly that once when we were going along the Bethlehemstrasse and passed the little synagogue, he said to me, "This shouldn't be here." As far as I know, Adolf Hitler was already a confirmed anti-Semite when he went to Vienna. And although his experiences in Vienna might have deepened this feeling, they certainly did not give birth to it.

In my opinion, Adolf Hitler's own version seeks to convey the following: In Linz, where the number of Jews was negligible, the question did not concern me. It was only in Vienna, where the Jews were more numerous, that I was forced to face this problem.

His attitude to the church is a somewhat different matter. *Mein Kampf* hardly mentions it at all, except for a description of his childhood experiences in Lambach.

As I had singing lessons at the Monastery in Lambach in my spare time, I had an excellent opportunity of revelling, again and again, in the festive splendour of the magnificent church ceremonies. Nothing was more natural than that I should see a most desirable ideal in the Abbot, as once my father had done in the little parish priest. This was so, at any rate, for some time.

Hitler's forebears were certainly religious, churchgoing people, as is natural with peasant folk. But Hitler's own parents were divided in this respect; his mother was pious and devout, his father liberal, a lukewarm Christian. It is certain that the question of the church interested his father more than the Jewish problem. As a servant of the state, in view of the close connection between state and church, he could not afford to be openly anti-clerical.

As long as the little Adolf remained close to his mother, he was completely influenced by her devout behaviour and receptive to all the grandeur and beauty of the church. The pale little choir boy was absorbed by his faith. Though Hitler devotes only a few words to the subject, what he does say means a lot. The magnificent monastery had become familiar to him. In his childish susceptibility he was attracted by the church and his mother certainly encouraged him. As he grew away from his childhood experience, with the passing of the years, and became closer to his father, the latter's liberalism gained in influence. The school in Linz also helped. Franz Sales Schwarz, who taught religion at the Technical School, was not the man to have any effect on these young people, for the pupils did not take him seriously.

My own recollections can be summed up in a few sentences: as long as I knew Adolf Hitler I never remember his going to church. He knew that I used to go every Sunday with my parents, and accepted this fact. He never tried to persuade me not to go, though he said occasionally that he couldn't understand me — his mother was also a religious woman, but nevertheless he would not let her drag him to church. Moreover he made these comments only by the way, with a certain tolerance and patience, which was not usual with him. But in this case, apparently, he was not even interested in imposing his own idea. I cannot remember that, when he used to meet me at the close of the Sunday service, he ever made any derogatory remarks about this Sunday churchgoing, or behaved improperly. To my astonishment, he never made this an occasion for an argument.

Yet one day he came to me full of excitement and showed me a book about witch trials, and another time about the Inquisition. But however worked up he got about the events described in these books, he never drew any political conclusions from them. Perhaps this was a case in which he did not consider me the right audience.

Every Sunday his mother went, with little Paula, to Mass. I can't remember that Adolf ever accompanied her, or that Frau Klara would have asked him to. Devout as she was herself, she was resigned to the fact that her son was different. It may be that in this case she was held back by the different attitudes of the father, whose precept and example was still her model for her son.

In conclusion, I would describe Hitler's attitude towards the church at that time as follows: he was by no means indifferent to the church, but the church could give him nothing.

To sum up, it can be said: Adolf Hitler became a Nationalist. I have seen with what absolute dedication, even as early as that, he gave himself to the people whom he loved. Only in this people could he live. He knew nothing other than this people.

Chapter 9 — Adolf Rebuilds Linz

While I was undecided whether to list my friend among the great musicians or the great poets of the future, he sprang on me the announcement that he intended to become a painter. I immediately remembered that I had seen him sketching, both at home and on our excursions. As our friendship progressed, I saw many samples of his work. In my job as an upholsterer, I had occasionally to do some sketches, which I always found difficult, so the more was I astonished by my friend's facility.

He habitually carried with him various types of paper. The start had always been the worst part for me; for him it was the other way round. He would take his pencil, and throwing a few bold strokes on the paper, would express his meaning. Where words failed him, the pencil would do the job. There was something attractive about these first rough lines — it thrilled me to see a recognisable design gradually emerge from their confusion. However, he wasn't so keen on finishing the rough draft.

The first time I went to visit him at home, his room was littered with sketches, drawings, blueprints. Here was "The New Theatre," there the Mountain Hotel on the Lichtenberg. It was like an architect's office. Watching him at work at the drawing board — he was more careful then and more precise in details than he used to be in moments of happy improvisation — I was convinced that he must long since have acquired all the technical and specialised skill necessary for his work. I simply could not believe that it was possible to set down such difficult things on the spur of the moment, and that everything I saw was improvised.

The number of these works is sufficient to allow one to form a judgment of Adolf Hitler's talents.

There is, in the first place, a water colour — rather, water colour is not the right term, as it is a simple pencil drawing coloured with tempera. But just the rapid catching of an atmosphere, of a certain mood, which is so typical of a water colour and which, with its delicate touch, imparts to it freshness and liveliness — this was missing completely in Adolf's work. Just here, where he might have worked with fast, intuitive strokes, he has daubed with painstaking precision.

All I can say about Adolf's artistic activity refers to his first attempts, and the only water colour of his I possess is one of these. It is still very clumsy, impersonal and really primitive, though perhaps this gives it a special attraction. In vivid colours it depicts the Pöstlingberg, the landmark of Linz. I still remember when Adolf gave it to me.

One cannot expect any artistic revelations from this water colour and the hundreds which followed it. His intention was not to express any of his own emotions, but just to paint pleasant little pictures. So he chose popular subjects, for preference architecture and, rarely, landscapes.

If these postcards and pictures had not been painted by Adolf Hitler, no one would have bothered about them.

His drawings are a different matter, but there are only a few of them in existence. Although he gave me several, only one of them is left, a purely architectural drawing with little meaning. It shows a villa at No. 7 Stockbauerstrasse. It had just been built and it appealed to Adolf. So he drew it and made me a present of it. Apart from revealing his love for architecture, it is of no significance.

Casting my thoughts back to those years, I have to say this: Adolf never took painting seriously; it remained rather a hobby outside his more serious aspirations. But building meant much more to him. He gave his whole self to his imaginary building and was completely carried away by it.

Once he had conceived an idea he was like one possessed. Nothing else existed for him — he was oblivious to time, sleep and hunger. Although it was a strain for me to follow him, those moments remain unforgettable. There he stood, with me, in front of the new Cathedral, this pallid, skinny youth, with the first dark brown showing on his upper lip, in his shabby pepper-and-salt suit, threadbare at the elbows and collar, with his eyes glued to some architectural detail, analysing the style, criticising or praising the work, disapproving of the material — all this with such thoroughness and such expert knowledge as though he were the builder and would have to pay for every shortcoming out of his own pocket. Then he would get out his drawing pad and the pencil would fly over the paper. This way, and no other, was the manner of solving this problem, he would say. I had to compare his idea with the actual work, had to approve or disapprove, and all this with a passion as though both our lives depended on it.

Here he could give full vent to his mania for changing everything, because a city always has good buildings and bad. He could never walk through the streets without being provoked by what he saw. Usually he carried around in his head half a dozen different building projects, and sometimes I could not help feeling that all the buildings of the town were lined up in his brain like a giant panorama. As soon as he had selected one detail, he concentrated on this with all his energy.

I remember one day when the old building of the bank for Upper Austria and Salzburg on the central square was demolished. With feverish

Chapter 9 — Adolf Rebuilds Linz

impatience he followed the rebuilding. He was terribly worried lest the new building should not fit into its surroundings. When, in the middle of the rebuilding, he had to leave for Vienna be asked me to give him periodical reports on the progress of the work. In his letter of July 21, 1908, he wrote, "As soon as the Bank is completed, please send me a picture postcard." As there was no picture postcard available, I got out of it by procuring a photograph of the new building and sending it to him. Incidentally, the building met with his approval.

There were a lot of such houses in which he took a constant interest. He dragged me along wherever there was a building going up. He felt responsible for everything that was being built.

But even more than with these concrete examples was he taken up with the vast schemes that he himself originated. Here his mania for change knew no limit. At first I watched these goings-on with some misgiving and wondered why he so obstinately occupied himself with plans which, I thought, would never come to anything. The more remote the realisation of a project was, the more did he steep himself in it. To him these projects were in every detail as actual as though they were already executed and the whole town rebuilt according to his design. I often got confused and could not distinguish whether he was talking about a building that existed or one that was to be created. But to him it did not make any difference; the actual construction was a matter of only secondary importance.

Nowhere is his unshakable consistency more evident. What the fifteen-year-old planned, the fiftyyear- old carried out, often, as for instance in the case of the new bridge over the Danube, as faithfully as though only a few weeks, instead of decades, lay between planning and execution.

The plan existed; then came influence and power and the plan became reality. This happened with uncanny regularity, as though the fifteen-year-old had taken it for granted that one day he would possess the necessary power and means. This is just too much for me to take in. I cannot conceive that such a thing is possible. One is tempted to use the word "miracle," because there is no rational explanation for it.

Indeed, the plans which that unknown boy had drawn up for the rebuilding of his home town Linz are identical to the last detail with the town planning scheme which was inaugurated after 1938. I am almost afraid of giving, in the following pages, my account of these early plans, lest my veracity should be suspected. And yet every single syllable of what I am going to recount is true.

On my eighteenth birthday, August 3, 1906, my friend presented me with a sketch of a villa.

Similar to that planned for Stefanie, it was in his favourite Italian Renaissance style. By good luck, I have preserved the sketches. They show an imposing, palazzo-like building, whose frontage is broken up by a built-in tower. The ground plan reveals a well-thoughtout arrangement of rooms, which are pleasantly grouped around the music room.

The spiral staircase, a delicate architectural problem, is shown in a separate drawing, and so is the entrance hall, with its heavy beamed ceiling. The entrance is outlined with a few brisk strokes in a separate sketch. Adolf and I also selected a fitting site for my birthday present; it was to stand on the Bauernberg. When, later, I met Hitler in Bayreuth, I took good care not to remind him of this imaginary house. He would have been capable of actually giving me a villa on the Bauernberg, which presumably would have been finer than the original idea, and very much in the taste of the epoch.

More impressive are two sketches still in my possession, samples of his numerous designs for a new concert hall in Linz. The old theatre was inadequate in every respect, and some art lovers in Linz had founded a society to promote the construction of a modern theatre. Adolf immediately joined this society and took part in a competition for ideas.. He worked for months on his plans and drafts and was seriously convinced that his suggestions would be accepted. His anger was beyond measure when the society smashed all his hopes by giving up the idea of a new building and, instead, had the old one renovated.

I refer to his biting remarks in the letters he sent me on August 17, 1908. "It seems they intend to patch up once more the old junk heap." Full of fury, he said that what he would like to do best would be to wrap up his manual of architecture and send it off to the address of this "Theatre - Rebuilding - Society - Committee - for - the - Execution - of - the - Project - for - the - Rebuilding - of - the - Theatre." How well did this monster title express his rage! My two sketches, on either side of one sheet, date from that period. The one side shows the auditorium. Columns break up the walls and the boxes are placed in between them. The balustrade is adorned by various statues.

A mighty domed ceiling covers the hall. On the back of this bold project, Adolf explained to me the acoustic conditions of the intended building, in which I, as a musician, was particularly interested. It clearly shows how the sound waves, rising from the orchestra, are reflected from the ceiling in such a way as to be, so to speak, poured over the audience below. Adolf took a great interest in acoustic problems. I remember, for instance, his suggestion to remodel the Volksgarten Hall, whose bad acoustics always annoyed us, by structural alterations of the ceiling.

Chapter 9 — Adolf Rebuilds Linz

And now for the rebuilding of Linz! Here his ideas were legion, yet he did not change them indiscriminately, and indeed held fast to his decisions once they were taken. That is why I remember so much about it. Every time we passed one spot or another, all his plans were ready immediately.

The wonderfully compact main square was a constant delight to Adolf, and his only regret was that the two houses nearest to the Danube disturbed the free vista on to the river and the range of hills beyond. On his plans, the two houses were pushed apart sufficiently to allow a free view on to the new, widened bridge without, however, substantially altering the former aspect of the square, a solution which later he actually carried out. The Town hall, which stood on the square, he thought unworthy of a rising town like Linz. He visualised a new, stately town hall, to be built in a modern style, far removed from that neo-Gothic style which at that time was the vogue for town halls, in Vienna and Munich, for instance. In a different way, Hitler proceeded in the remodeling of the old Castle, an ugly, boxlike pile which overlooked the old city. He had discovered an old print by Merian depicting the castle as it was before the great fire. Its original appearance should be restored and the castle turned into a museum.

Another building which never failed to rouse his enthusiasm was the Museum, built in 1892. We often stood and looked at the marble frieze which was 110 metres long and reproduced scenes from the history of the country in relief. He never got tired of gazing at it. He extended the museum beyond the adjoining convent garden and enlarged the frieze to 220 metres to make it, as he asserted, the biggest relief frieze on the Continent. The new cathedral, then in course of construction, occupied him constantly. The Gothic revival was, in his opinion, a hopeless enterprise, and he was angry that the Linzers could not stand up to the Viennese. For the height of the Linz spire was limited to 134 metres out of respect for the 138-metre-high St. Stephen's spire in Vienna.

Adolf was greatly pleased with the new Corporation of Masons which had been founded in connection with the building of the cathedral, as he hoped this would result in the training of a number of capable masons for the town. The railway station was too near the town, and with its network of tracks impeded the traffic as well as the town's development. Here, Adolf found an ingenious solution which was far ahead of his time. He removed the station out of the town into the open country and ran the tracks underground across the town. The space gained by the demolition of the old station was designated for an extension of the public park. Reading this, one must not forget that the time was 1907, and that it was an unknown youth of eighteen, without training or qualification, who propounded these projects which revolutionised town planning, and which proved how capable he was, even then, of brushing aside existing ideas.

In a similar way, Hitler also reconstructed the surroundings of Linz. An interesting idea dominated his plans for the rebuilding of Wildberg Castle. Its original state was to be restored and it was to be developed as a kind of open-air museum with a permanent population — quite a new idea.

Certain types of artisans and workmen were to be attracted to the place. Their trades had to be partly in the medieval tradition, but should also partly serve modern purposes, a tourist industry, for instance. These inhabitants of the Castle were to dress in ancient fashion. The traditions of the old guilds should rule, and a Master Singer School was to be established. This "Island where the centuries had stood still" (these were his very words) would become a place of pilgrimage for all those who wanted to study life as it was lived in a medieval stronghold. Improving upon Dinkelsbühl and Rothenburg, Wildberg would not only show architecture but real life. Visitors would have to pay a toll at the gates, and so contribute to the upkeep of the local inhabitants.

Adolf gave much thought to the choice of suitable artisans and I remember that we discussed the subject at great length. After all, I was just about to take my Master's examination and was, therefore, entitled to have my say.

Quite a different project, of absolutely modern design, was the tower on the Lichtenberg. A mountain railway should run up to the peak, where a comfortable hotel would stand. The whole was dominated by a tower three hundred metres high, a steel construction which kept him very busy. The gilded eagle on the top of St. Stephen's in Vienna could be seen on clear days through a telescope from the highest platform of the tower. I think I remember seeing a sketch of this project.

The boldest project, however, which put all the others in the shade, was the building of a grandiose bridge which would span the Danube at a great height. For this purpose he planned the construction of a high-level road. This would start at the Gugl, then still an ugly sandpit, which could be filled in with the town's refuse and rubbish, and provide the space for a new park. From there, in a broad sweep, the new road would lead up to the Stadtwald. (Incidentally, the city engineers went thus far some time ago, without knowing Hitler's plans. The road which has meanwhile been built corresponds exactly to Hitler's projects.) The Kaiser-Franz-Josef-Warte in the Jagermayerwald — it is still standing — was to be demolished and replaced by a proud monument. In a Hall of Fame there would be assembled the portrait busts of all the great men who had deserved well of

Chapter 9 — Adolf Rebuilds Linz

the Province of Upper Austria; from the top of the hall one would have a magnificent view over a vast expanse of country; and the whole edifice was to be crowned by a statue of Siegfried, raising aloft his sword, Nothung. (The Hall of Liberation at Kehlheim and the Hermann Monument in the Teutoburger Wald were obvious models.) From this spot the bridge sweeps in one arch to the steep slope of the opposite bank.

Adolf got his inspiration for this from the legend of a daring horseman who, pursued by his enemies, is said to have jumped from this point into the appalling depths below, to swim across the Danube and reach the other side. My imagination boggled at the dimensions of this bridge.

The span of the arch was calculated to be more than 500 metres. The summit was 90 metres above the level of the river. I much regret that no sketches of this really unique project survive..

This bridge across the deep valley, my friend declared, would give Linz an edifice without rival in the whole world. When we stood on one bank of the river, or the other, Adolf would explain to me all the details of the scheme. These bold, far-reaching plans made a strange impression on me, as I still clearly remember.

Although I saw in the whole thing nothing but a figment of the imagination, I could, nevertheless, not resist its peculiar fascination. What exercised my friend's mind, and was hastily jotted down on scraps of paper, was more than nebulous fantasticism; these apparently absurd conceptions contained something compelling and convincing — a sort of superior logic. Each idea had its natural sequel in another, and the whole was a clear and rational chain of thought. Purely romantic conceptions, such as the "Medieval Revival of Wildberg Castle," obviously betrayed Richard Wagner's paternity. They were linked to extremely modern technical devices, such as the replacement of level crossings by underground railway tracks. This was no unbridled wallowing in sheer fantasy, but a well-disciplined, almost systematic process. This "Architecture set to Music" attracted me, perhaps, just because it seemed fully feasible — although we two poor devils had no possibility of realising these plans. But this did not disturb my friend in the least, His belief, that one day he would carry out all his tremendous projects, was unshakable. Money was of no importance — it was only a matter of time, of living long enough. This absolute faith was too much for my rational way of thinking. What was our future? I might become, at best, a well-known conductor. And Adolf? A gifted painter or draughtsman, perhaps a famous architect. But how far distant were these professional goals from that standing and reputation, those riches and power necessary for the rebuilding of an entire city! And who knows whether my friend, with his incredible flights of fancy and impulsive temperament, would stop at the rebuilding of Linz, for he was incapable of keeping his hands off anything within reach. Consequently I had grave doubts and occasionally I dared to remind him of the undeniable fact that all our worldly possessions put together did not amount to more than a few crowns — hardly enough to buy drawing paper.

Usually Adolf brushed my objections impatiently aside, and I still remember his grim expression and his disdainful gesture on such occasions. He took it for granted that one day the plans would be executed with the greatest of exactitude, and prepared for this moment accordingly. Even the most fantastic idea was thought out in the greatest detail. How was the material to be transported for the bridge across the Danube? Should it be stone or steel? How were the foundations for the end abutments to be laid? Would the rock stand the weight?

These questions were, in part, quite irrelevant for the expert, in part, however, very much to the point. Adolf lived so much in his vision of the future Linz that he adapted his day-to-day habits to it; for instance, we would visit the Hall of Fame, the Memorial Temple or our "Medieval Open-air Museum."

One day when I interrupted the bold flow of his ideas for the National Monument and asked him soberly how he proposed to finance this project, his first reply was a brusque, "Oh, to hell with money!" But apparently my query had disturbed him. And he did what other people do who want to get rich quickly — he bought a lottery ticket. And yet there was a difference between the way Adolf bought a lottery ticket and the way other people did. For other people only hope, or rather, dream of getting the first prize, but Adolf was sure he had won from the moment of buying the ticket and had only forgotten to collect the money. His only possible worry was how to spend this not inconsiderable sum to the best advantage.

It was typical of him that he often mingled his most fantastic ideas with the coolest calculations, and the same thing happened with the purchase of the lottery ticket. While he was already, in his imagination, spending his winnings, he carefully studied the lottery conditions and worked out our chance with the greatest precision. Adolf invited me to go shares with him in this venture. He was quite systematic about it. The price of the ticket was ten crowns, of which I had to find five. He stipulated, however, that these five crowns should not be given to me by my parents, but I had to earn them myself. At that time I earned some pocket money and also got occasional tips from the customers. Adolf insisted on knowing exactly where these five crowns came from, and when he was satisfied that my contribution was really my own, we went together to the office of the State Lottery to buy the ticket. It took him a long time to make up his mind, and I still don't know what considerations prompted his choice. As he was absolutely skeptical about occultism and more than rational in these matters, his behaviour remained a mystery to me. But in the end he found his winner. "Here it is!" he said, and put the ticket carefully away in the little, black notebook in which he wrote his poems.

The time that elapsed before the draw was for me the happiest period of our friendship. Love and enthusiasm, great thoughts, lofty ideas, all that we bad already. The only thing that was lacking was money. Now we had that, too. What more could we want? Although the first prize represented a lot of money, my friend was by no means tempted to spend it thoughtlessly. On the contrary. He went about it in the most calculating and economical way. It would have been senseless to invest the whole sum in one of the projects, say the rebuilding of the museum, for this would only have been a small part within the framework of the great townplanning scheme. It was more reasonable to use the money for our own benefit, to help us to a standing in public life which would enable us to progress further towards our ultimate aims.

It would have been too expensive to build a villa for ourselves; it would have swallowed up so much of our fortune that we would have moved into this splendour quite penniless. Adolf suggested a compromise: we should rent a flat, he said, and adapt it to our purpose. After long and careful examination of the various possibilities, we selected the second floor of No. 2 Kirchengasse in Urfahr; for this house was in a quite exceptional position. Near the bank of the Danube, it had a view over the pleasant green fields which culminated in the Pöstlingberg. We crept into the house secretly, looked at the view from the staircase window, and Adolf made a sketch of the ground plan.

Then we moved in, so to speak. The larger wing of the flat should be for my friend, the smaller one was reserved for me. Adolf arranged the rooms so that his study was as far removed as possible from mine, so that he, at his drawing board, would not be disturbed by my practising.

My friend also saw to the furnishing of the rooms, drawing each single piece of furniture to scale on the ground plan. The furniture was of most beautiful and superior quality, made by the town's leading craftsmen, by no means cheap, mass-produced stuff. Even the decorations for the walls of each single room were designed by Adolf. I was only allowed to have a say about the curtains and draperies, and I had to show him how I. suggested dealing with the rooms he had given me.

He was certainly pleased with the self-assured manner in which I co-operated with the arrangement of the flat. We had no doubt that the first prize was ours. Adolf's own faith had bewitched me into believing as he did. I, too, expected to move into No. 2 Kirchengasse very soon.

Although simplicity was to be the keynote of our home, it was nevertheless imbued with a refined, personal taste. Adolf proposed to make our home the centre of a circle of art lovers. I would provide the musical entertainment. He would recite something, or read aloud, or expound his latest work. We would make regular trips to Vienna to attend lectures and concerts, and to go to the theatre. (I realised then that Vienna played an important part in my friend's world of ideas.

Strange that he had opted for the Kirchengasse in Urfahr.) Winning the first prize would not alter our mode of life. We would remain simple people, wearing clothes of good quality, but certainly not ostentatious. With regard to our dress, Adolf had a delicious idea which delighted me immeasurably. We should both dress in exactly the same way, he suggested, so that people would take us for brothers. I believe that, for me, this idea alone made it worthwhile to win the Lottery. It shows how our mere theatre acquaintance had ripened into a deep, romantic friendship.

Of course I would have to leave my parents' home and give up my trade. My future musical studies would leave me no time for such things; for as our studies progressed, our understanding for artistic experiences increased and engrossed us completely.

Adolf thought of everything, even the running of the household, which was necessary as the day of the draw was approaching. A refined lady should preside over our home and run it. It had to be an elderly lady, to rule out any expectations or intentions which might interfere with our artistic vocation. We also agreed on the staff that this big household would need. Thus, everything was prepared. This image remained with me for a long time to come: an elderly lady, with greying hair, but incredibly distinguished, standing in the brilliantly lit hall, welcoming, on behalf of her two young, gifted gentlemen of seventeen and eighteen years, the guests who formed their circle of select, lofty-minded friends.

During the summer months we were to travel. The first and foremost destination was Bayreuth, where we were to enjoy the perfect performances of the great master's music dramas. After Bayreuth, we were to visit famous cities, magnificent cathedrals, palaces and castles, but also industrial centres, shipyards and ports. "It shall be the whole of Germany," said Adolf. This was one of his favourite sayings.

The day of the draw arrived.

Chapter 9 — Adolf Rebuilds Linz

Adolf came rushing wildly round to the workshop with the list of results. I have rarely heard him rage so madly as then. First he fumed over the State Lottery, this officially organised exploitation of human credulity, this open fraud at the expense of docile citizens. Then his fury turned against the state itself, this patchwork of ten or twelve, or God knows how many nations, this monster built up by Hapsburg marriages. Could one expect other than that two poor devils should be cheated out of their last few crowns? Never did it occur to Adolf to reproach himself for having taken it for granted that the first prize belonged to him by right; and this in spite of the fact that he had brooded for hours over the conditions of the Lottery and calculated exactly how small our chances were in view of the number of tickets in existence and the number of prizes offered. I could find no explanation for this contradiction in his character. But there it was.

For the first time he had been deserted by his will power which always seemed to move matters that concerned him in the desired direction. This he could not bear, for it was worse than the loss of the money and having to give up the flat and the lady-housekeeper receiving our guests with distinguished nonchalance.

It seemed to Adolf more reasonable to rely on himself and build his own future, rather than trust government institutions like lotteries. This would spare him from such setbacks. Thus, after a short period of utter depression, he returned to his earlier projects.

One of his favourite plans was the replacement of the bridge which linked Linz and Urfahr. We used to cross this bridge daily, and Adolf was particularly fond of this walk. When the floods of May 1868 destroyed five supports of the old wooden bridge, it was decided to build an iron bridge, which was completed in 1872. This rather ugly bridge was far too narrow for the traffic, although in those days there were not even any motorcars; and it was always overcrowded to a frightening degree.

Adolf liked to listen to the cursing drivers, who with wild oaths and much cracking of the whip, would try to make a way for themselves. Although generally he showed little interest in the thing at hand and preferred to take the long view for his projects, he suggested here a provisional solution to remedy the existing state of affairs. Without altering the bridge itself, to either side should be added a footpath, two metres wide, which would carry the pedestrian traffic and thus relieve the roadway.

Naturally, nobody in Linz listened to the suggestions this young dreamer, who could not even produce decent school reports. All the more enthusiastically did Adolf now occupy himself with the complete rebuilding of the bridge.

The ugly iron structure must be demolished. The new bridge must be so proportioned as to give the visitor who approached the Danube from the main square the impression of seeing, not a bridge, but a broad, impressive street. Mighty statues would underline the artistic aspect of the whole.

It is greatly to be regretted that, so far as I know, none of the numerous sketches which Hitler then made for the new bridge has been preserved; for it would be very interesting to compare these sketches with the plans which, thirty years later, Adolf Hitler prepared for this bridge and ordered to be executed. We owe it to his impatience to see the new Linz built that, in spite of the outbreak of war in 1939, that structure, being the central project of the Linz town planning, actually was completed.

Chapter 10 — In That Hour It Began

It was the most impressive hour I ever lived through with my friend. So unforgettable is it, that even the most trivial things, the clothes Adolf wore that evening, the weather, are still present in my mind as though the experience were exempt from the passing of time.

Adolf stood outside my house in his black overcoat, his dark hat pulled down over his face. It was a cold, unpleasant November evening. He waved to me impatiently. I was just cleaning myself up from the workshop and getting ready to go to the theatre. Rienzi was being given that night. We had never seen this Wagner opera and looked forward to it with great excitement. In order to secure the pillars in the Promenade we had to be early. Adolf whistled, to hurry me up.

Now we were in the theatre, burning with enthusiasm, and living breathlessly through Rienzi's rise to be the Tribune of the people of Rome and his subsequent downfall. When at last it was over, it was past midnight. My friend, his hands thrust into his coat pockets, silent and withdrawn, strode through the streets and out of the city. Usually, after an artistic experience that had moved him, he would start talking straight away, sharply criticizing the performance, but after Rienzi he remained quiet a long while. This surprised me, and I asked him what he thought of it. He threw me a strange, almost hostile glance. "Shut up!" he said brusquely.

The cold, damp mist lay oppressively over the narrow streets. Our solitary steps resounded on the pavement. Adolf took the road that led up to the Freinberg. Without speaking a word, he strode forward. He looked almost sinister, and paler than ever. His turned-up coat collar increased this impression.

I wanted to ask him, "Where are you going?" But his pallid face looked so forbidding that I suppressed the question.

As if propelled by an invisible force, Adolf climbed up to the top of the Freinberg. And only now did I realize that we were no longer in solitude and darkness, for the stars shone brilliantly above us.

Adolf stood in front of me; and now he gripped both my hands and held them tight. He had never made such a gesture before. I felt from the grasp of his hands how deeply moved he was. His eyes were feverish with excitement. The words did not come smoothly from his mouth as they usually did, but rather erupted, hoarse and raucous. From his voice I could tell even more how much this experience had shaken him.

Gradually his speech loosened, and the words flowed more freely. Never before and never again have I heard Adolf Hitler speak as he did in that hour, as we stood there alone under the stars, as though we were the only creatures in the world.

I cannot repeat every word that my friend uttered. I was struck by something strange, which I had never noticed before, even when he had talked to me in moments of the greatest excitement. It was as if another being spoke out of his body, and moved him as much as it did me. It wasn't at all a case of a speaker being carried away by his own words. On the contrary; I rather felt as though he himself listened with astonishment and emotion to what burst forth from him with elementary force. I will not attempt to interpret this phenomenon, but it was a state of complete ecstasy and rapture, in which he transferred the character of Rienzi, without even mentioning him as a model or example, with visionary power to the plane of his own ambitions. But it was more than a cheap adaptation. Indeed, the impact of the opera was rather a sheer external impulse which compelled him to speak. Like flood waters breaking their dikes, his words burst forth from him. He conjured up in grandiose, inspiring pictures his own future and that of his people.

Hitherto I had been convinced that my friend wanted to become an artist, a painter, or perhaps an architect. Now this was no longer the case. Now he aspired to something higher, which I could not yet fully grasp. It rather surprised me, as I thought that the vocation of the artist was for him the highest, most desirable goal. But now he was talking of a mandate which, one day, he would receive from the people, to lead them out of servitude to the heights of freedom.

It was an unknown youth who spoke to me in that strange hour. He spoke of a special mission which one day would be entrusted to him, and I, his only listener, could hardly understand what he meant. Many years had to pass before I realized the significance of this enraptured hour for my friend.

His words were followed by silence.

We descended into the town. The clock struck three. We parted in front of my house. Adolf shook hands with me, and I was astonished to see that he did not go in the direction of his home, but turned again towards the mountains.

"Where are you going now?" I asked him, surprised. He replied briefly, "I want to be alone." In the following weeks and months he never again mentioned this hour on the Freinberg. At first it struck me as odd and I could find no explanation for his strange behavior, for I could not believe that he had forgotten it altogether. Indeed he never did forget it, as

Chapter 10 — In That Hour It Began

I discovered thirty-three years later. But he kept silent about it because he wanted to keep that hour entirely to himself. That I could understand, and I respected his silence. After all, it was his hour, not mine. I had played only the modest role of a sympathetic friend.

In 1939, shortly before war broke out, when I, for the first time visited Bayreuth as the guest of the Reichs Chancellor, I thought I would please my host by reminding him of that nocturnal hour on the Freinberg, so I told Adolf Hitler what I remembered of it, assuming that the enormous multitude of impressions and events which had filled these past decades would have pushed into the background the experience of a seventeen year old youth. But after a few words I sensed that he vividly recalled that hour and had retained all its details in his memory. He was visibly pleased that my account confirmed his own recollections. I was also present when Adolf Hitler retold this sequel to the performance of *Rienzi* in Linz to Frau Wagner, at whose home we were both guests. Thus my own memory was doubly confirmed. The words with which Hitler concluded his story to Frau Wagner are also unforgettable for me. He said solemnly, "In that hour it began."

Chapter 11 — Adolf Leaves for Vienna

I had been noticing for a long time that Adolf, whether he was talking about art, politics or his own future, was no longer satisfied with friendly and familiar, though Philistine Linz, and cast his eyes more and more frequently towards Vienna. Vienna, still a resplendent Imperial city and the metropolis of a State of forty-five million people, promised him fulfillment of all his hopes for the future.

At the time of which I speak, the summer of 1907, Adolf knew Vienna from a visit he had paid it in the previous year. In May and June, 1906, be had stayed there long enough to grow enthusiastic about everything that had specially attracted him — the Hof Museum, the Hof Opera, the Burg Theatre, the magnificent buildings on the Ring — but not long enough to observe the distress and misery which were concealed by the magnificent facade of the city. This deceptive picture, largely produced by his artistic imagination, held a powerful attraction for him. In his thoughts he was often no longer in Linz but already in Vienna, and his incredible capacity for ignoring the reality in f front of him, and for accepting as real what existed only in his imagination, now came here into full play.

I have to correct here a small error which Adolf Hitler made in *Mein Kampf* in regard to his first stay in Vienna. He is wrong when he says that he was then not yet sixteen years old, for actually he had just had his seventeenth birthday. For the rest, his account of it corresponds entirely with my own.

I well remember the enthusiasm with which my friend spoke of his impressions of Vienna. Details of his account, however, escape my memory. It is all the more fortunate that the postcards he wrote to me on this first visit are still preserved. There are, altogether, four postcards which, apart it from their biographical interest, are important graphological documents; for they are the earliest substantial examples of Adolf Hitler's handwriting still existing. It is a strangely mature, rather flowing hand, which one would hardly connect with a youth of barely eighteen, while the incorrect spelling not only bears witness to patchy schooling, but also to a certain indifference in such matters. All the picture postcards he sent me were, significantly enough, of buildings. A different kind of young man of his age would certainly have chosen a different kind of picture postcard for his friend.

The first of these cards — dated May 7, 1906 — is a masterpiece of the postcard production of the period and must have cost him a pretty

Chapter 11 — Adolf Leaves for Vienna

penny: it opens out into a kind of triptych, with a full view of the Karlsplatz, with the church — the Karlskirche — in the centre. The text is: "In sending you this postcard I have to apologise for not having written sooner. Well, I have safely arrived and am going around everywhere. Tomorrow I am going to the Opera, 'Tristan,' and the day after, 'The Flying Dutchman,' etc. Although I find everything very beautiful, I am longing for Linz. Tonight Stadt-Theatre. Greetings, your friend, Adolf Hitler." On the picture side of the card, the Conservatory is expressly marked, probably the reason for his choice of this particular view, for he was already playing with the idea that someday we would study together in Vienna, and never missed an opportunity of reminding me of this possibility in the most alluring form. On the lower margin of the picture, he adds: "Greetings to your esteemed parents." I would like to mention that the words "Although I find everything very beautiful, I am longing for Linz" do not refer to Linz but to Stefanie, for whom his love was all the greater the farther from her he was. It certainly satisfied his impetuous longing for her that he, a lonely stranger in this heartless metropolis, could write these words which only his friend who shared his secrets would understand.

On the same day, Adolf sent me a second postcard which depicts the stage of the Hof Opera House. Presumably this particularly successful photograph, which shows a part of the decor, had appealed to him. On it he wrote: "The interior of the edifice is not very stirring. If the exterior is mighty majesty, which gives the building the seriousness of an artistic monument, the inside, though commanding admiration, does not impress one with its dignity. Only when the mighty sound waves flow through the hall and when the whispering of the wind gives way to the terrible roaring of the sound waves, then one feels the grandeur and forgets the gold and velvet with which the interior is overloaded. Adolf H."

On the front of the card there is again added: "Greetings to your esteemed parents." Adolf is completely in his element here. The friend is forgotten, even Stefanie is forgotten; no greeting, not even a hint, so overwhelmed is he by his recent experience. His clumsy style clearly reveals that his power of expression is not sufficient to do justice to the depth of his feelings. But even his poor style, which sounds like the ecstatic stammering of an enthusiast, reveals the magnitude of his experience. After all, it had been the greatest dream of our boyhood in Linz to see, someday, a perfect production at the Vienna Opera House instead of the performances in our provincial theatre, which left so much to be desired. Certainly Adolf, with his glowing description, aimed at my own art-loving heart. For what could make Vienna more attractive to me than the enthusiastic echo of such artistic impressions? On the very next day, May 8, 1906, he wrote again; it is rather surprising that he wrote three times in the space of two days. His motive becomes clear from the contents of the postcard, which shows the exterior of the Vienna Opera House.

He wrote: "I am really longing for my dear Linz and Urfar. Want and must see Benkieser again.

What might he be doing, so I am arriving on Thursday on the 3.55 in Linz. If you have time and permission, meet me. Greetings to your esteemed parents! Your friend, Adolf Hitler." The word "Urfar," misspelt in the hurry, is underlined, although Adolf's mother was still living in Humboldtstrasse, and not in Urfahr. Of course, that remark referred to Stefanie, ie, and so did the agreed code word, Benkieser. The phrase "Want and must see Benkieser" is typical of Adolf's style and character. Also significant are the words, "If you have time and permission, meet me." Although it was a matter of urgency for him, he respects my duty of obedience towards my parents, nor does he omit to greet them on this card.

Unfortunately, I cannot verify whether Adolf really returned to Linz on the following Thursday, or if this indication was only intended to satisfy his unappeasable longing for Stefanie. His remark in *Mein Kampf* that his sojourn in Vienna lasted only a fortnight is incorrect. Actually, he stayed there about four weeks, as is evidenced by the postcard of June 6, 1906.

This card, which shows the Franzensring and House of Parliament, is on conventional lines: "To you and to your esteemed parents, I send herewith best wishes for the holidays and kind regards. Respectfully, Adolf Hitler." With this memory of his first stay in Vienna transfigured by his yearning for Stefanie, Adolf entered the critical summer of 1907. What he suffered in those weeks was in many respects similar to the grave crisis of two years earlier. Then, after much heart-searching, he had finally settled his accounts with the school and made an end of it, however painful this might be for his mother. A grave illness bad rendered the transition easier for him. But this transition led him only to the "hollowness of the life of leisure." Without school, with no career in mind, he had spent two years living with his mother and not earning a penny. These were by no means idle years. Having had daily contact with Adolf, I can testify how intensely my friend, studied and worked in those days, But this private study, as well as his artistic activity, had no determined goal. He felt himself that it couldn't continue. Something had to happen, a profound change would give a clear direction to his aimless, day-to-day mode of life.

Outwardly, this seeking for a new path showed itself in dangerous fits of depression. I knew only too well those moods of his, which were

Chapter 11 — Adolf Leaves for Vienna

in sharp contrast to his ecstatic dedication and activity, and realised that I couldn't help hint. At such times he was inaccessible, uncommunicative and distant. It might happen that we didn't meet at all for a day or two. If I tried to see him at home, his mother would receive me with great surprise. "Adolf has gone out," she would say, "he must be looking for you." Actually, Adolf would wander around aimlessly and alone for days and nights in the fields and forests surrounding the town. When I met him at last, he was obviously glad to have me with him. But when I asked him what was wrong, his only answer would be, "Leave me alone," or a brusque, "I don't know myself." And if I insisted, he would understand my sympathy, and then say in a milder tone, "Never mind, Gustl, but not even you can help me." This state lasted several weeks. One fine summer evening, however, when we were strolling beside the Danube, the tension began to ease. Adolf reverted to his old, familiar tone. I remember this moment exactly. As usual, we had been to see Stefanie pass by arm-in-arm with her mother.

Adolf was still under her spell. Even though he saw her, at this time, almost every day, these meetings never became something commonplace for him. While Stefanie had probably long since become bored by the silent, but strictly conventional adulation of the pale, thin youth, my friend lost himself increasingly in his wishful dreams the more he saw her. Yet he was past those romantic ideas of elopement or suicide. He explained to me in eloquent words his state of mind: the vision of the beloved pursued him day and night; he was unable to work or even to think clearly; he feared he would go mad if this state of affairs went on much longer, though he saw no way of altering the situation, for which Stefanie was not to blame, either. "There is only one thing to be done," he cried. "I must go away — far away from Stefanie." On our way home he explained his decision in greater detail. His relationship with Stefanie would become more bearable for him once he was living at a distance and could not meet her every day. It did not occur to him that in this way he might lose Stefanie altogether — so deeply convinced was he that he had won her forever.

The true situation was different. Adolf perhaps already realised that if he wanted to win Stefanie, he would have to speak to her or take some such decisive step — it is probable that even he began to find the exchange of glances on the Landstrasse a little childish. Nevertheless, he felt instinctively that it would abruptly destroy his life's dream if he actually made Stefanie's acquaintance. Indeed, as he said to me: "If I introduce myself to Stefanie and her mother, I will have to tell her at once what I am, what I have and what I want. My statement would bring our relations abruptly to an end." This awareness, and the simultaneous realisation that he had to put his relationship with Stefanie on a firm basis to avoid ridicule, were the horns of a dilemma for him, from which he saw only one way out — flight. He started at once to expound his plan to the last detail. I received precise instructions what to tell Stefanie if she asked, full of astonishment, what had become of my friend. (She never did!) Adolf himself realised that if he wanted to marry her, he would have to offer her a secure existence.

But this unsolved and, for a person of my friend's nature, insoluble problem of his relationship with Stefanie was only one of the many reasons which prompted him to quit Linz, although the most personal and therefore decisive. Another reason was that he was anxious to escape the atmosphere that prevailed at home. The idea that he, a young man of eighteen, should continue to be kept by his mother had become unbearable to him. It was a painful dilemma which, as I could see for myself, made him almost physically ill. On the one hand, he loved his mother above everything; she was the only person on earth to whom he felt really close, and she reciprocated his feeling to the same extent, although she was deeply disturbed by her son's unusual nature, however proud she was at times of him. "He is different from us," she used to say.

On the other hand, she felt it to be her duty to carry out the wishes of her late husband, and to prevail on Adolf to embark on a safe career. But what was "safe," in view of the peculiar character of her son? He had failed at school and had ignored all his mother's wishes and suggestions. A painter — that's what he had said he wanted to become. This could not seem very satisfactory to his mother, for, simple soul that she was, anything connected with art and artists appeared to her frivolous and insecure. Adolf tried to change her mind by telling her of his intention to study at the Academy.

That sounded better; after all, the Academy, of which Adolf spoke with increasing enthusiasm, was really a kind of school, where his mother thought he might make up for what he had missed in the Technical School. When listening to these domestic discussions, I was always surprised by the sympathetic understanding and patience with which Adolf tried to convince his mother of his artistic vocation. Contrary to his habit, he never became cross or violent on these occasions.

Often Frau Klara would also unburden herself to me, for she saw in me, too, an artistically gifted young man with high aims. Having a better understanding of musical matters than of her son's dabbling in drawing and painting, she frequently found my opinions more convincing than his, and Adolf was very grateful for my support. But in Frau Klara's eyes there was one important difference between Adolf and me: I had learnt an honest trade, finished my apprenticeship and passed my journeyman's examination.

Chapter 11 — Adolf Leaves for Vienna

I would always have a safe haven to shelter in, whereas Adolf was just steering into the unknown. This vision tormented his mother unceasingly.

Nevertheless, he succeeded in convincing her that it was essential for him to go to the Academy and study painting. I still remember distinctly how pleased he was over it. "Now mother will not raise any more objections," he told me one day. "I definitely go to Vienna at the beginning of September." Adolf had also settled with his mother the financial side of his plan. His living expenses and the Academy fees were to be paid out of the small legacy left him by his father and now administered by his guardian. Adolf hoped that, with great economy, he would be able to manage on this for a year. What would happen afterwards remained to be seen, he said. Perhaps he would earn something by the sale of some drawings and pictures.

The main opponent of this plan was his brother-in-law, Raubal, who, with his limited revenue official's horizon, was incapable of understanding Adolf's thoughts. That was rubbish, he said; it was high time that Adolf learned something respectable. Although Raubal, after some violent altercations with Adolf, in which he always came off worst, avoided any further argument with him, he tried all the harder to influence Frau Klara. Adolf found out most of this from "the kid," as he used to call his eleven-year-old sister.

When Paula told him that Raubal had been to see his mother, Adolf would fall into a rage. "This Pharisee is ruining my home for me," he once remarked to me furiously. Apparently Raubal had also got in touch with Adolf's guardian, for one day the worthy peasant Mayrhofer, who would have liked best to make a baker out of Adolf and had already found an apprenticeship for him, came from Leonding to see Frau Klara. Adolf was afraid that his guardian might induce her to hold back the legacy. This would have put a stop to his moving to Vienna. But the plan did not get so far, though for some time the decision was very much in doubt. By the end of this tough struggle, everybody was against Adolf — even, as happens in tenement buildings, the other tenants.

Frau Klara listened to this more or less wellmeant chatter and became completely confused by it all. Often, when Adolf had his fits of depression and was wandering through the woods, I used to sit with her in her little kitchen, listening sympathetically to her laments, trying hard to comfort the wretched woman without being unfair to my friend, and at the same time helping him where I could. I could easily put myself in Adolf's shoes. It would have been simple enough for him, with his great energy, just to pack up and go, if consideration for his mother had not prevented him. He had come to hate the Philistine world in which he had to live. He could hardly bear to return to that narrow world after lonely hours spent in the open. He was always in a ferment of rage, hard and intractable. I had a lot to put up with in those weeks. But the secret of Stefanie, which we shared, bound us inseparably together. The sweet magic which she, the unattainable, radiated calmed the stormy waves. So, as his mother was so easily influenced, the matter remained undecided, although Adolf had long since made up his mind.

On the other hand, Vienna was calling. That city had a thousand possibilities for an eager young man like Adolf, opportunities which might lead to the most sublime heights or to the most sombre depths. A city magnificent and at the same time cruel, promising everything and denying everything — that was Vienna. She demanded the highest stake from everyone who pledged himself to her. And that is what Adolf wanted.

No doubt Adolf had his father's example before. him. What would he have become if he hadn't gone to Vienna? A poor, haggard cobbler somewhere in the poverty-stricken Waldviertel. And see what Vienna made of this poor, orphaned cobbler's boy! Ever since his first visit in the spring of 1906, these rather vague ideas had assumed concrete form in Adolf's mind. He who had dedicated his life to art could develop his talents only in Vienna, for in that city were concentrated its most perfect achievements in every field. During his first short stay there he had already been to the Hof Opera House and seen *The Flying Dutchman*, *Tristan*, and *Lohengrin*. By these standards, the performance in the Linz Theatre appeared provincial and inadequate. In Vienna, the Burg Theatre, with its classic productions, awaited the young man. There was also the Vienna Philharmonic Orchestra which, with justification, was then considered the best in the world. Then the museums, with their immeasurable treasures, the picture galleries, the Hof Library, provided unending possibilities for study and self-improvement.

Linz had little more to offer Adolf. What rebuilding had to be done in this city he had already done, mentally, and no more large tempting problems were left for him to solve. And I was always there to report any further alterations to the town, such as the new building of the Bank of Upper Austria and Salzburg on the main square, or the projected new theatre. But he wanted to look at grander things — the magnificent buildings of the centre of Vienna, the vast, truly imperial layout of the Ringstrasse — rather than the humble little Landstrasse in Linz. Moreover, his growing interest in politics found no outlet in conservative Linz, where political life ran in well-defined grooves.

Simply nothing happened that might have had any political interest for a young man; there was no tension, no conflict, no unrest. It was a great

Chapter 11 — Adolf Leaves for Vienna

adventure to move from this absolute calm into the centre of the storm. All the energies of the Hapsburg State were concentrated in Vienna. Thirty nations struggled for their national existence and independence, and thus created an atmosphere like that of a volcano. How the young heart would rejoice at throwing itself unrestrainedly into this struggle! At long last the great moment arrived. Adolf, beaming with delight, came to see me at the workshop, where we were very busy at that time. "I'm leaving tomorrow," he said briefly. He asked me to accompany him to the station, as he didn't want his mother to come. I knew how painful it would have been for Adolf to take leave of his mother in front of other people. He disliked nothing more than showing his feelings in public. I promised him to come and to help him with his luggage.

Next day I took time off and went to the Blütengasse to collect my friend. Adolf had prepared everything. I took his suitcase, which was rather heavy with books he did not want to leave behind, and hurried away to avoid being present at the farewells. Yet I couldn't avoid them entirely. His mother was crying and little Paula, whom Adolf never bothered with much, was sobbing heart-rendingly. When Adolf caught up with me on the stairs and helped me with the suitcase, I saw that his eyes, too, were wet. We took the tram to the railway station, chatting about trivialities, as often happens when one wants to hide one's feelings. It moved me deeply to say goodbye to Adolf, and I felt miserable going home alone. It was a good thing that there was so much work waiting for me at the workshop.

Unfortunately, our correspondence of that period is lost. I only remember that for several weeks I had no news at all from him. And it was during those days that I felt most deeply how much he meant to me. Other young people of my age did not interest me, as I knew in advance that they would only turn out to be disappointing, with few interests other than their own shallow and superficial doings. Adolf was much more serious and mature than most people of his age. His horizon was wide and his passionate interest in everything had carried me along with it. Now I felt very lonely and miserable, and to find some comfort I went to the Blütengasse to see Frau Klara.

Talking to somebody so fond of Adolf would certainly make me feel better.

I thought that Adolf would already have written to his mother, for after all, it was a fortnight since he had left; and I would get his address and write to him, according to instructions, of all that had happened meanwhile. Actually, not much *had* happened, but for Adolf, every detail was important. I had seen Stefanie at the Schmiedtoreck, and indeed, she was surprised when she saw me there alone, for that much she knew about us, that in this "affair" I played only a secondary role. The chief protagonist was missing. That seemed strange to her. What could it mean?

Though Adolf was only a silent admirer, he was more persistent and tenacious than all the others. She did not want to lose this faithful adorer. Her enquiring glance caught me so unexpectedly, that I was almost tempted to address her. But Stefanie was not alone, being, as usual, accompanied by her mother, and moreover my friend had given me strict instructions to wait until Stefanie, herself asked me. Surely, as soon as she realised that he had gone for good, she would take the first opportunity of running over the bridge alone to entreat me impetuously to tell her what had become of my friend. Perhaps he had had an accident, or he was ill again as he was that time two years ago, or perhaps even dead. Unthinkable! Anyhow, though that conversation had not yet taken place, I had enough material to fill four pages of a letter.

But what on earth had happened to Adolf? Not a line from him. Frau Klara opened the door to me and greeted me warmly, and I could see that she had been .longing for me to come. "Have you heard from Adolf?" she asked me, still at the door. So he hadn't written to his mother either, and this made me feel anxious. Something out of the ordinary must have happened. Perhaps things hadn't gone according to plan in Vienna.

Frau Klara offered me a chair. I saw how much good it did her to be able to unburden herself. Ah, the old lament, which I had come to know by heart! But I listened patiently. "If only he had studied properly at the technical school he would almost be ready to matriculate. But he won't listen to anybody." And she added, "He's as pigheaded as his father. Why this crazy journey to Vienna? Instead of holding on to his little legacy, it's just being frittered away. And after that? Nothing will come of his painting. And story-writing doesn't earn anything either. And I can't help him — I've got the little one to look after. You know yourself what a sickly child she is, but just the same she must get some decent training. Adolf doesn't give it a thought, he goes his way, just as if he were alone in the world. I shall not live to see him making an independent position for himself. .." Frau Klara seemed more careworn than ever. Her face was deeply lined. Her eyes were lifeless, her voice sounded tired and resigned. I had the impression that, now that Adolf was no longer there, she had let herself go, and looked older and more ailing than ever. She certainly had concealed her condition from her son to make the parting easier for him, Or perhaps it was Adolf's impulsive nature that had kept up her vitality. Now, on her own, she seemed to me an old, sick woman.

Chapter 11 — Adolf Leaves for Vienna

I forget, unfortunately, what happened during the course of the following weeks. Adolf had briefly informed me of his address. He was living in the 6th District, at No. 29 Stumpergasse, Staircase II, second floor, door No. 17, in the flat of a woman with the curious name of Zakreys. That was all he wrote. But I guessed that there was more behind this obstinate silence, for I knew that Adolf's silences usually meant that he was too proud to talk.

I quote, therefore, from his own description in *Mein Kampf* of his second sojourn in Vienna, which by general consent is entirely truthful:

... I had gone to Vienna with the intention of taking the entrance examination for the Academy. I had set out, armed with a thick wad of drawings, convinced that it would be child's play to pass.

At the technical school I had been by far the best in my class at drawing, and since then my ability had developed quite extraordinarily; so I was quite satisfied with myself and this made me proudly and happily hope for the best ...

So here I was for the second time in the beautiful city, waiting impatiently, but hopefully, for the result of the entrance examination. I was so sure of success that the news of my rejection hit me like a bolt from the blue. Yet, that was what happened. When I went to see the Rector and asked to know the reasons why I had not been admitted to the general painting school of the Academy, I was told by this gentleman that the drawings I had submitted showed clearly that I had no aptitude for painting, my ability seemed rather to lie in the field of architecture, and I should not go to the painting school, but rather to the school of architecture of the Academy. That I had never been to a school for building, nor received any training in architecture, seemed to him hard to believe.

Defeated, I left the monumental building on the Schiller Square, for the first time in my young life at variance with myself. For what I had been told about my ability seemed to me to disclose in a flash of lightning a discord from which I had long suffered without, hitherto, clearly realising the why and wherefore.

In a few days, I knew myself that I would become an architect. Yet this was an incredibly difficult path, for what I had missed, out of obstinacy, in the technical school, now took its bitter revenge.

The attendance at the school of architecture of the Academy was dependent on the attendance at a technical school for building, and entrance to the latter required one to have passed the matriculation examination at a secondary school. I didn't fulfil any one of these conditions. As far as could be foreseen, therefore, the fulfilment of my dream to become an artist was impossible.

He had been refused by the Academy, he had failed even before he had got a footing in Vienna.

Nothing more terrible could have happened to him. But he was too proud to talk about it, and so he concealed from me what had happened. He concealed it from his mother, too. When later we met again, he had to some extent already lived down this hard verdict. He did not mention it at all.

I respected his silence and didn't ask him any questions, because I suspected that something had gone wrong with his plans. Not until the next year, when we were living together in Vienna, did all these circumstances gradually become clear to me.

Adolf's talent for architecture was so obvious that it would have justified an exception — how many less talented students were to be found at the Academy! This decision was therefore as biased and bureaucratic as it was unjust. Yet Adolf's reaction to this humiliating treatment was typical. He made no attempt to obtain exceptional treatment, or to humiliate himself in front of people who did not understand him. Then were neither revolt nor rebellion; instead came a radical withdrawal into himself, an obstinate resolve to cope alone with adversity, an embittered "Now, more than ever!" which he flung at the gentlemen of the Schillerplatz, just as, two years earlier, he had settled his account with his school teachers. Whatever disappointments life brought him, they were but a spur for him to brave all obstacles, and to continue on the path on which he had embarked.

In his book *Mein Kampf* he writes: "As the Goddess of Misery took me in her arms and so often threatened to break me, the Will to Resist grew, and in the end the Will triumphed."

Chapter 12 — His Mother's Death

I remember that Adolf's mother had to undergo a serious operation at the beginning of 1907. She was then in the Hospital of the Sisters of Mercy in the Herrenstrasse, and he visited her there daily. I forget what her illness was, but it was probably cancer of the breast. Although Frau Klara recovered sufficiently to run her household again, she remained very weak and ailing, and every now and then she had to take to her bed.

Yet, a few weeks after Adolf had left for Vienna, she seemed to be better, for I met her by chance on the Promenade, where at that time a street market used to be held, peasant women coming in from the country to sell eggs, butter and vegetables. "Adolf is right," she told me contentedly. "If only I knew what on earth he is studying! Unfortunately, he does not mention that at all.

However, I imagine that he is very busy." That was good news, which pleased me, too, for Adolf had not written to me about his activities in Vienna. Our correspondence was mainly concerned with "Benkieser" — otherwise Stefanie. But his mother, of course, must not be told of that. I asked Frau Klara how she was. Not at all well, she said; she had a lot of bad pain, and very often could not sleep at night. But she warned me not to write to Adolf about it, for perhaps she would soon be better. When we parted, she asked me to come to see her soon.

We were then very busy in the workshop, indeed business had never before been as good as in that year, and orders came in regularly and often. Yet in spite of this heavy work, I devoted every moment of leisure to my musical training, I played the viola both in the Music Society and the great Symphony Orchestra. So the weeks passed, and it was late in November when at last I found time to visit Frau Hitler. I was shocked when I saw her. How wilted and worn was her kind, gentle face! She was lying in bed and stretched out her pale, thin hand to me. Little Paula pushed a chair up beside her. She started at once to talk about Adolf and was happy about the hopeful tone of his letters.

I asked her if she had informed him of her illness, and offered to do so for her in case writing was too great an effort. But she hastily refused. If her condition did not improve, she said, she would have to send for Adolf from Vienna. She was sorry she had to tear him away from his hard work — but what else could she do? The little one had to go to school every day, Angela had enough worries of her own (she was expecting a second

The Young Hitler

baby) and on her son-inlaw, Raubal, she could not rely at all. Since she had taken Adolf's side and supported him in his decision to go to Vienna, Raubal had been angry with her and now never showed up; he had even prevented his wife from looking after her. So, she said, there was nothing left but to go to the hospital — as the doctor had advised.

The Hitler family's doctor was the very popular Dr. Bloch, known in the town as the "poor people's doctor," an excellent physician and a man of great kindness, who sacrificed himself for his patients. If Dr. Bloch had advised Mrs. Hitler to go to the hospital, her condition must be grave. I was wondering whether it was not, after all, my duty to inform Adolf. Frau Klara said how awful it was for her that Adolf was so far away. I never realised as clearly as on that visit how devoted she was to her son. She thought and planned for his welfare with all the strength that was left to her. In the end, she promised me that she would tell Adolf of her condition.

When I took leave of her that evening, I was very dissatisfied with myself. Was there no way of helping the poor woman? I knew how devoted Adolf was to his mother; something had to be done. If his mother really needed help, little Paula was too clumsy, too frightened to be of any use. When I got home, I talked to my mother. She offered at once to look after Frau Hitler, although she was a complete stranger. But this was vetoed by my father who, with his exaggerated ideas of correct behaviour, thought it was bad manners to offer one's help without being asked. A few days later I went again to see Frau Klara. I found her up, busy in the kitchen.

She felt somewhat better and she was already regretting that she had told Adolf about her illness.

I stayed with her a long time that evening; she was more talkative than usual and, quite contrary to her habit, she began to tell me about her life. Some of it I understood, and a lot I guessed at, though much was left unsaid; nevertheless, the story of a life of suffering was disclosed to a young man then in the full hopes of his nineteen years.

But in the workshop time was pressing, and my father was a strict boss. Even concerning my artistic ambitions he used to say: Work first — then music. And with a special performance coming on, there was one orchestral rehearsal after another. Sometimes I literally didn't know how to cram in everything. Then one morning, as I was energetically filling a mattress, Adolf suddenly appeared in the room. He looked terrible. His face was so pale as to be almost transparent, his eyes were dull and his voice hoarse. I felt that a storm of suffering must be hidden behind his icy demeanour. He gave me the impression that he was fighting for life against a hostile fate.

Chapter 12 — His Mother's Death

There was hardly a greeting, no question about Stefanie, nothing about what he had been doing in Vienna.

"Incurable, the doctor says" — this was all he could utter. I was shocked by the unequivocal diagnosis. Probably Dr. Bloch had told him of his mother's condition. Perhaps he had called in another doctor for consultation; and he couldn't reconcile himself to this cruel verdict.

His eyes blazed, his temper flared up. "Incurable — what do they mean by that?" he screamed.

"Not that the malady is incurable, but that the doctors aren't capable of curing it. My mother isn't even old. Forty-seven isn't an age where you give up hope. But as soon as the doctors can't do anything, they call it incurable." I was familiar with my friend's habit of turning everything he came across into a problem. But never had he spoken with such bitterness, with such passion as now. Suddenly it seemed to me as though Adolf, pale, excited, shaken to the core, stood there arguing and bargaining with Death, who remorselessly claimed his victim.

I asked Adolf if I could help him. He didn't hear me — he was too busy with this settling of accounts. Then he interrupted himself and declared in a sober, matter-of-fact voice: "I shall stay in Linz and keep house for my mother." "Can you do that?" I asked. "One can do anything, when one has to." And he said no more.

I went with him as far as the street. Now, I thought, he would certainly ask after Stefanie; perhaps he had not liked to mention her in the workshop. I would have been glad if he had, because I had carried out my instructions faithfully and could tell him a good deal, even though the expected conversation had not taken place. I also hoped that Adolf, in his deep spiritual affliction, would find comfort in the thought of Stefanie. And it certainly was so. Stefanie meant more to him in those dark weeks than ever before. But he stifled any mention of her, so deeply engrossed was he in his preoccupation with his mother.

I cannot recollect exactly when Adolf returned from Vienna. It was perhaps late in November, but possibly even December. But the weeks that follow remain indelibly in my memory; they were in a certain sense the most beautiful, the most intimate weeks of our friendship. How deeply these days impressed me can be gathered from the mere fact that from no other period of our association do so many details stand out in my memory. He was as though transformed. So far I had been certain that I knew him thoroughly and in all his aspects. After all, we had lived together for more than three years in an exclusive friendship that did not permit of any secrets. Yet in those weeks it seemed to me that my friend had become a different person.

Gone were the problems and ideas which used to agitate him so much, gone all thoughts of politics. Even his artistic interests were hardly noticeable. He was nothing but his mother's faithful and helpful son.

I had not taken Adolf very seriously when he said that he would now take over the household in the Blütengasse, for I knew Adolf's low opinion of such monotonous chores, necessary though they were. And so I was skeptical as to his good intentions and imagined that they would not exceed a few well-meant gestures.

But I was profoundly mistaken. I did not understand that side of Adolf sufficiently, and had not realized that his unbounded love for his mother would enable him to carry out this unaccustomed domestic work so efficiently that she could not praise him enough for it. Thus one day, on my arrival at the Blütengasse, I found Adolf kneeling on the floor. He was wearing a blue apron and scrubbing out the kitchen, which had not been cleaned for a long time. I was really immensely surprised and I must have shown it, for Frau Klara smiled in spite of her pain and said to me: "There, you see, Adolf can do anything." Then I noticed that Adolf had changed the furniture around. His mother's bed now stood in the kitchen because that was heated during the day.

The kitchen cupboard had been moved into the living room, and in its place was the couch, on which Adolf slept, so that he could be near her during the night as well. The little one slept in the living room. I could not refrain from asking how he managed the cooking. "As soon as I've finished the scrubbing, you can see for yourself," said Adolf. But, before I did, Frau Klara told me that every morning she discussed the dinner with Adolf. He always chose her favourite dishes, and prepared them so well that she herself couldn't have done better. She enjoyed her food immensely, she insisted, and she had never eaten with such good appetite as since Adolf came home, I looked at Frau Klara, who had sat up in bed. The fervour of her words had coloured her usually pale cheeks. The pleasure of having her son back and his devotion to her had transfigured the serious, worn face. But behind this mother's joy were the unmistakable signs of suffering. The deep lines, the drawn mouth and the sunken eyes showed how right the doctor had been.

To be sure, I should have known that my friend would not fail, even in this out-of-the-ordinary task, for whatever he did, he did thoroughly. Seeing the seriousness with which he carried out the running of the household, I suppressed a chaffing remark, although Adolf, who was always so punctilious about his neat dress, certainly looked comical in his old clothes with the apron tied around him. Nor did I utter a word of appreciation, so

Chapter 12 — His Mother's Death

touched was I by his changed attitude, knowing how much self-restraint this work was costing him.

Frau Klara's condition was changeable. Her son's presence improved her general state and cheered her up. Sometimes she would even get up in the afternoon and sit in the arm. chair.

Adolf anticipated her every wish and took the most tender care of her. I had never before seen in him such loving tenderness. I didn't trust my own eyes and ears. Not a cross word, not an impatient remark, no violent insistence on having his own way. He forgot himself entirely in those weeks, and lived only for his mother. Although Adolf, according to Frau Klara, had inherited many of his father's traits, I realised then how much his nature resembled his mother's. Certainly this was partly due to the fact that he had spent the last four years of his life alone with her. But, over and above that, there was a peculiar spiritual harmony between mother and son which I have never since come across. All that separated them was pushed into the background. Adolf never mentioned the disappointment which he had suffered in Vienna. For the time being, cares for the future no longer seemed to exist. An atmosphere of relaxed, almost serene contentment surrounded the dying woman.

Adolf, too, seemed to have forgotten everything that had preoccupied him. Only once, after I had said goodbye to Frau Klara, did he come to the door with me and ask me if I had seen Stefanie.

But this question was now put in a different tone. It no longer expressed the impatience of the impetuous lover, but the secret anxiety of a young man who feared that fate would now deprive him of the last thing that made life worth living. I gathered from his hasty question how much this girl meant to him in those grave days, more perhaps than if she had actually been as close to him as he would have wished. I reassured him; I often met Stefanie, with her mother, going over the bridge, and everything seemed unaltered.

December was cold and unfriendly. For days on end, damp, heavy mist hung over the Danube; the sun shone rarely, and when it did, so feebly as to give no warmth at all. His mother's condition deteriorated visibly and Adolf asked me to come. only every other day. As often as I entered the kitchen Frau Klara greeted me by lifting her hand a little and stretching it out towards me, and a faint smile would pass over her face, now distorted with pain. I remember a small but significant incident. Going through Paula's exercise books, Adolf had noticed that she was not getting on in school as well as her mother expected. Adolf took her by the hand and led her to their mother's bed and there made her swear always to be a diligent and well-behaved pupil. Perhaps Adolf wanted to show his mother by this little scene that he had meanwhile realised his own faults. If he had stayed on at the Technical School until matriculation, he would have avoided the disaster in Vienna. No doubt this decisive event which, as he said later, had for the first time put him at variance with himself was at the back of his mind during those terrible days and added to his depression.

When I returned to the Blütengasse two days later and knocked softly on the door, Adolf opened it immediately, came out into the corridor and closed the door behind him. He told me that his mother was not at all well and was in terrible pain. Even more than his words, his emotion made me realise the seriousness of the situation. I thought it better to leave and Adolf agreed with me.

We silently shook hands, and I departed.

Christmas was approaching. Snow had fallen at last and the town had assumed a festive garb.

But I didn't feel like Christmas. I walked across the Danube bridge to Urfahr. I learned from the people in the house that Frau Hitler had already received Extreme Unction. I wanted to make my visit as short as possible. I knocked, and Paula opened the door. I entered hesitantly. Frau Klara was sitting up in bed. Adolf had his arm around her shoulders to support her, as, while she was sitting up, the terrible pain was less severe.

I remained standing by the door. Adolf signed to me to go. As I was opening the door, Frau Klara waved to me with her outstretched hand. I shall never forget the words which the dying woman then uttered in a whisper. "Gustl," she said — usually she called me Mr. Kubizek, but in that hour she used the name by which Adolf always called me — "go on being a good friend to my son when I'm no longer here. He has no one else." With tears in my eyes I promised, and then I went. This was the evening of December 20.

The next day Adolf came to see us at home. He looked worn out and we could tell from his distraught face what had happened. His mother had died in the early hours of the morning, he said. It was her last wish to be buried by the side of her husband in Leonding. Adolf could hardly speak, so deeply shaken was he by the loss of his mother.

My parents expressed their sympathy, but my mother realised that the best thing was to turn to practical matters straight away. Arrangements had to be made for the funeral. Adolf had already seen the undertakers and the funeral was fixed for December 23 at 9 A.M. But there was much else to be seen to. The removal of the body to Leonding had to be arranged, the necessary documents procured and the funeral announcements printed. All

Chapter 12 — His Mother's Death

this helped Adolf to get over his emotional shock, and he calmly made the necessary preparations.

On December 23, 1907, I went with my mother to the house of mourning. The weather had changed; it was thawing and the streets were covered in slush. The day was damp and misty, and one could hardly see the river. We entered the apartment to take leave of the dead with flowers, as was customary. Frau Klara was laid out on her bed. Her waxen face was transfigured.

I felt that death had come to the dead woman as a relief from terrible pain. Little Paula was sobbing, but Adolf restrained himself. Yet a glance at his face was sufficient to know how he had suffered in those hours. Not only had he now lost both his parents, but with his mother he had lost the only creature on earth on whom he had concentrated his love, and who had loved him in return.

My mother and I went down into the street. The priest came. The body had been laid in the coffin, which was brought down to the hall. The priest blessed the dead and then the small cortège moved off. Adolf followed the coffin. He wore a long black overcoat, black gloves, and carried in his hand, as was customary, a black top hat. The dark clothing made his white face seem even paler. He looked stern and composed. On his left, also in black, was his brother-inlaw, Raubal, and between them the eleven-year-old Paula. Angela, who was well advanced in pregnancy, followed the mourners in a closed carriage. The whole funeral made a wretched impression on me. In addition to my mother and myself, there were only a few tenants of No. 9 Blütengasse, and a few neighbours and acquaintances from their former home in the Humboldtstrasse. My mother, too, felt how miserable this cortege was, but in the kindness of her heart she immediately defended those who had stayed away. Tomorrow was Christmas, she said, and it was quite impossible for many women, with the best will in the world, to get away.

At the church door the coffin was taken from the hearse and carried inside. After the Mass, the second blessing took place. As the body was to be taken to Leonding, the funeral cortege then went through the Urfahr Hauptstrasse. The church bells were ringing as it approached.

Instinctively, I raised my eyes to the windows of the house where Stefanie lived. Perhaps my ardent wish that she should not desert my friend in this, his gravest hour had called her. I can still see how the window opened, a young girl appeared, and Stefanie looked down, interestedly, at the little procession that was passing beneath. I glanced at Adolf; his face remained unchanged, but I did not doubt that he, too, had seen Stefanie. He told me, later, that this was indeed so, and confessed how much in that painful hour the sight of the beloved had comforted him. Was it by intention or was it by chance that Stefanie came to the window at that moment? Perhaps it was just that she had heard the church bells and wondered why they were ringing so early in the morning. Adolf, of course, was convinced that she wanted to show him her sympathy.

In the Hauptstrasse, a second closed carriage was waiting, which Adolf and Paula entered, while the procession broke up. Raubal joined his wife. Then the hearse and the two carriages started off to Leonding for the interment.

On the following morning, December 24, Adolf came to my house. He looked worn out, as though any minute he might collapse. He seemed to be desperate, quite empty, with no spark of life in him. As he felt how worried my mother was about him, he explained that he had not slept for days. My mother asked him where he was going to spend Christmas Eve. He said that the Raubals had invited him and his sister; Paula had already left, but he had not made up his mind yet whether he would go or not. My mother exhorted him to help to make Christmas a peaceful occasion, now that all the members of the family had suffered the same loss, Adolf listened to her in silence. But when we were alone he said to me brusquely: "I shall not go to Raubal's." "Where else will you go?" I asked him impatiently. "After all, it's Christmas Eve." I wanted to ask him to join us. But he did not even let me finish, and shut me up quite energetically, in spite of his sorrow.

Suddenly he pulled himself together and his eyes became bright.

"Perhaps I shall go to Stefanie," he said.

This answer was doubly characteristic of my friend: first, because he was capable of forgetting completely in such moments that his relationship with Stefanie was nothing but wishful thinking, a beautiful illusion, and secondly, because even when he realised this he would, after sober reflection, prefer to stick to his wishful thinking rather than unbosom himself with real people.

Later he confessed to me that he had really been determined to go to Stefanie, although he knew very well that such a sudden visit, without a previous appointment, without even having been introduced to her, and moreover on Christmas Eve, was contrary to good manners and social convention and would probably have meant the end of his relationship with her. But, he told me, on his way he had seen Richard, Stefanie's brother, who was spending his Christmas holiday in Linz. This unexpected meeting had made him give up the idea, for it would have been painful for him if Richard, as was inevitable, had been present at the interview. I did not ask any more questions; it really did not matter whether Adolf was deceiving himself with this pretext, or whether he only offered it to me as an excuse for his behaviour. Certainly I, too, had seen Stefanie at the window, and the sympathy which showed on her face was undoubtedly genuine.

However, I doubt very much if she recognised Adolf at all in his extraordinary attire and in these peculiar circumstances. But of course I did not express this doubt to him, because I knew that it would only have robbed my friend of his last hope.

I can well imagine what Adolf's Christmas Eve in the year 1907 was really like. That he did not want to go to Raubal I could understand. I could also understand that he did not want to disturb our quiet little family celebration, to which I had invited him. The serene harmony of our home would have made him feel his loneliness even more. Compared with Adolf, I considered myself fortune's favourite, for I had everything that he had lost: a father who provided for me, a mother who loved me and a quiet home which welcomed me into its peace.

But he? Where should he have gone that Christmas Eve? He had no acquaintances, no friends, nobody who would have received him with open arms. For him the world was hostile and empty.

So he went — to Stefanie. That is to say — to his dream.

All he ever told me of that Christmas Eve was that he had wandered around for hours. Only towards morning had he returned to his mother's home and gone to sleep. What he thought, felt and suffered, I never knew.

A 1906 watercolor by Hitler given to Kuzibek.

Kubizek at the time of the writing of his book.

Kubizek at the time of his friendship with Hitler.

The Young Hitler

A sketch by Hitler of the house he wanted to build for Kubizek.

A sketch by Hitler of the interior of house he wanted to build for Kubizek.

Illustrations

Stefanie, the young Hitler's true love. She was unaware of his devotion.

The Young Hitler

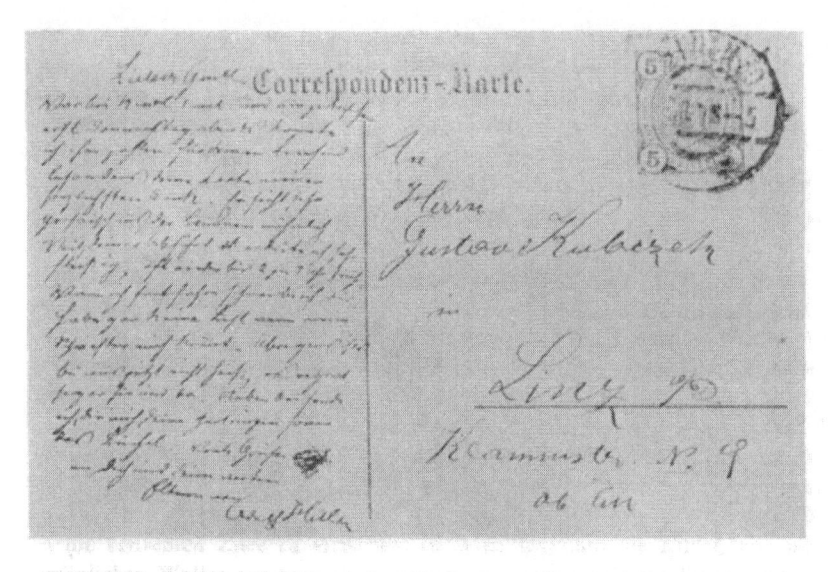

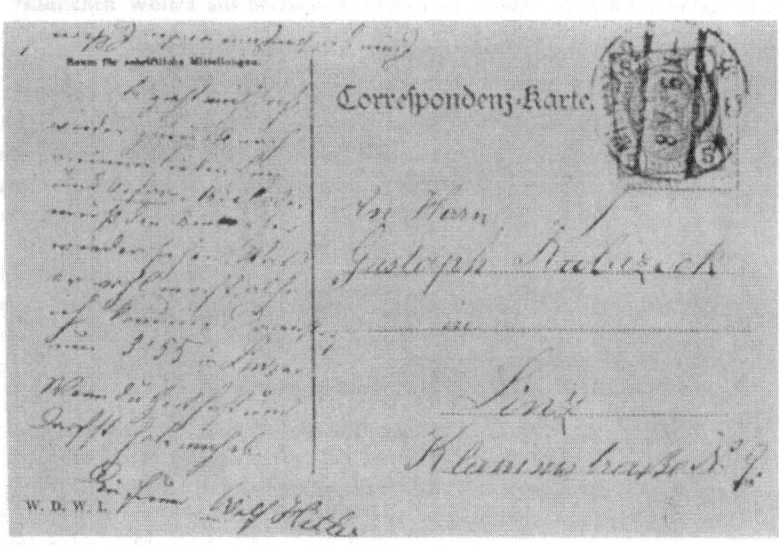

Postcards from Hitler to Kubizek from Vienna. The bottom card contains the codeword for Stefanie: "Benkieser." Hitler writes: "Must also see Benkieser again."

Illustrations

A postcard from Hitler to Kubizek from Vienna.

The Young Hitler

A postcard from Hitler to Kubizek from Weitra im Waldviertel, wishing him the best on his "naming day" (a German tradition separate from a birthday).

Illustrations

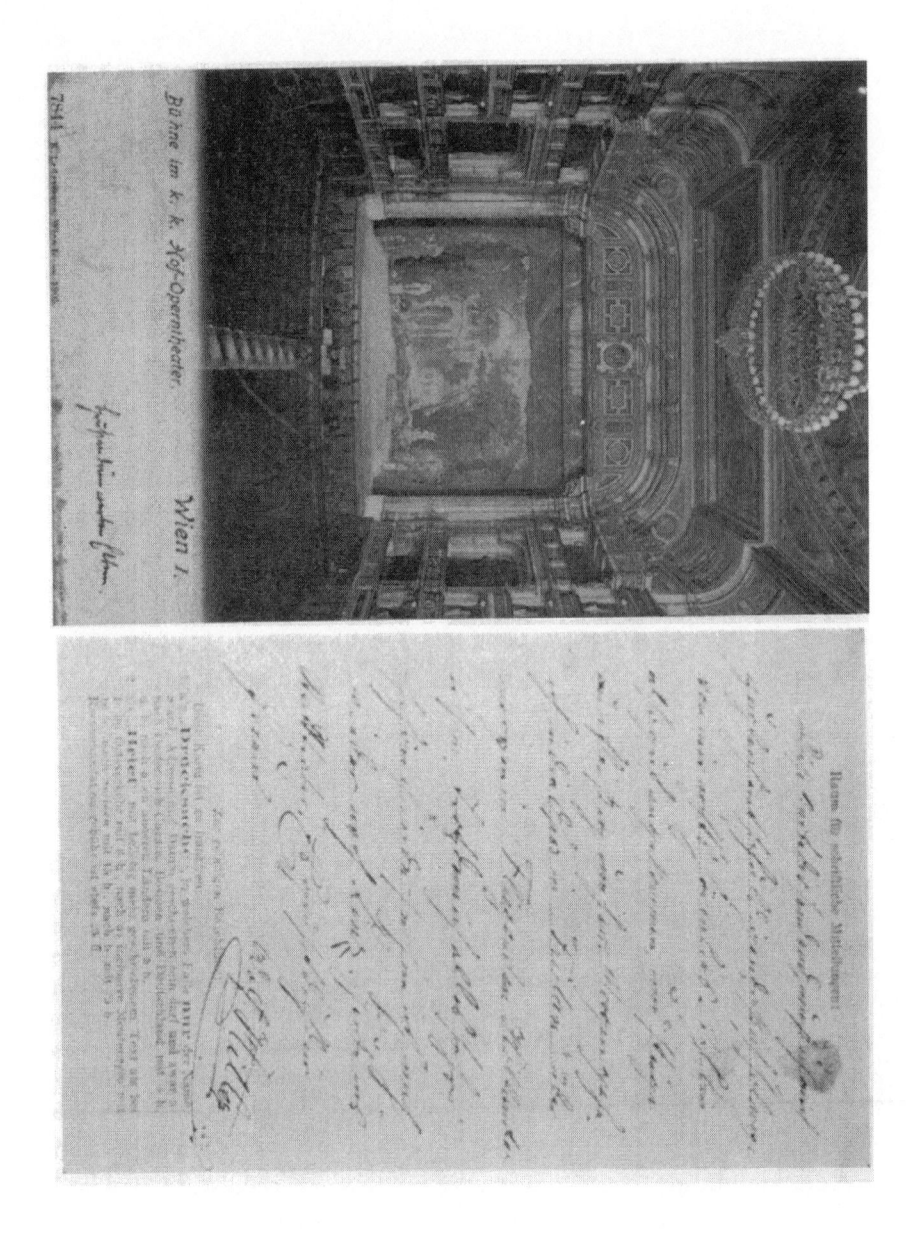

Postcard from Hitler to Kubizek 1906.

Postcard from Hitler to Kubizek when he was living in Vienna.

Illustrations

The first card that Kubizek received from Hitler in Vienna. The text describes the music conservatory and adds that Hitler wants to show his friend the wonderful buildings on the city's Ringstrasse.

Postcard to Kubizek from Hitler, 18 February 1908, in which he asks his friend to come to Vienna.

Letter from Hitler to Kubizek, written while he was traveling to Linz during the Easter weekend.

Letter from Hitler to Kubizek telling him that he would come back to visit his parents in Linz during the summer.

Illustrations

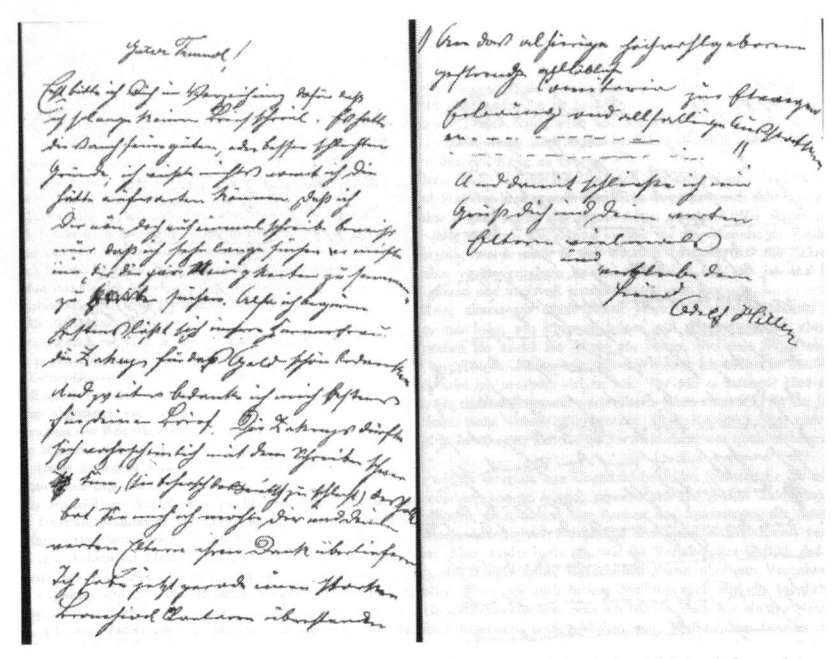

The last letter written by the young Hitler to Kubizek in 1908. After this, Hitler disappeared, plunged into poverty and too ashamed to be seen by his friend again.

Adolf Hitler   München, den 4.August 1933.
                                          Braunes Haus

```
            Mein lieber  Kubizek!

            Erst heute wird mir Dein Brief vom
2.Februar vorgelegt. Bei den Hunderttausenden von
Schreiben, die ich seit dem Januar erhielt, ist es
nicht verwunderlich. Umso grösser war meine Freude,
zum ersten Mal nach so vielen Jahren eine Nachricht
über Dein Leben und Deine Adresse zu erhalten. Ich
würde sehr gerne - wenn die Zeit meiner schwersten
Kämpfe vorüber ist - einmal persönlich die Erinnerung
an diese schönsten Jahre meines Lebens wieder wachru-
fen. Vielleicht wäre es möglich, dass Du mich besuchst.
            Dir und Deiner Mutter alles Gute wün -
schend bin ich in Erinnerung an unsere alte Freundschaft
            Dein
```

Letter to Kubziek from Hitler after he became Chancellor in 1933, saying that the time they spent together were the "best of our lives."

The Young Hitler

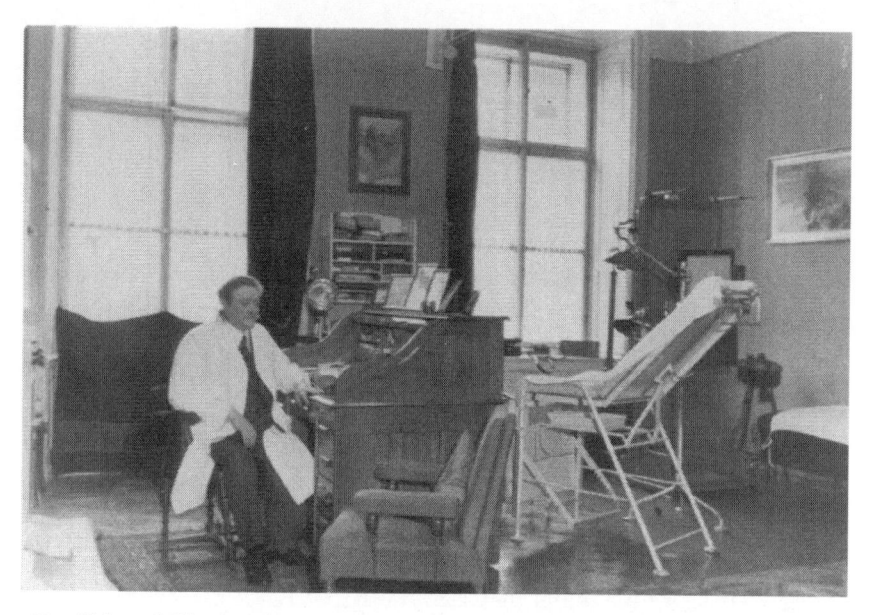

Dr. Eduard Bloch, who was Jewish, treated Hitler as a young man, along with his mother and other members of the Hitler family. This picture of Dr. Bloch in his office in Linz was taken in 1938 on order of Martin Bormann for Hitler's "personal film file." The inscription reads: "The Führer often sat on the chair beside the desk."

Klara Hitler, Adolf's mother, treated by Dr. Bloch.

Chapter 13 — "Come with me, Gustl!"

Adolf had often said these words jestingly when speaking of his intention of going to live in Vienna. But, later on, when he realised how impressed I was by his remarks, the idea grew in his mind that we would go there together, he to attend the Academy of Arts and I the Conservatory.

With his magnificent imagination he produced such a colourful picture of this life, so clear and so detailed, that I often did not know whether it was just wishful thinking or reality. For me, such fantasies had a more practical aspect. To be sure, I had learned my trade well and satisfied my father as well as our customers by my efforts. But the hours in the dusty workshop bad impaired my health, and our doctor, my secret ally, advised emphatically against my continuing to work as an upholsterer.

This meant for me that I would try to make my beloved music my profession, a desire which assumed a more and more concrete shape, although the obstacles were many. I had learned all that there was to be learned in Linz. My teachers, too, encouraged me in my decision to devote my life to music, but this meant my going to live in Vienna. Thus the "Come with me, Gustl" which my friend had at first uttered so lightheartedly took on the character of a firm invitation and a definite goal. Nevertheless, I feel that without Adolf's determined intervention, my unadventurous nature would not have allowed me to change my profession and go to live in Vienna.

Yet my friend certainly thought primarily of himself. He had a horror of going alone, because this, his third journey to Vienna, was a quite different proposition from his earlier visits. Then, he still had his mother, and though he was away, his home still existed. He was not then taking a step into the unknown, for the knowledge that his mother was waiting to welcome him with open arms at any time and in any circumstances gave a firm and reliable substance to his insecure life. His home was the quiet centre round which his stormy existence revolved. Now he had lost it. Going to Vienna would be the last and final decision from which there was no turning back-a jump into the dark.

During the months he had spent there last autumn, he had not succeeded in making any friends; perhaps he had no desire to do so. Relatives of his mother were living there with whom he had formerly had some contact and, unless I am mistaken, he had even stayed with them during his first visit. He never went to see them again and did not even mention them. It was quite understandable that he should have avoided his relatives, because he was afraid that they might question him about his work and livelihood. They would certainly have discovered then that the Academy had rejected him, and he would have suffered starvation and misery rather than have appeared to be in need of help. Nothing, therefore, was more natural than that he should take me with him, as I was not only his friend, but also the only person with whom he shared the secret of his great love. Since his mother's death, Adolf's "Come with me, Gustl" had begun to sound more like a friendly entreaty.

After New Year's Day, 1908, I went with Adolf to visit the grave of his parents. It was a fine winter day, cold and clear, which has forever remained in my memory. Snow covered all the familiar landmarks. Adolf knew every inch of our route, as for years this had been his way to school.

He was very composed, a change that surprised me for I knew that his mother's death had shaken him deeply, and had even caused him physical suffering that had brought him near to collapse from exhaustion. My mother had invited him to share our meals during Christmas, in order that he might recover his strength and leave for a while the empty, cold house in which everything reminded him of his mother. He had come, but had sat silent and serious at our table. It was not yet time to talk to him of future plans. Now, as he walked solemnly by my side, looking much older than I, much more mature and manly, he was still deeply immersed in his own affairs. Yet I was surprised how clearly and detachedly he spoke of them, almost as if it were of someone else's business. Angela had let him know that Paula could now live with them. Her husband had agreed to that, but had refused to receive Adolf into his family as he, Adolf, had behaved disrespectfully to him. Thus, he was relieved of his greatest worry, for the child at least had a secure home.

He himself had never intended to seek asylum with the Raubals. He had expressed his gratitude to Angela and had informed her that all his parents' furniture would go to Paula. The funeral expenses were paid out of his mother's estate. Incidentally, Angela had had a baby girl the day before, who was also to be christened Angela, and his guardian, he added, the Mayor of Leonding, had promised to settle the affairs connected with the inheritance and also to help him to apply for an orphan's pension.

All this sounded very sober and sensible. Afterwards, he began to talk of Stefanie. He was determined, he said, to bring the present state of affairs to an end. At the next opportunity, he would introduce himself to Stefanie and her mother, as this had not been possible during the Christmas holidays. It was high time, he said, to bring matters to a head.

Chapter 13 — "Come with me, Gustl!"

We were walking through the snow-covered village. There was a small one-storied house, No. 61, which had once belonged to Adolf's father; the big beehive, of which his father had been so proud, was still there, but now it was owned by strangers. Next to it was the cemetery. His father's grave, in which his mother had now been buried, was near the eastern wall, and the fresh little mound was covered with snow. Adolf stood in front of it with a stern, set face; he looked hard and severe, and there were no tears in his eyes. His thoughts were with his beloved mother. I stood by his side and prayed.

On our way back, Adolf said that he would probably stay in Linz throughout the month of January until the home was finally disposed of and the estate settled. He foresaw, he said, some heated arguments with his guardian. Certainly his guardian wanted to do his best for Adolf, but what use was this to him if the "best" was nothing more than an apprenticeship to a master baker in Leonding? Old Josef Mayrhofer, Hitler's guardian, now well advanced in years, still lives in Leonding.

Naturally, he has often been asked about his experiences with the young Hitler, and his impressions of him. In his simple, disinterested manner, he has replied to all questioners — first the enemies, then the friends, and then again the enemies of his ward — and his replies have always been the same, irrespective of the questioner's opinions.

One day in January, 1908, he would say, the Hitler-Adi, grown tall, with dark down on his upper lip and a deep voice, almost a grown man, came to see him to discuss the question of his inheritance. But his first sentence was: "I am going to Vienna again." All attempts to dissuade him failed — a stubborn fellow, like his father, the old Hitler.

Josef Mayrhofer still has in his possession the documents relating to these discussions. The application for an orphan's pension for himself and his sister which Adolf made at his guardian's request, reads as follows:

To the Respected Imperial and Royal Finance Administration. The respectfully undersigned herewith request the kind allocation of the Orphans' Pension due to them. Both of these applicants, after the death of their mother, widow of an Imperial and Royal Customs Official, on December 21, 1907, are now without either of their parents, are minors, and are incapable of earning their own living. The guardian of both applicants — Adolf Hitler, born on the 20th April, 1889, in Braunau-on-Inn, and Paula Hitler, born on the 21st January, 1898, in Fischlham, near Lambach, Upper Austria — is Mr. Joseph Mayrhofer, of Leonding, near Linz. Both applicants are domiciled in Linz.
    ADOLF HITLER —- PAULA HITLER

Incidentally, Adolf obviously signed the application for his sister Paula, for the name "Hitler" in both signatures shows the same downward-sloping tendency which was so characteristic of his signature in later years. Besides, he made a mistake in the date of birth of his sister; Paula was not born in 1898, but in 1896.

According to the legislation then in force regarding state officials, orphans of under twenty-four years of age, with no means of their own, were entitled to claim an orphan's pension amounting to one half of the widow's pension which their mother had been receiving. Frau Hitler had received a pension of 100 crowns a month since her husband's death; therefore, Adolf and Paula were entitled to a total of 50 crowns a month, and Adolf's share was thus 25 crowns a month.

This, of course, was not enough for him to live on: for example, he had to pay 10 crowns a month for his room at Mrs. Zakreys'.

The application was granted, and the first payment was made on February 12, 1908, when Adolf was already in Vienna. Incidentally, three years later he renounced his share in favour of his sister Paula, although he could have continued to claim it until he reached the age of twenty-four, i.e., in April, 1913. The document of renunciation, dated May 4th, 1911, is still in the possession of his guardian, Joseph Mayrhofer.

The document concerning the inheritance, which Adolf signed in the presence of his guardian before he left for Vienna, also mentioned his share in his father's estate, amounting to about seven hundred crowns. It is possible that he had already spent part of this money during his previous stay in Vienna, but in view of his very economical way of life — the only large item in his budget was books — he was left with enough to tide him over at least the beginning of his new sojourn there. As regards our future together, Adolf was more fortunate than I, not only because he had some capital and a fixed monthly income, however small — a matter which I had still to arrange with my parents — but also because, having prevailed over his guardian, he was free to make his own decisions, whereas my decisions were subject to my parents' confirmation.

For me, moreover, moving to Vienna meant giving up the trade I had learned, whereas Adolf could continue to lead there more or less his previous life. All these circumstances made it increasingly difficult for me to come to a decision; Adolf could not understand this for some time, although from the beginning he had taken the lead in this whole difficult affair. As far back as the beginning of our friendship, when I could still only visualise my future in the dusty, upholsterer's workshop, Adolf, though nearly a year younger than I, had made it abundantly clear to me that I

Chapter 13 — "Come with me, Gustl!"

ought to become a musician. Having put this idea into my head, he never gave up his efforts to persuade me. He comforted me when I despaired, he bolstered up my self-confidence when I was in danger of losing it, he praised, he criticised, he was occasionally rude and violent and railed at me furiously, but he never lost sight of the goal which he had set for me; and if sometimes we had such furious rows that I believed it was the end of everything, we would enthusiastically renew our friendship after a concert performance in which I had taken part.

By God, nobody on earth, not even my mother who loved me so much and knew me so well, was as capable of bringing my secret desires into the open and making them come true as my friend, although he had never had any systematic musical training.

In the winter of 1907, when work in our business was slackening and I had more time to myself, I took lessons in harmonics from the conductor of the Linz Theatre. My studies were as thorough as they were successful, and filled me with enthusiasm. Unfortunately, there was no scope in Linz for studying the other special subjects of musical theory, such as counterpoint, orchestration and the history of music. Nor was there a seminary for training in conducting and composition, much less any stimulus for free composition. This sort of training was only available at the Vienna Conservatory; besides, there I would have the opportunity of hearing firstclass performances of operas and concerts. Though I had made up my mind to go to Vienna, unlike my friend I lacked the necessary determination to carry out my decision against all odds. But Adolf had already prepared the ground. Without my knowledge, he bad succeeded in convincing my mother of my musical vocation; for what mother does not like to hear a brilliant career prophesied for her son as a conductor, especially when she herself is so devoted to music? Thus, she soon became our ally. And there was also her justifiable anxiety about my health, as my lungs could no longer stand the perpetual dust in the workshop. So my mother, who had grown fond of Adolf just as Frau Klara had become fond of me, was won over, and everything now depended on my father's consent. Not that he openly opposed my wish.

My father was in every respect the opposite of Adolf's father, as he had been described to me by my friend. He was always quiet, and apparently took no interest in what was going on around him. All his thoughts were devoted to the business which he had created out of nothing, had successfully steered through grave crises, and had now built up into a reputable, prosperous enterprise. He regarded my musical tastes as idle dilettantism, as he could not believe that it was possible to build a secure existence on more or less useless fiddling and strumming. To the last, he could not understand that I, knowing poverty and distress, was willing to renounce security in favour of a vague future.

How often did I hear him say "A bird in the hand is worth two in the bush," or bitterly, "What was the use of all my drudgery?" I was working harder than ever in the workshop, as I did not want it said that I was neglecting my trade for the sake of my musical studies. My father saw in my industry a sign that I wanted to remain in the trade and take over his business someday. My mother knew how devoted my father was to his work, and so kept silent in order not to upset him. So at the time when my musical future depended absolutely on my attending the Vienna Conservatory, things seemed to have reached a deadlock within our domestic circle: I worked feverishly in the workshop, and said nothing. My mother also said nothing, and my father, thinking that I had finally abandoned the plan, did the same.

At this juncture, Adolf came to see us. At one glance he realised what the situation was, and intervened immediately. To begin with, he brought me back into "form." During his stay in Vienna, he had made detailed enquiries about the study of music and now he gave me exact information on the subject, telling me, in his tempting way, how much he had enjoyed attending operas and concerts. My mother's imagination was also fired by these vivid descriptions, and so a decision became more and more imperative. It was, however, essential that Adolf himself should convince my father.

A difficult enterprise! What use was the most brilliant eloquence if the old master upholsterer had no regard for anything connected with art? He was quite fond of Adolf but, after all, he only saw in him a young man who had failed at school and thought too highly of himself to learn a trade.

My father had tolerated our friendship, but actually would have preferred a more sound companion for me. Adolf was, therefore, in a decidedly unfavorable position, and it is astonishing that he nevertheless managed to win over my father to our plan in so comparatively short a time. I would have understood it if there had been a violent clash of opinions; in that case, Adolf would have been in his element and able to play all the trump cards which he held. But that was not the case. I cannot recollect that any argument in the usual sense took place at all. Adolf treated the whole matter as of no great importance and, in particular, implied that the decision rested with my father alone. He accepted the fact that my father only half gave his consent, suggesting a temporary solution: as the current scholastic year at the Conservatory had already started in the previous autumn, I should go to Vienna for a trial period only to look around for a while. If the facilities for training came up to my expectations, I could then make a final decision,

Chapter 13 — "Come with me, Gustl!"

but failing this, I could return home and enter my father's business. Adolf, who hated compromise and with whom it was usually all or nothing, was, surprisingly enough, agreeable to this course. I was blissfully happy as never before in my life, for now I had achieved my purpose without upsetting my father, and my mother shared my joy.

At the beginning of February, Adolf returned to Vienna. His address remained the same, he told me when he left, as he had continued to pay his rent to Mrs. Zakreys, and I should write to him in good time announcing my arrival. I helped him carry his luggage to the station, four cases altogether unless I am mistaken, every one of them very heavy. I asked him what they contained, and he answered "All my belongings." They were almost entirely books.

At the station Adolf once again spoke of Stefanie. Unfortunately, he had had no opportunity to talk to her, he said, for he had never met her unaccompanied. What he had to tell Stefanie was for her ears only. "Perhaps I shall write to her," he added in conclusion. But I thought that this idea, expressed by Adolf for the first time, was merely a sign of embarrassment, or at the most, a cheap consolation. My friend entered the train and, standing at the window, shook me by the hand. As the train moved off, "Follow me soon, Gustl," he called out to me.

My good mother had already started preparing my clothes and linen for my journey to great, unknown Vienna. In the end, even my father wanted to contribute something; he made me a big wooden box which was reinforced with strong iron bands. I put into it my music, and my mother filled the remaining space with clothes and shoes.

In the meantime, a postcard arrived from Adolf, dated February 18, 1908, showing a view of the Armour Collection at the Vienna Museum of the History of Art: "Dear Friend" it began-and this form of address proved how much our relationship had deepened since his mother's death. "Dear Friend, am anxiously expecting news of your arrival. Write soon so that I can prepare everything for your festive welcome. The whole of Vienna is awaiting you, therefore come soon. I will, of course, come and meet you." On the back of the postcard he wrote: "Now the weather here is improving. I hope you will have better weather too. Well, as I said before, at first you will stay with me. Later we shall see. One can get a piano here in the so-called 'Dorotheum' for as little as 50/60 Fls. Well, many regards to you and your esteemed parents, from your friend, Adolf Hitler." Then a postscript. "Beg you again, come soon."

Adolf had addressed the card as usual to "Gustav" Kubizek. He spelt Gustav sometimes with a "v" and sometimes with a "ph." He heartily disliked my first name, August, and always called me "Gustl," which was more like Gustav than August. He would probably have preferred it had I formally changed my first name. He even addressed me as Gustav when he wrote to me on my Saint's day, the feast of Saint Augustine, August 28. Under my name there is the abbreviation "Stud.", and I remember that he liked to refer to me as "Stud. Mus." This postcard, unlike the previous ones, is much more cheerful. Typical of Adolf's mood is his humour, which permeates it. "The whole of Vienna is awaiting you," he says, and he intends to prepare a "festive welcome." All this indicates that, after the dark and depressing days which he had spent in Linz following his mother's death, he was feeling relaxed and free in Vienna, however uncertain the future might be. Nevertheless, he must have been very lonely. The "anxiously" in the first sentence of his card was no doubt meant seriously, and the fact that he repeats the "come soon," even in the form "beg you again to come soon," proves how much he was looking forward to my arrival. Even the information as to the cheap piano was intended to encourage me to come without delay. He may have feared secretly that my vacillating father would change his mind at the last moment.

The day of my departure arrived. In the morning I went to church with my mother; I felt how painful my departure was for her, although she stuck tenaciously to her resolve. Yet I also remember a typical remark which my father made when he saw my mother weeping. "I can't understand why you are so depressed, Mother," he said. "We haven't asked Gustl to leave his home; he wanted to himself." My mother, in her grief at our parting, concentrated on my creature comforts, giving me a nice piece of roast pork; and the dripping, which was to be spread on my bread, was put into a special container. She baked some buns for me, gave me a large piece of cheese, a jar of jam and a bottle of coffee. My brown canvas bag was full to overflowing with food.

So off I went to the station after my last dinner at home, well provided for in every respect. My parents saw me off; my father shook my hand and said "Always remain honest." But my mother, with tears in her eyes, kissed me and, as the train started, made the sign of the Cross on my forehead. For a long time I felt her tender fingers there as they traced the Cross.

Chapter 14 — 29 Stumpergasse

My first impression on arriving in Vienna was one of noisy and excited confusion. I stood there, holding my heavy case, so bewildered that I did not know which way to turn. All these people! And this noise and tumult! This was terrible. I was almost inclined to turn tail and go straight home again. But the crowds, thrusting and complaining, were jostling me through the barrier where the ticket inspectors and police stood, till I found myself in the Station Hall looking round for my friend. I shall always remember this first welcome in Vienna. While I stood there, still overwhelmed by all the shouting and hustling, recognisable from a mile away as a country bumpkin, Adolf behaved as a perfectly acclimatised city dweller. In his dark, good-quality overcoat, dark hat and the walking stick with the ivory handle, he appeared almost elegant. He was obviously delighted to see me and greeted me warmly and, as was then the custom, kissed me lightly on the cheek.

The first problem was the transport of my bag for, thanks to my mother's presents, this weighed very heavily. As I was looking around for a porter, Adolf grabbed one of the handles and I took the other. We crossed the Mariahilferstrasse — with people everywhere, coming and going about their affairs, and such a terrible noise that one could not hear oneself speak; but how thrilling were the electric arc-lights that made the station yard as bright as day.

I still remember how glad I was when Adolf soon turned into a side street, the Stumpergasse.

Here it was quiet and dark. Adolf stopped in front of a fairly new-looking house on the right side, No. 29. As far as I could see, it was a very fine house, most imposing and distinguished looking, perhaps too distinguished for such youngsters as we were, I thought. But Adolf went straight through the entrance and crossed a small courtyard. The house on the far side of this courtyard was much humbler. We went up a dark staircase to the second floor. There were several doors opening on this floor — ours was No. 17.

Adolf unlocked the door. An unpleasant smell of kerosene greeted me, and ever since, this smell has been connected, for me, with the memory of that apartment. We seemed to be in a kitchen, but the landlady was not about. Adolf opened a second door. In the small room that he occupied, a miserable kerosene lamp was burning. I looked around me.

The first thing that struck me were the sketches that lay around on the table, on the bed, everywhere. Adolf cleared the table, spread a piece of newspaper on it and fetched a bottle of milk from the window. Then he brought sausage and bread. But I can still see his white, earnest face as I pushed all these things aside and opened the bag. Cold roast pork, stuffed buns, and other lovely things to eat. All he said was, "Yes, that's what it is to have a mother!" We ate like kings. Everything tasted of "home." After all the commotion, I began to collect myself. Then came the inevitable question about Stefanie. When I had to confess that I had not been for the evening stroll on the Landstrasse for some considerable time, Adolf told me that I ought to have gone for his sake. Before I could reply there was a knock on the door. A little old woman, withered, and altogether of a rather comic appearance slipped inside.

Adolf rose and introduced me in his most formal manner: "My friend, Gustav Kubizek, of Linz, a music student." "Pleased to meet you, pleased to meet you," the old woman repeated several times, and announced her own name: Maria Zakreys. From the singsong tone and the peculiar accent, I realised that Frau Zakreys was not a real Viennese. Or rather, she was a Viennese, perhaps even a typical one, but she had not first seen the light of day in Hernals or Lerchenfeld but rather in Stanislau or Neutitschein. I never asked and never found out, and after all, it made no difference. In any case, Frau Zakreys was the only person in this city of millions with whom Adolf and I ever had any dealings, Tired as I was this first evening, I remember that Adolf showed me around the city How could a person who had just come to Vienna go to bed without having seen the Opera House? So I was dragged to the Opera House. The performmace was not yet over. I admired the entrance hall, the magnificent staircase, the marble balustrade, the deep, soft carpets and the gilded decorations on the ceiling. Once away from the humble abode in the Stumpergasse, I felt as though I had been transported to another planet, so overwhelming was the impression.

Now it was I who insisted on seeing the St. Stephen's Spire. We turned into the Kärntnerstrasse.

But the evening mist was so thick that the spire was lost to view. I could just see the heavy, dark mass of the nave stretching up into the grey monotony of the mist, almost unearthly, as though not built by human hands. In order to show me something else special, Adolf took me to the Maria am Gestade Church, which, compared with the overpowering bulk of St. Stephen's, seemed to me like a delicate Gothic chapel.

When we got home we each had to pay the grumpy concierge whom we had awakened a *Sperrsechserl* (a penny for unlocking) for opening the big door of the house. Mrs. Zakreys had made me up a primitive bed on the floor of Adolf's room. Although midnight was long past, Adolf still

Chapter 14 — 29 Stumpergasse

kept talking excitedly. But I stopped listening — it was just too much for me. The moving farewell from my home, my mother's sad face, the journey, the arrival, the noise, the clamour, the Vienna of the Stumpergasse, the Vienna of the Opera House — worn out, I fell asleep.

Of course, I could not stay at Frau Zakreys'. Anyhow, it was impossible to put a grand piano in the little room. So the next morning, when Adolf finally got up, we set out to look for a room. As I wanted to stay as near as possible to my friend, we wandered at first along the nearby streets.

Once more I saw this alluring city, Vienna, from the "other side." Gloomy courtyards, narrow, ill-lit tenements and stairs, ever more and more stairs. Adolf paid Frau Zakreys ten crowns, and that was what I reckoned to pay. But the rooms we were shown at that price were mostly so small and wretched that it would have been impossible to get a grand piano into them, and when we did find a room that would have been big enough, the landlady would not hear of having a lodger who played the piano.

I was very depressed and low-spirited and full of home sickness. What kind of big city was this Vienna? Full of indifferent, unsympathetic people — it must be awful to live here. I walked, despairing and miserable, with Adolf along the Zollergasse. Once more we saw a notice "Room to Let." We rang the bell and the door was opened by a neatly dressed maid, who showed us into an elegantly furnished room containing magnificent twin beds. "Madame is coming immediately," said the maid, curtsied, and vanished. We both knew at once that it was too stylish for us. Then "Madame" appeared in the doorway, very much a lady, not so young, but very elegant.

She wore a silk dressing gown and slippers trimmed with fur. She greeted us smilingly, inspected Adolf, then me, and asked us to sit down. My friend asked which room was to let. "This one," she answered, and pointed to the two beds. Adolf shook his head and said curtly, "Then one of the beds will have to come out, because my friend must have room for a piano." The lady was obviously disappointed that it was I and not Adolf who wanted a room, and asked whether Adolf already had a room. When he answered in the affirmative, she suggested that I, together with the piano I needed, should move into his room and he should take this one. While she was animatedly suggesting this to Adolf, through a sudden movement the belt which kept the dressing gown together came undone. "Oh, excuse me, gentlemen," the lady exclaimed, and immediately fastened the dressing gown together again. But that second had sufficed to show us that under her silk covering she wore nothing but a brief pair of panties.

Adolf turned as red as a peony, gripped my arm, and said, "Come, Gustl." I do not remember how we got out of the house. All I remember is Adolf furiously exclaiming as we got into the street again, "What a Mrs. Potiphar." Apparently, such experiences, too, were part of Vienna.

Adolf must have realised how hard it was for me to find my way around in this bewildering city, and on our way home he suggested that we should take a room together. He would speak to Frau Zakreys; perhaps she would fix up something in her own house.

In the end he succeeded in persuading Frau Zakreys to move into his little room and let us take over the somewhat bigger room that she occupied. We agreed on a rent of twenty crowns a month. She had nothing against my playing the piano, so this was an excellent solution for me.

The next morning, while Adolf was still asleep, I went to register at the Conservatory. I produced my references from the Linz Music School and was immediately examined. First came an oral examination, then I had to sing something at sight, and finally, a test in harmony. All went well, and I was asked to go to the Administration Office, Director Kaiser — and for me he was really the Emperor-congratulated me, and told me about the curriculum. He advised me to register as an extramural student at the University and to attend lectures in the history of music. Then he introduced me to the conductor, Gustav Gutheil, with whom I should study, among other things, the practical side of conducting. In addition to this, I was accepted as viola player in the Conservatory's orchestra. All this was quite straightforward and soon, in spite of the initial bewilderment, I felt on firm ground. As so often happened in my life, I found help and consolation in music; even more, it now became my whole life. I had finally escaped from the dusty upholsterer's workshop and could devote myself entirely to my art.

In the nearby Liniengasse I discovered a piano store, called Feigl. I inspected the instruments for hire; of course, they were not particularly good ones, but I did finally find a grand piano that was fairly good and I hired it for ten crowns a month. When Adolf came home in the evening — I did not yet know how he spent his days — he was astonished to see the grand piano. For that comparatively small room an upright model would have been more suitable. But how was I to become a conductor without a grand piano! Admittedly, it was not as easy as I had thought.

Adolf immediately took a hand to try out the best place to put it. He agreed that to get enough light, the piano had to stand near the window. After much experiment, the contents of the room—two beds, a night chest, a wardrobe, a washstand, a table and two chairs, were distributed to the best

Chapter 14 — 29 Stumpergasse

advantage. In spite of this, the instrument took up the whole space of the right-hand window.

The table was pushed into the other window enclosure. The space between the beds and the piano, as well as that between the beds and the table, was hardly more than one foot wide. And for Adolf, room to stride up and down was every bit as important as playing the piano was for me.

At once he tried it out. From the door to the curve of the piano — three steps! That was enough, because three steps one way, and three steps the other made six, even though Adolf in his continual pacing up and down had to turn so often that it became almost a case of moving around his own axis.

The bare, sooty rear side of the house in front was all we could see from our room. Only if you stood very close to the free window, and looked sharply upwards, would you see a narrow slice of the firmament, but even this modest bit of sky was generally hidden by smoke, dust or fog. On exceptionally lucky days the sun would shine through. To be sure it shone hardly at all on our house, much less in our room. But on the rear of the house in front streaks of sunshine were to be seen for a couple of hours, and this had to compensate us for the sun that we so sorely missed.

I told Adolf that I had got through the entrance examination at the Conservatory quite well and was glad that I was now firmly settled down to my studies. Adolf remarked baldly, "I had no idea I had such a clever friend." This did not sound very flattering, but I was used to such remarks from him. Apparently he was at a very critical period, was very irritable, and shut me up brusquely when I began to talk about my studies. He finally reconciled himself to the piano.

He could practise a bit too, he remarked. I said I was willing to teach him — but here again I had put my foot into it. Ill-temperedly he snarled at me: "You can keep your scales and such rubbish. I'll get on by myself." Then he calmed down again and said, in a propitiating tone, "Why should I become a musician, Gustl? After all, I have you!" Our circumstances were modest in the extreme. I certainly could not do much with the monthly allowance my father made me. Regularly at the beginning of each month, Adolf received a certain sum from his guardian. I do not know how much this was, perhaps only the twenty-five crowns orphan's pension, of which he had immediately to pay out ten to Frau Zakreys; perhaps it was more, if his guardian was paying out of capital in installments whatever his parents may have left.

Perhaps relatives helped to support him, for instance, the humpbacked Aunt Johanna; but I do not know. I only know that even then

Adolf often went hungry, although he would not admit this to me. What did Adolf have for an ordinary day's meals? A bottle of milk, a loaf of bread, some butter.

For lunch he often bought a piece of poppyseed cake or nutcake to add to it. That is what he made do with. Every fortnight my mother sent a food parcel, and then we feasted. But in money matters Adolf was very precise. I never knew how much, or rather, how little, money he had.

Doubtless he was secretly ashamed of it. Occasionally, anger got the better of him and he would shout with fury, "Isn't this a dog's life?" Nevertheless, he was happy and contented when we could go once more to the opera, or listen to a concert, or read an interesting book.

For a long time I could not find out where he ate his lunch. Any enquiries about it he would crossly dismiss — these were not subjects one discussed. As I had some spare time in the afternoon, sometimes I used to come home directly after lunch; but I never found Adolf at home.

Perhaps he was sitting in the Soup Kitchen in the Liniengasse where I sometimes had my midday meal. No, he was not there, I went to the "Auge Gottes." Neither was he there. When I asked him in the evening why he never came to the Soup Kitchen, he made a long speech about the contemptible institution of these soup kitchens which only symbolise the segregation of the social classes.

As an extramural student of the university I was permitted to eat in the canteen — it was still the old canteen, for the new one erected by the German Schools Society did not then exist — and I could also procure cheap meal tickets for Adolf, and finally he consented to come with me. I knew how much he liked sweets, so, as well as the main dish, I got some cakes, I thought he would enjoy this because you could see from his face how hungry he was, but as he sulkily gulped it down, he venomously hissed at me, "I don't understand how you can enjoy anything among such people!" Of course, there used to gather in the canteen students from all the nations of the realm, together with several Jewish students. That was reason enough to stop him going there. But, to tell the truth, in spite of all his determination, he let hunger get the better of him. He squeezed himself in next to me in the canteen, turned his back on the rest and greedily wolfed down his favourite nutcake. Many a time, in my political indifference, was I secretly amused to see him swinging between anti-Semitism and his passion for nutcake.

For days on end he could live on milk and bread and butter only. I certainly was not spoilt, but this was beyond me. We did not make any acquaintances. Adolf would never have permitted me time for anybody but

Chapter 14 — 29 Stumpergasse

himself. More than ever did he regard our friendship as one that excluded any other relationship.

Once, as a result of pure chance, he treated me to a very explicit reproof in this respect. Harmony was my hobbyhorse; in Linz, too, I had shone at it, and here I got on swimmingly. One day Professor Boschetti called me to the office and asked me whether I would like to do some coaching in the subject. Then he introduced me to my future pupils. The two daughters of a brewer in Kolomea, the daughter of a landowner in Radautz, and also the daughter of a businessman in Spalato.

I was most depressed by the startling differences between the good-class boardinghouse in which these young ladies lived and our wretched hole that always stank of kerosene. Usually, at the end of the lesson, I partook of a tea so substantial that it served me for supper as well. When there was added to the group the daughter of a cloth manufacturer from Jägerndorf in Silesia and the daughter of a magistrate in Agram, my half-dozen pupils together represented every corner of the widespread Hapsburg Empire.

And then the unexpected happened. One of them, the girl from Silesia, found she could not get on with a piece of written homework, and came round to me in the Stumpergasse to ask for my help. Our good old landlady raised her eyebrows when she saw the pretty young girl. But that was all right; I was indeed only concerned with the musical example which she had not understood, and I explained it to her. As she copied it down quickly, Adolf came in. I introduced him to my pupil, "My friend from Linz, Adolf Hitler." Adolf said nothing. But hardly had the girl got outside when he went for me wildly — for since his unfortunate experience with Stefanie he was a woman hater.

Was our room, already spoilt by that monster, that grand piano, to become the rendezvous for this crew of musical women, he asked me furiously? I had a job to convince him that the poor girl was not suffering from the pangs of love, but from examination-pains. The result was a detailed speech about the senselessness of women studying. Like blows the words fell upon me, as though I were the cloth manufacturer or the brewer who had sent his daughter to the Conservatory. Adolf got himself more and more involved in a general criticism of social conditions. I cowered silently on the piano stool while he, enraged, strode the three steps along and the three steps back and hurled his indignation in the bitterest terms, first against the door, and then against the piano.

Altogether, in these early days in Vienna, I had the impression that Adolf had become unbalanced. He would fly into a temper at the slightest thing. There were days when nothing I could do seemed right to him, and he made our life together very hard to bear. But I had known Adolf now for over three years. I had gone through terrible days with him after the wreck of his scholastic career, and also after his mother's death. I did not know to what this present mood of deep depression was due, but I thought that sooner or later it would improve.

He was at odds with the world. Wherever he looked, he saw injustice, hate and enmity. Nothing was free from his criticism; nothing found favour in his eyes. Only music was able to cheer him up a little, as, for instance, when we went on Sundays to the performances of sacred music in the Burgkapelle. Here, one could hear at no expense soloists from the Vienna Opera House and the Vienna Boys' Choir. Adolf was particularly fond of this famous Boys' Choir, and he told me again and again how grateful be was for that early musical training he had received at Lambach. But in other ways, to remember, just at that time, his carefree childhood was particularly painful to him.

All this time he was ceaselessly busy. I had no idea what a student at the Academy of Arts was supposed to do. In any case, the subjects must have been exceedingly varied; one day he would be sitting for hours over books, then again he would sit writing till the small hours, or another day would see the piano, the table, his bed and mine, and even the floor, completely covered with designs. He would stand, staring tensely down at his work, move stealthily on tiptoe among the drawings, improve something here, correct something there, muttering to himself all the time and underlining his rapid words with violent gestures. Woe betide me if I disturbed him on these occasions. I had great respect for this difficult and detailed work, and said I liked what I saw of it.

When, getting impatient, I would open the piano, he would shuffle the sheets quickly together, put them in a cupboard, grab up a hook and make off to Schönbrunn. He had found a quiet bench there among the lawns and trees, where no one ever disturbed him. Whatever progress he made with his studies in the open air was accomplished on this seat. I, too, was fond of this quiet spot, where one could forget one lived in a metropolis. Often in later years I visited this lonely bench.

It would seem that a student in architecture could spend much more time in the open air and work more independently than could a Conservatory student. On one occasion, when he had once more written till all hours of the night — the ugly little smoky kerosene lamp had nearly burnt out and I was still awake — I asked him bluntly what was going to be the end of all this work. Instead of answering, he handed me a couple of hastily scribbled sheets. Astounded, I read: "Holy Mountain in

Chapter 14 — 29 Stumpergasse

the background, before it the mighty sacrificial block surrounded by huge oaks; two powerful warriors hold the black bull, which is to be sacrificed, firmly by the horns, and press the beast's mighty head against the hollow in the sacrificial block. Behind them, erect in light-coloured robes, stands the priest. He holds the sword with which he will slaughter the bull. All around, solemn, bearded men, leaning on their shields, their lances ready, are watching the ceremony intently." I could not see any connection between this extraordinary description and the study of architecture, so I asked what it was supposed to be.

"A play," replied Adolf.

Then, in stirring words, he described the action to me. Unfortunately, I have long since forgotten it. I only remember that it was set in the Bavarian mountains at the time of the bringing of Christianity to those parts. The men who lived on the mountain did not want to accept the new faith. On the contrary! They had bound themselves by oath to kill the Christian missionaries. On this was based the conflict of the drama.

I would have liked to have asked Adolf whether his studies in the Academy left him so much free time that he could write dramas, too, but I knew how sensitive he was about everything appertaining to his chosen profession. I could appreciate his attitude, because certainly he had struggled hard enough to get his chance to study. I suppose that is what made him so touchy in this respect. But, nevertheless, there seemed to me something not quite right about it all.

His mood worried me more and more as the days went by. I had never known him torment himself in this way before. On the contrary! In my opinion, he possessed rather too much than too little self-confidence. But now things seemed to have changed round. He wallowed deeper and deeper in self-criticism. Yet it only needed the slightest touch — as when one flicks on the electric light and everything becomes brilliantly clear — for his self-accusation to become an accusation against the times, against the whole world; choking with his catalogue of hates, he would pour his fury over everything, against mankind in general who did not understand him, who did not appreciate him and by whom he was persecuted. I see him before me, striding up and down the small space in boundless anger, shaken to his very depths. I sat at the piano with my fingers motionless on the keyboard and listened to him, upset by his hymn of hate, and yet worried about him, for his ranting at the bare walls was heard only by me, and perhaps by Frau Zakreys working in the kitchen, who would be worrying about whether the crazed young man would be able to produce his next month's rent. But those at whom these burning words were directed, they did not hear him at all. So of what use was all the great display? Suddenly, however, in the middle of this hate-ridden harangue where he challenged a whole epoch, one sentence revealed to me how deep was the abyss on whose edge he was tottering.

"I shall give up Stefanie." These were the most terrible words he could utter, for Stefanie was the only creature on God's earth whom he excepted from this infamous humanity — a being who, made radiant by his glowing love, gave his tormented existence sense and purpose. His father dead, his mother dead, his only sister still a child, what was there left to him? He had no family, no home; only his love, only Stefanie in the midst of all his sufferings and catastrophes had remained steadfastly by his side — admittedly only in his imagination. Until now this imagination had been strong enough to be a help to him. But in the spiritual convulsion through which he was now passing, apparently even this obstinately held conviction had broken down.

"I thought you were going to write to her?" I interposed, meaning to help him by this suggestion.

He brushed my remark away with an impatient gesture (it was only forty years later that I learned that he really had written to her then), and then came words that I had never before heard him utter: "It's mad to wait for her. Certainly Mama has already picked out the man for Stefanie to marry.

Love? They won't worry about that. A good match, that's all that matters. And I'm a poor match, at least in the eyes of Mama." Then came a furious reckoning with the "Mama," with everybody who belonged to these fine circles who, through cleverly arranged marriages among themselves, continue to enjoy their unmerited social privileges.

I gave up the attempt to practise the piano, and went to bed, while Adolf became absorbed in his books. I still remember how shocked I was then. If Adolf could no longer cling to the thought of Stefanie, whatever would become of him? My feelings were divided: on the one hand, I was glad that he was finally released from this hopeless love for Stefanie, and on the other hand, I knew that Stefanie was his only ideal, the only thing that kept him going and gave his life an aim.

The next day, for a trifling reason, there was a bitter row between us. I had to practise, Adolf wanted to read. As it was raining he could not go off to Schönbrunn.

"This eternal strumming," he shouted at me, "One's never safe from it." "It's quite simple," I answered, and getting up took my timetable out of my music case, and with a drawing pin fixed it on the cupboard door.

Chapter 14 — 29 Stumpergasse

Now he could see exactly when I was out, when not, and just when my hours for practising were. "And now hang your timetable under it," I added.

Timetable! He didn't need any such thing. He kept his timetable in his head. That was good enough for him and it had to be good enough for me.

I shrugged my shoulders doubtfully. His work was anything but systematic. He worked practically only at night; in the morning he slept.

I had quickly settled into the life of the Conservatory, and my teachers were satisfied with my work — more than satisfied, as was shown by their offering me the extra coaching. Naturally, I was proud of it, and certainly a bit conceited. Music is perhaps the one art where a lack of formal education does not seem to matter so much. So, pleased with myself, and contented, I set off happily every morning for the Conservatory. But just this sureness of purpose, this certainty of success, awoke in Adolf the most bitter comparisons, although he never mentioned it.

So now, the sight of the timetable stuck on the wall, which must have seemed to him like an officially accredited guarantee for my future, brought about an explosion.

"This Academy," he screamed, "a lot of old-fashioned fossilized civil servants, bureaucrats, devoid of understanding, stupid lumps of officials. The whole Academy ought to be blown up!" His face was livid, the mouth quite small, the lips almost white. But the eyes glittered. There was something sinister about them. As if all the hate of which he was capable lay in those glowing eyes! I was just going to point out that those men of the Academy on whom he so lightly passed judgment in his measureless hatred were, after all, his teachers and professors, from whom he could certainly learn something. But he forestalled me.

"They rejected me, they threw me out, they turned me down." I was shocked. So that was it. Adolf did not go to the Academy at all. Now I understood a good deal that had puzzled me about him.

I felt his hard luck deeply, and asked him whether he had told his mother that the Academy had not accepted him.

"What are you thinking of?" he replied. "How could I burden my dying mother with this worry?" I could not help but agree.

For a while we were both silent. Perhaps Adolf was thinking of his mother. Then I tried to give the conversation a practical turn.

"And what now?" I asked him.

"What now, what now," he repeated irritably. "Are you starting too — what now?" He must have asked himself this question a hundred times and more, because he had certainly not discussed it with anyone else.

"What now?" he mocked my anxious inquiry again, and instead of answering, sat himself down at the table and surrounded himself with his books. "What now?" Then he adjusted the lamp, took up one of the books, opened it and began to read.

I made to take the timetable down from the cupboard door. He raised his head, saw it and said calmly, "Never mind."

Chapter 15 — Adolf Rebuilds Vienna

We often saw the old Emperor when he rode in his carriage from Schönbrunn through the Mariahilferstrasse to the Hofburg. On such occasions Adolf did not make much ado about it, neither did he refer to it later, for he was not interested in the Emperor as a person but only in the State which be represented, the Austro-Hungarian monarchy.

All my recollections of life in Vienna are sharpened by contrasts, and are thus more clearly etched in my memory. Indeed, in the course of the turbulent year 1908, there took place two political events which agitated the people.

On the one hand, there was the Emperor's Diamond Jubilee. On the other, there was the annexation of Bosnia, decreed in connection with the Jubilee, a matter which caused heated arguments among the citizens. This extension of the external power of the country only revealed its weakness within, and soon all the signs were of war. In fact, the events which took place in 1914 might easily have happened then, six years earlier. It was no mere coincidence that the 1914/18 war actually had its origins in Sarajevo.

The people of Vienna, among whom we two unknown youngsters were living, were at that time torn between loyalty to the old Emperor and anxiety about the threatening war.

Everywhere we noticed a deep chasm between the social classes. There was the vast mass of the lower classes who often had not enough to eat and merely existed in miserable dwellings without light or sun. In view of our standards of living, we unhesitatingly included ourselves in this category. It was not necessary for us to go out to study the mass misery of the city — it was brought into our own home. Our own damp and crumbling walls, bug-infested furniture and the unpleasant odour of kerosene were typical of the surroundings in which hundreds of thousands of people in this city lived. When we went with empty stomachs into the centre of the city, we saw the splendid mansions of the nobility with garishly attired servants in front, and the sumptuous hotels in which Vienna's rich society — the old nobility, the captains of industry, landowners and magnates — held their lavish parties; poverty, need, hunger on the one side, and reckless enjoyment of life, sensuality and prodigal luxury on the other.

I was too homesick to draw any political inferences from these contrasts. But Adolf, homeless, rejected by the Academy, without any chance of changing his miserable position, developed during this period an ever growing sense of rebellion. The obvious social injustice which caused him almost physical suffering also roused in him a demoniacal hatred of that unearned wealth, presumptuous and arrogant, which we saw around us. Only by violently protesting against this state of affairs was he able to bear his own "dog's life." To be sure, it was largely his own fault that he was in this position; but this he would never admit. Even more than from hunger, he suffered from the lack of cleanliness, as he was almost pathologically sensitive about anything concerning the body. At all costs, he would keep his linen and clothing clean. No one, meeting this carefully dressed young man in the street, would have thought that he went hungry every day, and lived in a hopelessly bug-infested back room in the Sixth District.

It was more the lack of cleanliness in the surroundings in which he was forced to live than the lack of food which provoked his inner protests against the prevailing social conditions. The old Imperial City, with its atmosphere of false glamour and spurious romance and its now evident inner decay, was the ground on which his social and political opinions grew. All that he later became was born of this dying Imperial Vienna. Although he wrote later, "The name of this city of lotus eaters represents for me five years of misery and distress," this statement shows only the negative side of his experience in Vienna. The positive side was that his constant revolt against the existing social order produced his political philosophy to which little was added in later years.

In spite of his sympathetic interest in the poverty of the masses, he never sought direct contact with the inhabitants of the Imperial City. He profoundly disliked the typical Viennese. To begin with, he could not stand their soft, though melodious accent, and he even preferred the clumsy German spoken by Frau Zakreys. Above all, he hated the subservience and dumb indifference of the Viennese, their eternal muddling through, their reckless improvidence. His own character was just the opposite. As far as I can remember, Adolf was always very reserved, simply because he disliked any physical contact with people; but within him everything was in a ferment and urged him on to radical and total solutions. How sarcastic he was about the Viennese partiality to wine, and how he despised them for it! Only once did we go to the Prater pleasure gardens, and this only out of curiosity. He could not understand why people wasted their precious time with such nonsense.

When he heard people laughing uproariously at some sideshow, he would shake his head, full of indignation at so much stupidity, and ask me angrily if I could understand it. In his opinion, they must have been laughing at themselves, which he could well understand. In addition, he was

Chapter 15 — Adolf Rebuilds Vienna

disgusted at the medley of Viennese, Czechs, Magyars, Slovaks, Rumanians, Croats, Italians and God knows what else which surged through the Prater. To him, the Prater was nothing but a Viennese Babel. There was here a strange contradiction which always struck me: all his thoughts and ambitions were directed towards the problem of how to help the masses, the simple, decent, but underprivileged people, with whom he identified himself — they were ever-present in his thoughts. But in actual fact he always avoided any contact with people. The motley crowd in the Prater was physically repugnant to him; however much he felt for the little man, he always kept him at the greatest possible distance.

On the other hand, the arrogance of the ruling classes was equally alien to him, and he understood even less the apathy and resignation which in those years was gaining a hold on the leading intellectuals. The knowledge that the end of the Hapsburg State was inevitable had bred, especially among the traditional upholders of the Monarchy, a kind of fatalism which accepted whatever might befall, with the typically Viennese "there's nothing one can do about it."

This bittersweet tone of resignation prevailed also among Vienna's poets; for instance, Rilke, Hofmannstahl, Wildgans — names which never reached us, not because we had no appreciation of the words of a poet, but because the mood which prompted the work of those poets was foreign to us; we had come from the country and were nearer to nature than were the townsfolk.

In addition, we were of a different generation from those weary and resigned people. While the hopeless social conditions in their apparent inevitability produced in the older generation nothing but apathy and complete indifference, they forced the younger generation into racial criticism and violent opposition. And Adolf, too, felt the urgent need to criticise and counterattack. He did not know what resignation meant. He who resigned, he thought, lost his right to live. But he dissociated himself from his contemporaries, who were at that time very arrogant and turbulent, and went his own way, refusing to join any of the then existing political parties. Although he always felt a sense of responsibility for everything that happened he was always a lonely and solitary man, determined to rely upon himself only, and to reach his goal.

One other thing should be mentioned — Adolf's visit to the typical working-class district of Meidling. Although he never told me exactly why he went there, I knew that he wanted to study personally the housing and living conditions of the workers' families. He was not interested in any individual; he only wanted to know the ways of the class as a whole. He, therefore, made no acquaintances in Meidling, his aim being to study a cross section of the community quite impersonally.

However much he avoided close contact with people, he had nevertheless grown fond of Vienna as a city; he could have lived quite happily without the people, but never without the city. Small wonder, then, that the few people whom he came later to know in Vienna thought of him as a lone wolf and an eccentric, and regarded as pretence or arrogance his refined speech, his distinguished manners and his elegant bearing, which belied his obvious poverty. In fact, the young Hitler made no friends in Vienna.

All the more enthusiastic was he about what people had built in Vienna. Think only of the Ringstrasse! When he saw it for the first time, with its fabulous buildings, it seemed to him the realisation of his boldest artistic dreams, and it took him a long time to digest this overwhelming impression. Only gradually did he find his way about this magnificent exhibition of modern architecture. I often had to accompany him on his strolls along the Ring. Then he would describe to me at some length this or that building, pointing out certain details, or he would explain to me its origins. He would literally spend hours in front of it, forgetting not only the time but all that went on around him. I could not understand the reason for these long drawn out and complicated inspections; after all, he had seen everything before, and already knew more about it than most of the inhabitants of the city. When I occasionally became impatient, he shouted at me rudely, asking whether I was his real friend or not; if I was, I should share his interests. Then he continued with his dissertation. At home he would draw for me ground plans and sectional plans, or enlarge upon some interesting detail. He borrowed books on the origin of various buildings, the Hof Opera, the House of Parliament, the Burg Theatre, the Karlskirche, the Hof Museums, the Town Hall; he brought home more and more books, among them a general handbook of architecture. He showed me the various architectural styles, and particularly pointed out to me that some of the details on the buildings of the Ringstrasse demonstrated the excellent workmanship of local craftsmen.

When he wished to study a certain building, the external appearance alone did not satisfy him. I was always astonished how well informed he was about side doors, staircases, and even back doors and little-known means of access. He approached a building from all sides; he hated nothing more than splendid and ostentatious facades intended to conceal some fault in the layout. Beautiful facades were always suspect, Plaster, he thought, was an inferior material that no architect should use. He was never deceived, and

Chapter 15 — *Adolf Rebuilds Vienna*

often was able to show me that some construction which aimed at mere visual effect was just bluff. Thus, the Ringstrasse became for him an object by which he could measure his architectural knowledge and demonstrate his opinions.

At that time also, his first schemes for the replanning of large squares emerged. I distinctly remember his expositions: for instance, he regarded the Heldenplatz, between Hofburg and Volksgarten, as an almost ideal spot for mass meetings, not only because the semicircle of the adjacent buildings lent itself in a unique way to holding the assembled multitude, but also because every individual in the crowd would receive a great monumental impression whichever way he looked. I thought these observations were the idle play of an overheated imagination, but nevertheless I always had to take part in such experiments. The Schwarzenbergplatz was also very much beloved by Adolf. We sometimes went there during an interval at the Hof Opera in order to admire in the darkness the fantastically illuminated fountains. That was a spectacle after our own hearts. Incessantly the foaming water rose, coloured red, yellow and blue in turn by the various spotlights. Colour and movement combined to produce an incredible abundance of light effects, casting an unreal and unearthly spell over the whole square.

To be sure, Adolf, influenced by the Ringstrasse architecture, was also interested in great projects during his time in Vienna: concert halls, theatres, museums, palaces. exhibitions. But gradually his style of planning changed. In the first place, these monumental buildings were in a certain sense so perfect that even he, with his unbridled will to build, could find no room for change or improvement. Linz had been quite different in this respect.

With the exception of the massive pile of the old Castle, he had been completely dissatisfied with every building he had seen in Linz. Small wonder, therefore, that he planned a new and more dignified successor to the old town hall of Linz which was rather narrow and, squeezed in among the houses of the main square, was not very imposing; and that in the end, during our strolls through the town, he rebuilt the whole city. Vienna was different, not only because it was difficult for him to conceive as a unit the enormous dimensions of the city, but also because with growing political understanding, he became increasingly aware of the necessity for healthy and suitable housing for the masses of the population. In Linz it had never been a matter of great concern to him how these people, who would be affected by his great building projects, would react to them. In Vienna, however, he began to build for people. What he explained to me in long, nocturnal discussions, what he drew and planned, was no longer, as it had been in Linz, building for building's sake, but conscientious planning which took into account the needs and requirements of the occupiers. In Linz, it was still purely architectural building; in Vienna, social building; that is how one could describe his progress. This was also due to the merely external factor that Adolf had been fairly comfortable in Linz, especially in the pleasant apartment in Urfahr. Now, in contrast, in the gloomy sunless back room of the Stumpergasse in Vienna, he felt every morning when he awoke, looking at the bare walls and depressing view, that building was not, as he had thought hitherto, mostly a matter of show and prestige, but rather a problem of public health, of how to remove the masses from their miserable hovels.

Adolf had told me that during the past winter when he was still alone in Vienna, he had often been to warmed public rooms in order to save fuel, of which his inadequate stove consumed large quantities without giving much heat. There, one could sit in a warmed room without payment, and there were plenty of newspapers available. I suppose that Adolf, in his conversations with the people who frequented these places, gained his first depressing insight into the scandalous housing conditions of the metropolis.

In our hunt for lodgings which, so to speak, heralded my entry into Vienna, I had had a foretaste of the misery, distress and filth that awaited us. Through dark, foul-smelling backyards, up and down stairs, through sordid and filthy hallways, past doors behind which adults and children huddled together in a small sunless room, the human beings as decayed and miserable as their surroundings — this impression has remained unforgettably with me, just as the reverse side of the medal, that in the one house which might have come up to our sanitary and aesthetic standards, we met that acme of viciousness which, in the person of the seductive "Mrs. Potiphar," seemed to us more repulsive than the wretchedness of the poor people. There followed those nocturnal hours in which Adolf, striding up and down between door and piano, explained to me in powerful words the causes of these squalid housing conditions.

He started with the house in which we ourselves were living. On an area which was hardly large enough for an ordinary garden, there were tightly packed three buildings, each in the others' way and robbing each other of light, air and elbow room.

And why? Because the man who bought the ground wanted to make as large a profit as possible.

He therefore had to build as compactly as possible and as high as possible, because the more of these boxlike compartments he could pile one on top of the other, the more income he received.

Chapter 15 — Adolf Rebuilds Vienna

The tenant, in his turn, has to get from his apartment as much value as he can, and therefore sublets some of the rooms, usually the best ones; take, for instance, our good Frau Zakreys. And the subtenants crowd together in order to have room available for a lodger. So each one wants to make a profit out of the other, and the result is that all except the landlord have not enough living space. The basement flats are also a scandal, getting no light, sun or air. If this is unbearable for grownups, for children it is deadly. Adolf's lecture ended in a furious attack on the real estate speculators and the exploiting landlords. One word which I heard for the first time on that occasion still rings in my ears: These "professional landlords" who make a living from the awful housing condition of the masses. The poor tenant usually never meets his landlord, as the latter does not live in these tenements he owns — God forbids — but somewhere in the suburbs, in Hietzing or Grinzing, in luxurious villas where they enjoy in abundance that of which they deprive others.

Another day Adolf made his observations from the tenant's angle. What were such a poor devil's minimum needs for a decent home? Light- the houses must be detached. There must be gardens, playgrounds for the children — air — the sky must be visible; something green, a modest piece of nature. But look at our back building, he said. The sun shines only on the roof. The air — of that we would rather not speak. The water — there is one single tap outside on the landing, to which eight families have to come with their pails and jugs. The whole floor has one highly unsanitary lavatory in common, and it is almost necessary to take one's turn in a queue. And on top of all that, the bugs! When, during the weeks that followed — I had learned in the meantime that he had been rejected by the Academy — I asked Adolf occasionally where he was during the day, he answered: "I am working on the solution of the housing problem in Vienna, and I am doing certain research for this purpose; I therefore have to go around a lot." During that period he would often pore over his plans and drawings throughout the night, but he never spoke about it, nor did I ask him any more questions. But suddenly, I think it was towards the end of March, he said: "I shall be away for three days." He returned on the fourth day, dead tired. Goodness knows where he had been, where he had slept and how hungry he had been!

From his scanty reports I gathered that he had approached Vienna from some outlying point, perhaps from Stockerau or from the Marchfeld, to gain an idea of the land available for the purpose of relieving the city's congestion. He worked all night again, and then, at long last, he showed me the project. In the first place, some simple ground plans, workers' flats with the minimum requirements: kitchen, living room, separate bedrooms for parents and children, water laid on in the kitchen, lavatory and, at that time an unheard-of innovation, a bath. Then Adolf showed me his plans for various types of houses, neatly sketched in India ink. I remember them so clearly because for weeks these sketches were hanging on our walls, and Adolf returned repeatedly to the subject. In our airless and sunless subtenants' existence, I realised more sharply the contrast between our own surroundings and Adolf's attractive light and airy houses. For, as my glance wandered away from these pretty sketches, it fell on the crumbling, badly distempered wall which still showed traces of our nightly bug hunt.

This vivid contrast has indelibly printed on my memory the vast and grandiose plans of my friend.

"The tenements will be demolished." With this pithy pronouncement Adolf began his work. I should have been surprised had it been otherwise, as in everything he planned, he went all out and detested half measures and compromise — life itself would bring these. But his task was to solve the problem radically — that is to say, from the roots. Private speculation in land would be forbidden. Areas along both banks of the Danube would be added to the open spaces resulting from the demolition of the working-class districts, and wide roads would be laid across the whole.

The vast building area would be provided with a network of railway lines. Instead of big railway stations, there would be suitably scattered over the whole territory, and connected with the town centre, a series of small local stations which would cater for specified districts and offer favourable speedy communication between home and place of work. The motorcar at that time had not been envisaged as an important means of transport. The streets of Vienna were still dominated by the horsedrawn *fiacre*. The bicycle was only slowly becoming a cheap and practical means of travel. Only the railways were, is those days, able to provide transport for the masses.

Adolf's design was by no means concerned with the one. family or owner-occupier type of house, as is being built today, nor was he interested in "settlement." His idea was still based on the old type of tenement house, carved up into fractions. Thus came into being as his smallest unit the fourfamily house, a one-storied, well-proportioned structure, containing two flats on the ground floor and two on the first floor. This basic unit was the prevailing type. Where conditions required, from four to eight of these units were to be combined to form housing blocks for eight or sixteen families, but these blocks, too, remained "near the ground," that is to say, they still consisted of one story only, and were surrounded by gardens, playing grounds and groups of trees. The sixteen-family house was the limit.

Chapter 15 — Adolf Rebuilds Vienna

Having designed the types of house necessary to relieve the congestion in the town, my friend could now turn his attention to the problem itself. On a big map of the town, which was too large for the table and had to be spread out on the piano, Adolf laid out the network of railways and roads. Industrial centres were marked, residential districts suitably located. I was always in his way when he was engaged on this vast planning job. There was, indeed, not a square foot of space in the room that was not utilised for this task. If Adolf had not pursued his course with such grim determination, I would have regarded the whole thing as an interesting but idle pastime.

Actually, I was so depressed by our own bad housing that I became almost as fanatical as my friend, and that is no doubt the reason why so many details have remained in my memory.

In his way, Adolf thought of everything. I still remember that he was preoccupied with the problem of whether inns would be necessary or not in this new Vienna. Adolf was as radically opposed to alcohol as he was to nicotine. If one neither smoked nor drank, why should one go to an inn? In any case, he found for this new Vienna a solution which was as radical as it was bold: a new popular drink! On one occasion in Linz I had to redecorate some rooms in the office building of the firm of Franck, who manufactured a coffee substitute. Adolf came to see me there. The firm provided the workers with an excellent iced beverage which cost only one heller a glass.

Adolf liked this drink so much that he mentioned it again and again. If one could provide every household, he said, with this cheap and wholesome beverage, or with similar nonalcoholic drinks, one could do without the inns. When I remonstrated that the Viennese, from my knowledge of them, would be most unlikely to give up their wine, he replied brusquely, "You won't be asked!" as much as to say in other words "Nor will the Viennese either."

Adolf was particularly critical of those countries, and Austria was one of them, which had established a tobacco monopoly. In this way, he argued, the State ruined the health of its own subjects; therefore all tobacco factories must be closed and the import of tobacco, cigars and cigarettes forbidden. But he did not find a substitute for tobacco as a companion to his "People's Drink." Altogether, the nearer Adolf came in his imagination to the realisation of his projects, the more utopian did the whole business become. As long as it was only a matter of the basic principles of his planning, everything was quite reasonable; but when he thought out the details of its execution, Adolf juggled with ideas which seemed to me completely nebulous. Having to pay ten of my father's hardearned crowns for a half share in a bug-ridden room, I had the fullest sympathy with the idea that in his new Vienna there should be no landlords and tenants.

The ground was to be owned by the state, and the houses were to be not private property but administered by a sort of housing cooperative. One would pay no rent but instead a contribution to the building costs or the house, or a kind of housing tax. So far I could follow him. But when I timidly asked him, "Yes, but in this way you cannot finance such an expensive building project. Who is going to pay for it?" I provoked his most violent opposition. Furiously, Adolf flung replies at me, of which I understood but little. Besides, I can hardly remember details of these explanations, which consisted almost entirely of abstract conceptions. But what remains in my memory were certain regularly recurring expressions which, the less they actually meant, the more they impressed me.

The principal problems of the whole project were to be solved, as Adolf put it, "in the Storm of the Revolution." It was the first time that in our wretched dwelling this ponderous word was uttered. I do not know if Adolf picked it up from his copious reading. At any rate, at the moment when his flight of ideas would come to a standstill, regularly the bold words "Storm of the Revolution" would crop up and give a new fillip to his thoughts, though he never paused to explain the phrase. It could mean, I found out, either nothing or everything. For Adolf it was "everything," but for me "nothing," until he, with his hypnotic eloquence, had convinced me, too, that it only needed a tremendous revolutionary storm to break over the tired old earth to bring about all that which had long since been ready in his thoughts and plans, just as a mild rain in late summer brings the mushrooms springing up everywhere.

Another ever recurring expression was the "German Ideal State," which, together with the conception of the "Reich," was the dominating factor in his thinking. This "Ideal State" was in its basic principles, both national and social, social above all in respect of the poverty of the masses of the working class. More and more thoroughly, Adolf worked on the idea of a state which would give its due to the social requirements of our times. But the idea remained vague and was largely determined by his reading. Thus he chose the term, "Ideal State" — most likely he had read it in one of his many books — and left it to the future to develop the details of this ideal state, for the time being only sketched in general outline, but, of course, with the "Reich" as its final aim.

Also in connection with his bold building projects, Adolf first adopted a third expression which had already become a familiar formula

Chapter 15 — Adolf Rebuilds Vienna

in that period: "Social Reform." This expression, too, embraced much that was still swirling around in his brain in a very unformed state. But the eager study of political literature and visits to the House of Parliament, to which he dragged me, too, gradually lent the expression "Social Reform" a concrete meaning.

One day, when the Storm of the Revolution broke and the Ideal State was born, the long overdue Social Reform would become reality. This would be the moment to tear down the tenements of the "professional landlords," and to begin with the building of his model houses in the beautiful meadows behind Nussdorf.

I have dwelt so long on these plans of my friend's because I regard them as typical of the development of his character and his ideas during his sojourn in Vienna. To be sure, I realised from the beginning that my friend would not remain indifferent to the misery of the masses of the metropolis, for I knew that he did not close his eyes to anything and that it was quite contrary to his nature to ignore any important phenomenon. Yet I would never have believed that these experiences in the suburbs of Vienna would have stirred up his whole personality so enormously.

For I had always thought of my friend as, basically, an artist, and would have understood if he had grown indignant in the face of the masses, who appeared to be hopelessly perishing in their misery, yet remained aloof from all this, so as not to be dragged down into the abyss by the city's inexorable fate. I reckoned with his susceptibility, his aestheticism, his constant fear of physical contact with strangers — he shook hands rarely and then only with a few people — and I thought this would be sufficient to keep him at a distance from the masses. This was only true of personal contacts. But with his whole, overflowing heart, he stood then in the ranks of the underprivileged.

It was not sympathy, in the ordinary sense, he felt for the disinherited. That would not have been sufficient. He not only suffered with them, he lived for them and devoted all his thoughts to the salvation of these people from distress and poverty. No doubt this ardent desire for a total reorganisation of life was his personal response to his own fate, which had led him, step by step into misery. Only by his noble and grandiose work, which was intended "for everybody" and appealed to "all," did he find again his inner equilibrium. The weeks of dark visions and grave depressions were past; he was again full of hope and courage.

But for the time being, good old Maria Zakreys was the only person who occupied herself with these plans. To be exact, she did not really occupy herself with them, for she had given it up as a bad job to try to bring order into this mess of plans, drawings and sketches. She was satisfied as long as the two students from Linz paid their rent punctually.

As far as Linz was concerned, Adolf had not contemplated more than to transform it into a fine, attractive town whose distinguished buildings should raise it from its low, provincial standing. But Vienna he wanted to transform into a modem residential town in which distinction and prestige did not matter — this he left to the Imperial Vienna: what mattered was that the uprooted masses, who had become estranged from their own soil and their own people, should again settle down on firm ground.

The old Imperial City changed, on the drawing board of a nineteen-year-old youth who lived in a dark back room of the Mariahilf suburb, into a spacious, sunlit and exuberant city, which consisted of four- eight- and sixteen-family houses.

Chapter 16 — Solitary Study and Reading

There can be no doubt that Adolf was, at that time, convinced that he was destined to become an architect. How he would ever find his way into practice, even with this thorough private study, unable as he was to produce any testimonials and diplomas — this never caused him any worry.

We hardly ever spoke about it, for my friend was absolutely sure that by the time he had concluded his studies, circumstances would have changed (either peacefully or with violence, as a consequence of his Storm of the Revolution) to such an extent that formal qualifications would no longer matter, but only actual ability.

Thus, Adolf saw his future clearly before him. Back in Linz he had already defeated what he called his school's biased, unjust and idiotic treatment of him, by throwing himself heart and soul into the study of a subject of his own choosing, so he had no difficulty in doing the same here in Vienna, where a similar situation confronted him. He cursed the old-fashioned, fossilized bureaucracy of the Academy where there was no understanding for true artistry.

He spoke of the trip-wires which had been cunningly laid — I remember his very words! — for the sole purpose of ruining his career. But he would show these incompetent, senile fools that he could go ahead without them! From his salvoes of abuse of the Academy, I gained the impression that these teachers, by rejecting the young man, had involuntarily engendered in him more eagerness and energy than their teaching would ever have done.

But my friend had to face another problem: What was he to live on during his years of study? Many years would pass before he could make himself a position as an architect. Personally, I doubted if, indeed, anything would ever come of my friend's private studies. Admittedly he studied with incredible industry and a determination which one would have thought beyond the strength of his undernourished and weakened body. But his pursuits were not directed towards any practical goal.

On the contrary, every now and again he got lost in vast plans and speculations. Drawing a comparison with my musical studies, which were progressing absolutely according to plan, I could only conclude that Adolf was casting his nets far too wide and dragging in anything that had even the remotest connection with architecture; and he did it, moreover, with the greatest thoroughness and precision. How could all that ever lead to any conclusion — not to mention the fact that more and more new ideas assailed him and distracted him from his professional training.

The contrast between his boundless, unsystematic labours and my precisely regulated studies at the Conservatory did nothing to help our friendship, if only because our respective work at home necessarily led to friction. When, on top of this, Professor Boschetti sent me some private pupils, our disagreements became sharper. Now one could see, he said, that bad luck was pursuing him; there was a great conspiracy against him-he had no possibility of earning any money.

One evening — I suppose it was after a pupil of mine had been in for a lesson-I seized the opportunity to try to persuade him to look around for some remunerative work. Of course, if one is lucky, one can give lessons to young ladies, he began. I told him that without my taking the initiative, Professor Boschetti had sent me these pupils — it was a pity that they had to be taught harmonics rather than architectture. Incidentally, I went on more firmly, if I were as gifted as he was, I would have long since looked around for some part-time job.

He listened with interest, almost as though the whole thing did not refer to him at all, and then I let him have it: drawing, for instance, that was something he really could do, as even his teachers had admitted. What about looking for a job with a newspaper or in a publishing firm? Perhaps he could illustrate books, or do sketches for newspapers. He answered evasively that he was glad I credited him with such skill, but anyhow this kind of newspaper illustration was best left to the photographers, for not even the best artist could be as quick as a photographer.

Then what about a job as a dramatic critic, I continued? This was a job which he was actually doing, because after every visit to the theatre he came home to me with a very severe and radical, yet interesting and comprehensive review. Why should I remain the only inhabitant of Vienna ever to hear his opinions? He should try to get in touch with an influential paper. But he would have to take care not to show too much bias. What did I mean by that, he wanted to know? The Italian, Russian and French operas, too, had their right to exist, I replied. One had to accept foreign composers as well, for art has no national frontiers. We started a heated argument, as whenever music was the topic under discussion I stood my ground; for I did not speak for myself alone, but felt that I was the representative of the Institute whose pupil I was.

Although I fully shared Adolf's enthusiasm for Richard Wagner, I could nevertheless not bring myself to reject all the rest. But he stuck uncompromisingly to his point. I still remember well that in my excitement

Chapter 16 — *Solitary Study and Reading*

I flung at Adolf the words from the final Chorus of Beethoven's Ninth Symphony, "Seid umschlungen Millionen, diesen Kuss der ganzen Welt." The work of the artist must belong to the whole world. So there was trouble even before he took the job of an opera critic, remarked Adolf. And so this plan, too, was buried.

Adolf wrote a great deal during this period. I had discovered that it was mainly plays, dramas actually. He took the plots from the Germanic Mythology or German history. But hardly any of these plays were really finished. Nevertheless, it might have been possible to make some money out of them. Adolf showed me some of his drafts, and I was struck by the fact that he attributed much importance to magnificent staging. Except for the drama about the coming of Christianity, I cannot remember any one of these plays, but only that they all required an enormous production.

Wagner had accustomed us to the idea of pretentious productions, but Adolph's ideas dwarfed anything devised by the Master. I knew a thing or two about operatic production and was not slow to utter my doubts. With his settings ranging through Heaven and Hell, I explained to him, no producer would accept any one of his plays. He should be much more modest in all that concerned his scenery. Altogether it would be best for him not to write operas at all, but rather simple plays, comedies perhaps, which were popular with the public. The most profitable thing would be to write some unpretentious comedy. Unpretentious? This was all that was needed to make him furious. So this attempt, too, ended in failure.

Gradually I came to realise all my efforts were wasted. Even if I had managed to persuade Adolf to submit his drawings or his literary work to a newspaper editor or a publisher, he would soon have quarrelled with his employer, for he could never tolerate any interference with his work, and it would presumably make no difference that he was getting paid for it. He simply could not bear taking orders from people, for he received enough orders from himself.

So I chose another way. Through the generosity of my parents and through the private lessons I gave, I was financially better off than he was, and therefore I helped him wherever I could, preferably without his realising it at all, for he was very touchy and sensitive in these matters, Only on our walks and excursions did he consent to be my guest.

Later, when we had already parted, Adolf found, in Vienna, a very characteristic solution for this problem, which enabled him to make a modest living and still remain his own master. As his talent was best suited to drawing works of architecture rather than the human figure, he made most accurate and neat sketches of famous Vienna buildings, such as the

Karlskirche, the House of Parliament and similar subjects, coloured them and sold them whenever he could.

Having no expert knowledge, I cannot give any opinion on the special studies Adolf was then pursuing. Moreover, I was too busy myself to get any real idea of his work. What I noticed, however, was that he surrounded himself increasingly with technical books. I recall especially a big history of architecture because he loved to choose one of its pictures at random, cover the caption, and tell me what it was, Chartres Cathedral, for instance, or the Palazzo Pitti in Florence.

His memory was prodigious; it never failed him and was, of course, a great advantage in his work.

He worked tirelessly on his drawings. I had the impression that he had already learnt, in Linz, the basic principles of draughtsmanship, though only from books. I do not remember Adolf ever having tried to apply in practice what he had learnt, or ever attending classes in architectural drawing He never showed any desire to mix with people who shared his own professional interests, or to discuss with them common problems. Rather than meet people of specialised knowledge, he would sit alone on his bench in the Schönbrunn Park, holding imaginary conversations with himself about the subject matter of his books. This extraordinary habit of studying a certain subject and penetrating deeply into its very essence, while anxiously avoiding any contact with its practical application, this peculiar self-sufficiency, reminded me of Adolf's relationship with Stefanie. His boundless love of architecture, his passionate interest in building remained fundamentally a mere intellectual pastime. Just as he used to rush to the Landstrasse to see Stefanie when he needed some tangible confirmation of his feelings, so he would escape from the overpowering effects of his theoretical studies into the Ringstrasse, and recover his inner equilibrium among its splendours.

As time went on, I came to understand my friend's one-sided preference for the Ringstrasse, although, to my mind, the impact of such buildings as St. Stephen's, or the Belvedere — older and more original in their style — was stronger and more convincing. But Adolf altogether disliked Baroque, as it was too ornate for his taste. The Ringstrasse buildings had been constructed after the demolition of the city's fortifications; that is to say, in the second half of the past century, and were anything but uniform in style. On the contrary! Almost every style was represented. The House of Parliament was in the Classic, or rather pseudo-Hellenic style, the Town Hall neo-Gothic, and the Burg Theatre, an object of Adolf's special admiration, late Renaissance. Yet they had one thing in common which was

Chapter 16 — *Solitary Study and Reading*

especially attractive for my friend-their ostentation. But the real motive for his unceasing preoccupation with these buildings, his use of the Ringstrasse as his professional training ground, was the fact that these buildings of the preceding generation enabled him to study without difficulty the history of their construction, to redraw their plans, to reerect, so to speak, by his own effort every single structure, and to recall the life and achievements of the great architects of that epoch — Theophil Hansen, Semper, Hasenauer, Siccardsburg and van der Null.

I discovered with apprehension that new ideas, experiences and projects disorganised my friend's professional studies. As long as these new interests had some connection with architecture, they became just part of his general education, but there was much that was diametrically opposed to his professional plans, and, moreover, politics gained an increasingly firm hold on him. I asked Adolf, occasionally, what connection there was between the remote problems which we encountered during our visits to Parliament and his professional preparation.

He would answer, "You can build only when you have first created the political conditions for it." Sometimes his answers were rather rude. Thus I remember him once answering my question as to how he proposed to solve a certain problem, "Even if I had found the solution to this problem, I wouldn't tell it to you because you wouldn't understand it." But although he was often brusque, moody, unreliable and far from conciliatory, I could never be angry with him because these unpleasant sides of his character were overshadowed by the pure fire of an exalted soul.

I stopped asking him questions about his profession. It was much better for me to go quietly my own way and show him my own ideas of how to reach one's goal. After all, I had not even reached the lower classes of the technical school and had only been to a council school, but just the same, I was now a student at the Conservatory, as good as any boy who had matriculated.

But my friend's studies took just the opposite course to mine. While normally, training for a profession grows more and more specialised in the course of time, Adolf's studies became more general, more diffuse, more abstract and remote from anything practical. The more tenaciously he repeated his own slogan, "I want to become an architect," the more nebulous did this goal become in reality. It was the typical attitude of a young man who would actually be hindered by a profession in reaching what he feels is his true vocation. That was always the case with my friend.

Books were his whole world. In Linz, in order to procure the books he wanted, he had subscribed to three libraries. In Vienna he used the Hof

Library so industriously that I asked him once, in all seriousness, whether he intended to read the whole library through, which of course earned me some rude remarks. One day he took me to the library and showed me the big reading room. I was almost overwhelmed by these enormous masses of books, and I asked him how he managed to get what he wanted. He began to explain to me the use of the catalogue, which confused me even more.

Hardly anything would disturb him when he was reading. But sometimes be disturbed himself, for as soon as he opened a book he started talking about it, and I had to listen patiently whether I was interested in the subject or not. Every now and then, in Linz even more frequently than in Vienna, he would thrust a book into my hands and demand that I, as his friend, should read it. It did not matter so much to him that I should widen my own horizon as that he should have somebody with whom he could discuss the book, even though that somebody was only a listener.

As I have mentioned before, outstanding among his books were the German heroic legends.

Whatever his mood or external circumstances, he always came back to them and read them again, although he already knew them all by heart. The volume which he had in Vienna was, I believe, entitled *Legends of Gods and Heroes: the Treasures of Germanic Mythology*.

Already in Linz, Adolf had started to read the classics. Of Goethe's *Faust* he once remarked that it contained more than 'the human mind could grasp. Once he saw, at the Burg Theatre, the rarely performed second part, with Joseph Kainz in the title role. Adolf was very moved and spoke of it for a long time. It is natural that, of Schiller's works, *Wilhelm Tell* affected him most deeply.

On the other hand, strange to relate, he did not like *Die Räuber* very much. He was profoundly impressed by Dante's *Divine Comedy* although, to my mind, he was much too young when he read it. I know that be was interested in Herder, and we saw together Lessing's *Minna von Barnhelm*. He liked *Stifter*, partly perhaps because he encountered in his writings the familiar picture of his native landscape, while *Rosegger* struck him, as he once put it, as too "popular."

Every now and then he would choose books which were then in vogue, but in order to form a judgment of those who read them rather than of the books themselves. Ganghofer meant nothing to him, while he greatly praised Otto Ernst, with whose works he was familiar. Of modem plays we saw Frank Wedekind's *Frühlingserwachen*, and *Der Meister von Palmyra* by Wilbrandt. Adolf read Ibsen's plays in Vienna without being very much impressed by them.

Chapter 16 — Solitary Study and Reading

As for philosophical works, he always had his Schopenhauer by him, later Nietzsche, too. Yet I knew little about these, for he regarded these philosophers as, so to speak, his own personal affair — private property which he would not share with anybody. This reticence was possibly also due to the fact that we shared a love of music and this provided us with common ground more rewarding than that of philosophy, which for me was rather a remote subject.

In conclusion I should like to stress the same point with regard to my friend's reading that I have mentioned before, in describing his professional studies: he read prodigiously and, with the help of his extraordinary memory, stored up an amount of knowledge which was far above the normal standard of a twenty-year-old-but he avoided any factual discussion about it.

When he urged me to read a certain book he knew in advance that I would never be his equal in any argument, and it is even possible that he selected the books which he recommended me to read with this thought in mind. He was not interested in "another opinion," nor in any discussion of the book.

His attitude to books was the same as his attitude to the world in general. He absorbed with fervour everything he could lay his hands on, but he took great care to keep at a safe distance from anything that might put him to the test.

He was a seeker, certainly, but even in his books he found only what suited him. One day when I asked him if he really intended to complete his studies by the aid of books alone, he looked at me, surprised, and barked: "Of course, you need teachers, I can see that. But for me they are superfluous." In the further course of this conversation he called me an "intellectual scrounger" and a "parasite at other people's tables." I never felt, and particularly not in those days when we were living together in Vienna, that he was seeking anything concrete in his piles of books, such as principles and ideas for his own conduct; on the contrary, he was looking only for confirmation of those principles and ideas he already had. For this reason his reading, except perhaps the German Mythology, was not a matter of edification, but a sort of check-up on himself.

I remember him in Vienna expounding his many problems and usually winding up with a reference to some book, "You see, the man who wrote this is of exactly the same opinion."

Chapter 17 — Nights at the Opera

The high spots of our friendship were our visits together to the Hof Opera, and memories of my friend are inseparably connected with these wonderful experiences. The theatre in Linz saw the beginning of our youthful friendship, and this was reaffirmed whenever we visited the foremost Opera House in Europe. As we grew older, the contrasts between us made themselves increasingly noticeable and the difference in our family backgrounds, our professional aspirations and our attitude to public and political life separated us more and more. Yet our fervent enthusiasm for everything that was beautiful and noble, which found its highest artistic expression in the performances of the Vienna Opera, linked us ever more closely. In Linz our relationship had been smooth and harmonious. But in Vienna the conflicts and tensions grew, largely owing to our living together in a single room. It was fortunate that at the same time the influence of our common artistic experience fortified our friendship.

True to tradition, we humble poverty-stricken students had to fight hard for the chance of seeing those performances. It is true that in theory there existed cheap tickets for the Promenade which, in Vienna, as in Linz, used to be our aim; but we never got one, not even through the Conservatory. So we had to pay the full price — two crowns — a lot of money, when one thinks that Adolf, after having paid his rent, was left with fifteen crowns for the whole month. And although we paid full price, we had to fight hard to get these tickets, the sale of which started only one hour before the performance began.

Having finally secured the ticket, there started a rush towards the Promenade, which fortunately was not far from the box office. It was below the Imperial box and one could hear excellently.

Women were not admitted to the Promenade, which pleased Adolf hugely, but on the other hand it had the disadvantage of being split up into two halves by a bronze railing, one for civilians, one for the military. These young lieutenants who, according to my friend, came to the Opera less for the sake of the music than for social reasons, paid only ten hellers for their tickets, while we poor students were fleeced twenty times that amount. This always made Adolf very wild. Looking at these elegant lieutenants who, ceaselessly yawning, could hardly wait for the interval to display themselves in the foyer as though they had just come out of their box, he said that among the visitors to the Promenade, artistic understanding varied in

Chapter 17 — Nights at the Opera

inverse proportion to the price of the tickets. Moreover the military half of the Promenade was never full, while in the civilian half students, young employees and artisans trod on each others' toes.

One disadvantage was that the Promenade was usually the haunt of the claque, and this often spoilt our pleasure. The usual procedure was very simple: a singer who wanted to be applauded at a certain point would hire a claque for the evening. Its leader would buy their tickets for his men and, in addition, pay them a sum of money. There existed professional claqueurs who "worked" at a fixed rate. So it would often happen that, at a most unsuitable moment, roars of applause would break out around us. This made us boil with indignation. I remember once, during Tannhäuser, that we silenced a group of claqueurs by our hissing. One of them, who continued to shout "Bravo" although the orchestra was still playing, was punched in the side by Adolf. On leaving the theatre, we found the leader of the claque waiting for us with a policeman. Adolf was interrogated on the spot and defended himself so brilliantly that the policeman let him go, but he was in time to catch up with the claqueur in question in the street and give him a sound box on the ears.

As nobody was admitted to the Promenade in hat and coat, we left them behind when we went to the Opera, to save the cloakroom fee. To be sure, it was often bitterly cold, coming out of the overheated theatre into the night. But what did that matter after Lohengrin or Tristan? What was most annoying for us was that we had to be home by ten o'clock at the latest if we wanted to save the Sperrsechserl (the tip for the concierge). It took us, according to Adolf's precise calculations, at least fifteen minutes to walk home from the Opera, and so we had to leave there at a quarter to ten. The consequence was, that Adolf never succeeded in hearing the end of those operas which finished later and I had to play for him on the piano what he had missed.

Richard Wagner's music dreams were still the object of our undivided love and enthusiasm. For Adolf, nothing could compete with the great mystical world that the Master conjured up for us.

Thus, for instance, when I wanted to see some magnificent Verdi production in the Hof Opera, he would bully me until I gave up my Verdi and went with him to the People's Opera in Währing, where they were doing Wagner. He preferred a mediocre Wagner performance a hundred times to a first-class Verdi. I thought differently, but what was the use? I had to yield, as usual, for when it was a question of a Wagner performance, Adolf would tolerate no opposition. No doubt he had heard a much better performance of the work in question — I do not remember whether it was Lohengrin or

Tristan — at the Hof Opera. But this was not the point at issue. Listening to Wagner meant to him, not a simple visit to the theatre, but the opportunity of being transported into that extraordinary state which Wagner's music produced in him, that trance, that escape into a mystical dream world which he needed in order to endure the tensions of his turbulent nature.

The standard of the cast and orchestra at the People's Opera was remarkably high and much superior to anything we had been accustomed to in Linz. Another advantage was that one could get a cheap seat there without having to line up at the box office. What displeased us was the cold, modernistic style of the building, and the dull, unimaginative inside of the theatre, which was matched by the lack of glamour in its productions. Adolf used to call this theatre the Soup Kitchen.

Our theatregoing in Linz had given us the grounding for the full enjoyment in Vienna of the immortal Master's work. We were thoroughly familiar with his operas, without having been spoilt, and consequently the Hof Opera and even the more modest theatre in Währing seemed to create anew for us Richard Wagner's world.

Of course, we knew by heart Lohengrin, Adolf's favourite opera-I believe he saw it ten times during our time together in Vienna-and the same is true of the Meistersinger. Just as other people quote their Goethe or Schiller, we would quote Wagner, preferably the Meistersinger. We know, of course, that Wagner intended to immortalise his friend Franz Liszt in the figure of Hans Sachs, and to attack his bitter enemy Hanslick, in the person of Beckmesser. Adolf often quoted from the third scene of the second act.

"And still I don't succeed. I feel it and yet I cannot understand it. I can't retain it, nor forget it, and if I grasp it, I cannot measure it." In this, my friend saw the unique, eternal formula with which Richard Wagner castigated the want of comprehension of his contemporaries and which, so to speak, applied to his own fate; for his father, his family, his teachers, although they certainly had "felt" that there was something outstanding about him, for the love of God could not understand it. And when people had, at long last, grasped what he wanted, they still remained incapable of "measuring" the extent of his will.

These lines were for him a daily exhortation, a never failing comfort which helped him in his dark hours.

We studied, with libretto and score, those works of Wagner that we had not seen in Linz. So Wagnerian Vienna found us well prepared and, naturally enough, we entered at once the ranks of his worshipers, and wherever we could we acclaimed the work of the Master of Bayreuth with fervent enthusiasm.

Chapter 17 — Nights at the Opera

What had been for us the height of artistic experience in Linz was reduced to the level of poor, well-intentioned provincial performances after we had seen the perfect Wagner interpretations by Gustav Mahler at the Vienna Hof Opera. But Adolf would not have been Adolf if he had contented himself with regretful memories. He loved Linz, which he always thought of as his home town, although both his parents were dead and there was only one human being left there to whom he was passionately devoted, Stefanie, who still did not know what she meant to the pale youth who had stood and waited for her day after day at the Schmiedtoreck. The cultural life of Linz had to be brought to a level commensurate with that of Vienna: with savage determination Adolf set to work.

On leaving Linz, he had put great hopes in the Theatre Building Society, of which he had become an enthusiastic member. But these worthies who had got together to give Linz a new, dignified theatre apparently were making no headway. Nothing was ever heard of it and Adolf's impatience grew. So he started working on his own. He took pleasure in applying to his own home town that style of monumental architecture that he had become familiar with in Imperial Vienna.

He had already removed from the central area of the town the railway station with its ugly workshops, smoke-stained sheds and cumbersome railway tracks and transferred it to the outskirts. This enabled him to enlarge the Park and add a Zoo, a Palm House and, of course, an illuminated fountain. It was in the centre of this well-tended park that the new Linz Opera House should be erected, smaller in size than the Vienna Hof Opera, but its equal in technical equipment. The old theatre was to become a Playhouse and was to be put under the same direction as the Opera.

In this way my friend got over the deplorable conditions of his home town and all the greater was the enjoyment that he derived from Vienna's artistic attractions.

We saw almost all Richard Wagner's works. *The Flying Dutchman, Lohengrin, Tannhäuser, Tristan and Isolde, Die Meistersinger* have remained unforgettable to me, as has *The Ring,* and even *Parsifal.*

Occasionally, of course, Adolf saw other operas as well, but they never meant as much to him as Wagner's. In Linz we had already seen a surprisingly good Figaro, which had filled Adolf with delight. I still remember him saying, on our way home, that the Linz theatre should in future concentrate on operas which, like Figaro, were within their scope. A production of *The Magic Flute,* on the other hand, was a complete failure, and Weber's *Freischütz* was so bad that Adolf never wanted to see it again. But in

Vienna, of course, everything was different. We saw perfect performances, not only of the Mozart operas, but also of Beethoven's *Fidelio*. Italian opera never attracted Adolf, although Italian composers like Donizetti, Rossini, Bellini and especially Verdi, as well as Puccini, who was then still very modern, were highly appreciated in Vienna and played to full houses.

The Verdi operas we saw together were *The Masked Ball*, *Il Trovatore*, *Rigoletto* and *La Traviata*, but *Aïda* was the only one which he liked at all. For him, the plots of Italian operas laid too much emphasis upon theatrical effect. He objected to trickery, knavery and deception as the basic elements of a dramatic situation. He said to me once, "What would these Italians do if they had no daggers?" He found Verdi's music too unpretentious, relying too much on melody. How rich and varied by comparison was Wagner's range! One day when we heard an organ grinder playing *La donna e mobile*, Adolf said, "There's your Verdi!"

When I replied that no composer was safe from such profanation of his works, he barked at me furiously, "Can you imagine *Lohengrin's* narration on a barrel organ?" Neither Gounod, whose Faust he regarded as vulgar, nor Tchaikovsky, nor Smetana met with his approval. No doubt he was handicapped here by his obsession with German mythology. He rejected my contention that music should appeal to all races and nations. For him nothing counted but German ways, German feeling and German thought. He accepted none but the German masters. How often did he tell me that he was proud to belong to a people who had produced such masters.

When he listened to Wagner's music he was a changed man; his violence left him, he became quiet, yielding and tractable. His gaze lost its restlessness; his own destiny, however heavily it may have weighed upon him, became unimportant.

He no longer felt lonely and outlawed, and misjudged by society. He was intoxicated and bewitched. Willingly he let himself be carried away into that mystical universe which was more real to him than the actual workaday world. From the stale, musty prison of his back room, he was transported into the blissful regions of Germanic antiquity, that ideal world which was the lofty goal for all his endeavours.

Thirty years later, when he met me again in Linz, his friend whom he had last seen as a student of the Vienna Conservatory, he was convinced that I had become an important conductor; but when I appeared before him as a humble municipal employee, Hitler, then Reichs Chancellor, said to me, "So you have become a pen-pusher? But you are an artist. We'll talk about it." With these words, he was probably alluding to the possibility of my assuming the direction of an orchestra.

Chapter 17 — Nights at the Opera

I declined, gratefully. I no longer felt up to the task. When he realised that he could not help his friend with this generous offer, he recalled our common experiences in the Linz Theatre and in the Vienna Hof Opera, which had elevated our friendship from the commonplace to the sacred sphere of his own world, and invited me to come to Bayreuth.

I should never have thought that those outstanding artistic experiences of my Vienna student days could still be surpassed. And yet this was the case. For what I experienced in Bayreuth as the guest of the friend of my youth was the culmination of everything that Richard Wagner had ever meant in my life.

Chapter 18 — Adolf Writes an Opera

Soon our life together in Vienna showed its drawbacks because of the different subjects that Adolf and I were studying. In the morning, when I was at the Conservatory, my friend was still asleep; and in the afternoon when Adolf wanted to work, my practising disturbed him. This led to frequent friction.

Conservatory, fiddlesticks! What did he have his books for? He wanted to prove to me that, even without the Conservatory he could equal my achievements in the musical field. For it was not the Professor's wisdom that counted, he said, but genius.

This ambition led him to a most extraordinary experiment and I am still at a loss to say whether this experiment was of any value or not. Adolf harked back to the elementary possibilities of musical expression. Words seemed to him too complicated for this purpose, and he tried to discover how isolated sounds could be linked to notes of music; and with this musical language he combined certain colours.

Sound and colour were to become one and form the foundation of that which would finally appear on the stage as an opera. I, myself, convinced of the truth of what I had learnt at the Conservatory, rejected these experiments somewhat disdainfully, which annoyed him very much. He busied himself for some time with these abstract experiments, perhaps because he hoped to strike at the roots of my superior academic knowledge, I was reminded of my friend's essays in composition when a few years later a Russian composer caused some sensation in Vienna by similar experiments.

In those weeks Adolf wrote a lot, mainly plays, but also a few stories. He sat at his table and worked until dawn, without telling me very much about what he was doing. Only now and then would he throw onto my bed some closely written sheets of paper or would read out to me a few pages of his work, written in a strangely exalted style.

I knew that almost everything he was writing was set in the world of Richard Wagner; that is to say, in Germanic antiquity. One day I remarked, casually, that I had learned, during lectures on the History of Music, that the outline of a music drama about Wieland, the Smith, had been found among Wagner's posthumous writings. It was, in fact, only a short, hastily sketched text, and no drafts for a stage version existed, nor was anything known about the musical treatment of the material. Adolf immediately turned up the Wieland legend in his book on gods and heroes. Strangely enough, my

Chapter 18 — Adolf Writes an Opera

friend did not object at all to the plot of the Wieland legend, although King Nidur's action was entirely motivated by avarice and greed. The hunger for gold, so important an element in Germanic mythology, produced in him neither a negative nor a positive response. Nor was he at all impressed by the fact that Wieland kills his sons out of vengeance, rapes his daughter, and drinks from beakers fashioned out of the skulls of his sons. He started to write that same night. I was sure that in the morning he would surprise me with the draft of his new drama, Wieland, the Smith.

Yet things turned out differently. In the morning — nothing happened. But when I returned for lunch I found Adolf, to my great surprise, sitting at the piano. The scene that followed has remained in my memory.

Without any further explanation, he greeted me with the words, "Listen, Gustl, I am going to make the Wieland into an opera." I was so surprised that I was struck dumb.

Adolf enjoyed my reaction to his announcement and went on playing the piano, or what for him passed for "playing." Old Prewratzky had taught him something in his day, undoubtedly, but not enough to "play the piano" as I understood it.

When I had recovered, I asked Adolf how he imagined he would set about it.

"Quite simple — I shall compose the music, and you will write it down." Adolf's plans and ideas always moved more or less on a plane above normal comprehension — I had long since grown used to that. But now, when my own special domain, music, was in question, I really could not keep up with him. With all due respect to his musical gifts, he was no musician; he was not even capable of playing an instrument. He had not the slightest idea of musical theory. How could he dream of composing an opera? I only remember that my pride as a musician was hurt, and I walked out without uttering a word, and went to a small cafe nearby to do my homework.

However, my friend was not in the least offended by my behaviour, and when I returned home in the evening he was somewhat calmer. "Now, the prelude is ready — listen!" And he played, from memory, what he had thought up as the prelude to his opera.

I cannot recall, of course, a single note of this music. But one thing remains in my memory: it was a sort of illustration of the spoken word, by means of natural, musical elements, and he intended to have it performed on old instruments. As this would not have sounded harmonious, my friend decided in favour of a modern symphony orchestra, reinforced by Wagnerian tubas. At any rate, that was music which one could follow. Each separate musical theme in itself made sense, and if the whole impressed one as so primitive, it was only because Adolf could not play better; that is to say, he was incapable of expressing his ideas more clearly.

The composition was, of course, entirely influenced by Richard Wagner. The whole prelude consisted of a sequence of single themes. But the development of these themes, however well chosen they were, had been beyond Adolf's ability. After all, where should he have acquired the necessary knowledge? He entirely lacked any training for such a task.

Having finished his playing, Adolf wanted to hear my judgment. I knew how highly he valued it and what my praise in musical matters meant to him. But this was no simple problem.

The basic themes were good, I said, but he had to realise that with these themes alone it was impossible to write an opera, and I declared my readiness to teach him the necessary theoretical knowledge.

This roused his wrath, "Do you think I'm mad?" he shouted at me. "What have I got you for? First of all you will put down exactly what I play on the piano." I knew only too well my friend's mood when he spoke fn this manner, and realised that it was no good arguing. So I wrote down as faithfully as possible what Adolf had played. But it was late, Frau Zakreys was knocking on the door, and Adolf had to stop.

Next morning I left early, and when I returned for lunch, Adolf reproached me for having run away "in the middle of working on his opera." He had already prepared the music paper for me and immediately began to play. As Adolf stuck neither to the same time nor to a uniform key, it was hard to take down what I heard. I tried to make it clear to him that he had to keep to one key.

He ranted, "Who is the composer, you or I?" All I had to do was to write down his musical thoughts and ideas.

I asked him to start again. He did, and I wrote. Thus we made some progress; yet for Adolf it was too slow. I told him that, to begin with, I wanted to play through what I had taken down. He agreed, and I sat down at the piano, and it was his turn to listen.

Curiously enough, I liked what I was playing better than he did, perhaps because he had a very precise idea of his composition in his head and neither his own poor playing nor my notation and playing corresponded to it.

Nevertheless, we concentrated for several days, or rather nights, on this prelude. I had to put the whole thing into a suitable metric form. But whatever I did, Adolf was not satisfied. There were periods in the course of his composition in which the time changed from one bar to the next. I

Chapter 18 — Adolf Writes an Opera

succeeded in convincing Adolf that this was impossible; but as soon as I tried to render the whole section in one time, he protested again.

Today I can understand what brought him to the edge of despair during those strenuous nights and tested our friendship to the uttermost. He carried this prelude in his head as a finished composition, just as he had had ready the plan for a bridge or a concert hall even before he put pencil to paper. But, while he was complete master of the pencil and could give form to his idea till the drawing was completed, such means were denied him in the musical field. His attempt to make use of me made the whole thing even more complicated, for my theoretical knowledge only hindered his intuition. It reduced him to utter despair that he had an idea in his head, a musical idea which he considered bold and important, without being able to pin it down. There were moments in which he doubted his vocation, in spite of his pronounced self-conceit.

But soon he found a way out of the dilemma between passionate will and insufficient ability. It was as ingenious as it was original: he would compose his opera, he declared determinedly, in the mode of musical expression corresponding to that period in which the action was set, that is to say in Germanic antiquity. I intended to object that the audience, in order to "enjoy" the opera properly, should be composed of old Teutons, rather than people of the twentieth century. But even before I had raised this objection, he was already working fervently on his new solution. I had no opportunity to dissuade him from this experiment which I considered quite impossible.

Besides he would probably have succeeded in convincing me that his solution was feasible, by insisting that the people of our century would just have to learn to listen property.

He wanted to know if there was anything preserved of the German music.

"Nothing," I replied briefly, "except the instruments," "And what were they?" I told him that drums and rattles had been found, and in some places in Sweden and Denmark also a kind of flute, made of bones. Experts had succeeded in restoring these strange flutes and in producing with them some not very harmonious sounds. But most important were the Luren, wind instruments made of brass, almost two metres long and curved like a horn. They probably served only as bugles between homesteads, and the crude sounds they produced could hardly be called music.

I thought that my explanation, which he had followed with careful attention, would suffice to make him give up his idea, for you could not orchestrate an opera with rattles, drums, bone flutes and Luren. But

I was wrong. He started talking about the Skalds, who had sung to the accompaniment of harplike instruments, something I had really forgotten.

It should be possible, he went on, to deduce, from the kind of instruments the Germanic tribes had, what their music was like.

Now my book learning came into its own. "That has been done," I reported, "and it has been shown that the music of the Teutons had a vertical structure, and possessed some sort of harmony; they even had, perhaps, some inkling of major and minor keys. To be sure, these are only scientific assumptions, so-called hypotheses . . ." This was sufficient to induce my friend to start composing for nights on end. He surprised me with ever new conceptions and ideas. It was hardly possible to write down this music, which did not fit into any scheme. As the Wieland legend, which Adolf arbitrarily interpreted and extended, was rich in dramatic moments, a wide scale of sentiments had to be translated into the musical idiom.

To make the thing at all "tolerable" for the human ear, I finally persuaded Adolf to give up the idea of using the original instruments from the Germanic tombs, and to replace them by modem instruments of a similar type. I was content, when after nights of work, at long last the various Leitmotifs of the opera were established.

We then agreed on the characters, of whom only Wieland, the hero of the opera, had so far any substance. Thereupon Adolf divided the whole action into acts and scenes. In the meantime, he designed the scenery and costumes and made a charcoal sketch of the winged hero.

As my friend did not make any progress with the libretto, which was supposed to be in verse, I suggested that he should finish the prelude first, to which he agreed after several rather heated arguments. I gave him a lot of help with it, and consequently the prelude turned out quite presentable. But my suggestion that the composition should be orchestrated, and played by an orchestra as soon as an opportunity arose, was rejected by him out of hand. He refused to have the prelude classed as program music, and would not hear of an "audience" — which was in any case problematical. And yet he worked feverishly on it, as though an impatient opera producer had allowed him too little time and was waiting to snatch the manuscript from his hands.

He wrote and wrote and I worked on the music. When I fell asleep, overwhelmed by fatigue, Adolf roused me roughly. I had hardly opened my eyes and there he was in front of me, reading from his manuscript, the words tumbling over each other in his excitement. It was past midnight and he had to speak softly. This, in its contrast to the scenes of volcanic violence described in his verse, lent to his impassioned voice a sound of strange

Chapter 18 — *Adolf Writes an Opera*

unreality. I had long since known this behaviour of his, when a self-imposed task engrossed him completely and forced him to unceasing activity; it was as though a demon had taken possession of him.

Oblivious of his surroundings, he never tired, he never slept. He ate nothing, he hardly drank. At the most he would occasionally grab the milk bottle and take a hasty gulp, certainly without being aware of it, for he was too completely wrapped up in his work. But never before had I been so directly impressed by this ecstatic creativeness. Where was it leading him? He squandered his strength and talents on something that had no practical value. How long would this weakened, delicate body stand this overstrain? I forced myself to stay awake and to listen, nor did I ask him any of the questions that filled me with anxiety. It would have been easy for me to take as an excuse one of our frequent quarrels to move out. The people at the Conservatory would have been only too pleased to help me find another room. Why did I not do it? After all, I had often admitted to myself that this strange friendship was no good for my studies. How much time and energy did I lose in these nocturnal activities of my friend? Why, then, did I not go? Because I was homesick, certainly, and because Adolf represented for me a bit of home. But, after all, homesickness is something a young man of twenty can overcome. What was it then? What held me? Frankly, it was just hours like those through which I was now living which bound me even more closely to my friend. I knew the normal interests of young people of my age: flirtations, shallow pleasures, idle play and a lot of unimportant meaningless thoughts. Adolf was the exact opposite.

There was an incredible earnestness in him, a thoroughness, a true passionate interest in everything that happened and, most important, an unfailing devotion to the beauty, majesty and grandeur of art. It was this that attracted me especially to him and restored my equilibrium after hours of exhaustion. All this was well worth a few sleepless nights and those more or less heated quarrels to which, in my quiet, sensible way, I had become accustomed.

I still remembered that some of the opera's more dramatic scenes haunted me for weeks in my dreams. Only some of the pictures which Adolf designed still stand out in my memory. Pen and pencil were too slow for him and he used to draw with charcoal. He would outline the scenery with a few bold, quick strokes. Then we would discuss the action: first, Wieland enters from the right, then his brother Egil from the left, and then, from the back, the second brother Slaghid.

I have still before my eyes the Wolf Lake, where the first scene of the opera was laid. From the Edda, a book that was sacred for him, he knew

Iceland, the rugged island of the North, where the elements which formed the world meet now, as they did in the days of Creation: the violent storm, the bare, dark rock, the pale ice of the glaciers, the flaming fire of the volcanoes. There he laid the scene of his opera, for there Nature herself was still in those passionate convulsions which inspired the actions of gods and human beings. There, then, was the Wolf Lake on whose banks Wieland and his brothers were fishing, when one morning three light clouds, borne along by the winds, floated towards the men. There were three Valkyries in glittering coats of mail and shining helmets. They wore white, fluttering robes, magic garments which enabled them to float through the air. I remember what headaches these flying Valkyries caused us, as Adolf categorically refused to do without them. Altogether there was a lot of "flying" in our opera. In the last act, Wieland, too, had to forge himself a pair of wings, with which he would have to fly, a flight on wings of metal, which moreover had to be accomplished with the utmost ease in order to remove any doubts about the quality of his workmanship. This was for us, the creators of this opera, one more technical problem, which attracted Adolf in particular, perhaps because just in those days the first "heavier than air" machines were being flown by Lilienthal, the Wright brothers, Farman and Blériot. The "Flying Valkyries" married Wieland, Egil and Slaghid. Mighty horns summoned the neighbours to the wedding feast at the Wolf Lake.

It would take too long were I to recount the various episodes of the old saga; besides, I can no longer tell whether we followed it word for word in our work. But the impression of dramatic events driven on by wild, unbridled passion, expression in verses that inexorably engraved themselves on the heart, carried by just such inexorably severe and elemental music is still vivid in my memory.

I do not know what became of our opera. One day new, pressing problems confronted my friend, which required immediate solution; as even Adolf, in spite of his immense capacity for work, had only one pair of hands, he had to put aside the half-finished opera. He spoke less and less of it, and in the end did not mention it at all. Perhaps the insufficiency of his endeavours had meanwhile dawned on him. To me, it had been obvious from the beginning that we would never succeed in our attempt to write an opera, and I took good care not to raise the subject. "Wieland, the Smith," Adolf's opera, remained a fragment.

Chapter 19 — The "Mobile Reichs Orchestra"

My friend's interest in music was gratifyingly broadened in Vienna. Having previously been interested in opera only, he now turned increasingly to concerts. To be sure, even in Linz he had frequented the symphony concerts organised by the Music Society, and must have heard in those years altogether, say, six or seven concerts. But he came less for the sake of the music than for my sake, as I was playing in the orchestra, a fact that was important to him. With my quiet, compliant nature he did not think me capable of playing in public, and each time he was eager to see the result. At any rate, I remember that after the performances, he used to speak much more about me than about the concert.

Vienna changed all this, helped by the fact that at the Conservatory I was given two or sometimes three concert tickets every week. Adolf always got one of these, sometimes even two or all three, when I was prevented from going by my evening practice. As these free tickets were usually for good seats, this was not such a strain as going to the Hof Opera.

In discussing these concerts with him, I noticed to my surprise that Adolf was developing a taste for symphonic music. This pleased me because it created for us a new common interest.

The head of the Conductors' School of the Conservatory, Gustav Gutheil, was also the conductor of the Vienna Concert Society. But our special favourite was Ferdinand Loewe, the director of the Conservatory, who occasionally conducted the Vienna Philharmonic Orchestra; he was a great admirer of Bruckner. The musical life of Vienna at that time was still dominated by the Brahms-Bruckner controversy, although both masters had been dead for over ten years. Eduard Hanslick, the formidable music critic, whom we always called "Beckmesser," was also dead, but his pernicious influence was still noticeable. Hanslick who was our declared enemy, if only because he had attacked Richard Wagner violently and not always fairly, had firmly supported Brahms and fought furiously against Anton Bruckner. In Ferdinand Loewe, on the other hand, Bruckner had an inspired partisan; and also Franz Schalk, later director of the Vienna Opera, was a Bruckner supporter.

For our part, we had no difficulty in making up our minds in this controversy. I loved Bruckner and Adolf, too, was thrilled and moved by his symphonies. Besides, Bruckner came from our part of the country, and in exalting his work, we were exalting our homeland. Yet this was no reason for us to reject Brahms. In this dispute, we regarded ourselves as representatives of the younger generation, paid our tribute to both masters and smiled at the zeal of the older people, which seemed to us utterly superfluous. As for Adolf, he went even further. Just as Bayreuth had become the centre of Richard Wagner's most impressive work, he said, so Linz should become the shrine of Anton Bruckner's works. The Linz Concert Hall, plans for which he had just finished, should be consecrated to Bruckner's memory.

Apart from the great symphonies by the classical masters, Adolf liked especially the music of the Romanticists, Carl Maria von Weber, Franz Schubert, Felix Mendelssohn-Bartholdy and Robert Schumann. He was sorry that Richard Wagner had written only for the stage and not for the concert hall, so that usually only the overtures or some of his operas were performed.

I must not forget Edward Grieg, of whom Adolf was particularly fond and whose Piano Concerto in A Minor always delighted him.

In general Adolf was not very partial to virtuoso performances by soloists. But certain concertos he never missed, such as Mozart and Beethoven's piano and violin concertos, Mendelssohn's Violin Concerto in E Minor and, above all, Schumann's Piano Concerto in A Minor.

But there was something about his frequent visits to concerts, which made Adolf restless. For a long time I could not understand what it was. Any other young man would have been more than content with these performances; not so my friend.

There he sat in his free seat in the Concert Hall blissfully enjoying Beethoven's brilliant Violin Concerto in D Major and was happy and contented. Yet, on looking round the hall, he could count only four or five hundred people who had come to hear the concert. How puny was this number in comparison with the thousands who could not hear it. No doubt there were many, not only among the students, but also among the artisans and workers who would have been as happy as he was to be able to hear this immortal music either without payment, or at a price they could afford. And it was not Vienna alone one had to consider, for in Vienna it was comparatively easy for music lovers to go to concerts. But outside Vienna, the small places, the provincial towns. Oh! he had seen it himself in Linz, how little was done to satisfy the cultural needs of these places. This must be changed. The enjoyment of concerts should no longer be the privilege of the lucky few. The system of free tickets was no cure, however much he benefited from it personally; a radical remedy was called for.

This kind of thinking was typical of Adolf. Nothing could happen around him from which he would not draw some general conclusions. Even

Chapter 19 — The "Mobile Reichs Orchestra"

purely artistic experiences, like listening to a concert, which others accepted passively, roused his active interest and became problems of universal concern, for nothing was allowed to remain unimportant in the "Ideal State" of his dreams. The "Storm of the Revolution" must fling wide open the gates of Art, which hitherto had been locked to so many — "social reform" even in the field of artistic enjoyment.

No doubt, many young people thought as he did in those years. His protest against the privileged position of certain classes with regard to art was by no means isolated. On the contrary. Not only were there fanatical pioneers of the idea of bringing art to the people, but also societies, organisations and institutions which worked towards that aim, and not without success. What was unique, however, was the manner in which my friend was trying to remedy this sorry state of affairs. While others were content to apply modest measures and to approach their goal step by step, Adolf disdained half measures and strove for a total solution regardless of when and where it could be realised. As far as he was concerned, it was reality from the very moment when he first pronounced the basic idea.

And another characteristic of his: he was not content with simply stating this idea, but started immediately to elaborate it in all detail exactly as though he had received orders from "higher quarters." This detailed planning was for him, so to speak, as good as the actual realisation.

Once an idea had been thoroughly thought out and elaborated in detail, it would only need a command to carry it out. However, this command was never given during the course of our friendship and that is why I, in my heart of hearts, regarded Adolf as a visionary, however much I was convinced of the "reasonableness" of his words. He himself was even then absolutely certain that one day he, personally, would give this command, whereby the hundreds and thousands of plans and projects which he had at his fingertips would be carried out. To be sure, he mentioned them only rarely and then only to me, because he knew that I believed in him. I have often heard him, when an idea took possession of him, developing it to such an extent that the listener would be compelled to ask, "All well and good, but who is going to pay for it?"

When we were still in Linz, I was indeed often careless enough to utter this question because it seemed to me so obvious and all-important. In Vienna I had learned to be more cautious and refrained from discussing finance too frankly. Adolf's replies to these questions, which appeared to him superfluous, changed. In Linz, his standard reply was, "The Reich," which I thought was no answer at all. In Vienna he was a little more explicit: "That's a matter for the financial experts." But it also happened that he would shut me up rudely with, "You will be the last person to be consulted on this matter, for you don't know anything about it." Or even more briefly, "Please let this be my worry."

The first indication that he was working on a particular idea was always some peculiar phrase that would crop up in his diatribes, or in our discussions, some special expression which he had never used before. So long as he had not firmly decided what was the purpose of his idea, his phrase would keep changing. Thus, during the weeks of his frequent concert-going, he would speak at first only of "that orchestra which tours the provinces." I thought that there really did exist such an orchestra in Vienna, and that Adolf was speaking of an actual fact. Later, however, I discovered that this "mobile orchestra," as he came to call it (because the word "touring" reminded him too much of second-rate theatrical companies), existed only in his imagination. As he was never satisfied with half measures, he soon made of it a "mobile Reichs orchestra." I still remember that Adolf, after we had laid down the plans for this organisation, was so enthusiastic about his creation that he planned to set up and send out ten such orchestras, so that even the remotest corner of the Reich could enjoy Beethoven's Violin Concerto in D Major.

One evening when he was speaking for the first time at greater length of this orchestra, I asked him why on earth it was just musical matters to which he devoted his attention. I thought he was intending to become an architect? His reply was short and to the point, "Because, for the time being, I have you around." By which he meant that as long as I was at hand, he could always take advantage of my advice and of my special knowledge as a future conductor. This, of course, flattered me. But when I took my courage into both hands and hopefully asked him to whom he would entrust the direction of his orchestra, he immediately saw through me, laughed sarcastically and exclaimed, "Certainly not you!" But, serious once again, he added that perhaps he might actually contemplate making me the conductor of the mobile Reichs orchestra.

However, I was offended and replied that I could do without this honour, for I was interested in becoming the conductor of an orchestra which actually existed, not a nebulous dream orchestra.

That was enough to bring on an outburst of fury, for he could not bear it if one doubted that his plans would be realised. "You will be only too glad if I appoint you to such a post," he screamed at me.

I recall all the details concerning the mobile Reichs orchestra better than many other projects of Adolf's, because it was essentially my own sphere. Naturally, I was allowed to have a much bigger say than usual, even

Chapter 19 — The "Mobile Reichs Orchestra"

more than on the occasion of his attempt to supplement Richard Wagner's music dramas by a new opera, Wieland, the Smith. How thoroughly we tackled this task can be gathered from the fact that one evening we had a quarrel about the double-action harp. Certainly, the "mobile Reich's orchestra" needed a double-action harp. But Adolf insisted on three of these very expensive instruments, which moreover were frightfully difficult to transport.

"To what purpose?" I said. "An experienced conductor can manage with only one double-action harp." "Ridiculous," Adolf exclaimed angrily. "How can you play the Fire Music with only one double-action harp in the orchestra?" "Then the Fire Music won't be included in the repertoire," I replied. "You bet it will," Adolf insisted. I made a last effort. "Don't forget that a double-action harp costs eighteen thousand florins." That would make him change his mind, I thought. But I was wrong. "Oh, to hell with money," he exclaimed. That settled the matter. The mobile Reichs Orchestra was equipped with three double-action harps.

Today I cannot help smiling when I think of the heat with which we argued about matters that only existed in our own imagination, and yet those were wonderful times when we got more excited over nebulous dreams than over the reality of everyday life. I marvelled at my friend's uncanny imagination, which enabled him to find his way in his dream world better than in the real world.

Yet, what was for me only idle fantasy was much more important for him. The basic idea of this mobile Reichs orchestra was very plausible, and I had often thought about the problem myself. Adolf's solution was both brilliant and simple: an orchestra under a gifted conductor would be organised, capable of performing classic, romantic and modern symphonic music and sent out to the country according to a pre-established plan. Adolf asked me what size, in my view, this orchestra should be. The mere fact that he asked my advice, instead of looking it up in his books, filled me with pride. I can still see us building up this orchestra, the strings, the woodwinds, the brass and the percussion and remember how Adolf wanted to be informed about every trivial detail, how he questioned me about the peculiar orchestration of symphonic works, so that he would not overlook anything and would make the orchestra perfect in every respect.

This was the strange, enigmatic trait in his character, a contradiction that I could not explain: he would build projects on a foundation of thin air, but at the same time make them quite unassailable in themselves. The more the whole plan was only a matter of wishful taking, the more elaborate had to be its details.

The night was half over before we had finished our work, The orchestra which we had built up consisted of a hundred players, a respectable body of sound, which would be able to compete with any one of the big orchestras. Equipment was the next problem. Adolf was rather startled when I enumerated the requirements. Not only first-class instruments, whose careful transport had to be safeguarded, but an ample music library, and moreover desks, chairs and so forth. He agreed that a first-class cellist could not sit every night on a different chair. Finally he asked me to approach the Secretary of the Orchestra Society for further information about these purchases, and to make enquiries at the Musicians' Union about the engagement of musicians, and then work out a budget. Adolf was satisfied with the result of my inquiries. He dismissed the high amount of the budget with a disdainful gesture; but we had a heated argument about a uniform dress for the orchestra. Naturally the orchestra had to be pleasing to the eye. I suggested a suitable uniform, but Adolf was against it. We agreed in the end on a dark outfit, distinguished but unobtrusive.

A grave problem was the transport of the orchestra, for there were parts of the country that were inaccessible by railway. And these were the regions that mattered. But there were running in the streets those newfangled motorcars. In those days people still stopped and stared at these vehicles which raced up and down the Ring, noisy and smelly, at the "murderous" speed of ten miles per hour. What about loading our Reich's orchestra on such vehicles? No doubt these would increase the mobility of the orchestra and, consequently, its range. I forget to what point we developed this idea, which I personally disliked; for I could not imagine that an orchestra which arrived with such a devilish din could make people more receptive to harmonious sounds.

Well! The orchestra arrives, is ceremoniously greeted by the Mayor and makes its way through the festively decorated streets. First question: Where should it perform? Only a few towns possess a hall which can accommodate an orchestra of one hundred players and an audience of several hundred. "We shall play in the open," said Adolf. "Concerts under the starlit sky are certainly very impressive," I interjected, "provided, however, that the starlit sky will last throughout the duration of the concert." Besides, these concerts would be more for the benefit of the stars than of the audience because of the acoustical conditions. The whole plan almost foundered on this hard fact. Adolf pondered a while and then said, "There are churches everywhere. Why don't we play in the churches?" From the musical point of view there could be no objection. Adolf suggested I should ask the ecclesiastical authorities whether they would put the churches at the

Chapter 19 — The "Mobile Reichs Orchestra"

disposal of the mobile Reichs orchestra for concerts. This, in my opinion, was going a bit too far.

But I kept silent, and Adolf forgot to ask me what the results of my inquiries had been.

We differed strongly over the planning of the program. Adolf wanted to know how much rehearsal time an orchestra would need for a symphony, and was annoyed that no fixed rules could be applied. He categorically refused to accept my view that there were no earlier German composers — and on German composers solely he positively insisted — than Bach, Gluck and Handel, and perhaps Heinrich Schütz. "And what was before that?" he inquired. "Nothing suitable for an orchestra," I replied. "Who says so?" he shouted. I told him, calmly, that in this instance he could safely rely on my answer, unless he wanted to study the history of music himself. "And so I will," he said, angrily. And that brought our discussion to an end.

I had not taken his words seriously, for the study of the history of music is not a simple matter, apart from being outside the range of his professional interests. Moreover, he knew that I was really well versed in this field, as I was attending lectures at the University. I was the more surprised when on the next day I found him immersed in a heavy volume, *The Development of Music in the Course of Time*. He was quite unapproachable for a few days, but the book did not quite satisfy him. He asked me for other writings on the history of music and ploughed steadily through them.

"The Chinese had good music as early as two thousand years ago," he remarked; "why should we not have had the same? After all, one instrument certainly existed already — the human voice.

Because those learned gentlemen are fumbling in the dark about the origins of music, that is to say, know nothing about it, that does not mean to say that nothing existed." I had great respect for my friend's thoroughness. But sometimes I was driven to despair by his mania to get to the roots of everything. He did not give up until he had reached complete deadlock, and even then he would not accept defeat, and remained sceptical. I could well imagine how this attitude of his would have driven all the Professors of the Academy crazy.

At any rate, it was now established that we should start the program of the Mobile Reich's Orchestra with Johann Sebastian Bach and follow up with Gluck and Handel, to Haydn, Mozart and Beethoven. Then should come the Romanticists, with all the symphonies of Anton Bruckner as the culminating point. As far as the Moderns were concerned-the young, still unknown composers — Adolf himself wished to be sole arbiter of these.

He had no intention of being guided by the judgments of the Viennese music critics, whom he lost no opportunity of assailing, calling them "mere experts" and "specialists." From the time when we first set up the mobile Reichs orchestra, Adolf prepared himself a special notebook, which I quite well remember. It was a small book, easy to slip in the pocket, in which, after every concert he attended, he wrote the titles of the works, the name of the composers and the name of the conductor, as well as his own opinion of them. It was the highest praise a work could earn if he said, "This will be included in our program." For a long time to come I thought about the "mobile Reichs orchestra." It is true the gramophone already existed. To be sure it was a pitiable, scratchy monster of a thing but, with it, the path to "mechanical" music was already opened, Wireless telegraphy was still in its infancy. Meanwhile, in spite of the fact that records and radio have since triumphed to such an extent that it looks as though "performed" music only exists to supply the needs of "mechanical" music, the basic question which my friend tried to solve with the help of the mobile Reichs orchestra still remains for all intelligent, genuine art lovers: How to bring to the people who appreciate it fine music, perfectly performed, directly — that is to say without any mechanical aids — wherever they may live.

Chapter 20 — Unmilitary Interlude

One fine day — it must have been the beginning of April — I received a letter. As Adolf never got any letters, I used to be discreet about mine to spare his feeling, but he noticed at once that this letter must have some special significance. "What's the matter, Gustl?" he asked, sympathetically.

I replied simply, "Here, read it." I can still see how his face changed colour, how his eyes took on that extraordinary glitter which used to herald an outburst of rage. Then he started raving.

"You are not to register, on any account, Gustl," he screamed. "You're a fool if you go there. The best thing to do is to tear up this stupid bit of paper!" I jumped up and snatched my calling-up papers away from him, before he in his fury tore them to pieces.

I was so upset myself that Adolf soon calmed down. Striding angrily between door and piano, he immediately drew up a plan to help me out of my present predicament.

"It's not even certain, yet, whether you will be passed as fit," he remarked more calmly. "After all, it's only a year since you nearly went under with that bad attack of pneumonia. If you are unfit, as I hope, all this excitement will have been in vain." Adolf suggested that I should go to Linz and present myself before the medical board according to instructions. In case I should be passed as fit, I should forthwith cross the border into Germany secretly, at Passau. On no account was I to serve in the Austro-Hungarian army. This moribund Hapsburg Empire did not deserve a single soldier, he declared. As my friend was nine months younger than I, he did not expect his call-up until the following year, 1909. But, as was now evident, he had already made up his mind in this respect and was determined not to serve in the Austrian army. Perhaps he was quite pleased to use me as a guinea pig and find out how his suggested solution would really work in practice.

The next morning I went to the Director of the Conservatory and showed him my call-up papers. He explained to me that, as a member of the Conservatory, I was entitled to serve only one year, but he advised me, as the only son of a businessman, to register with the Reserve. There, I should only have to do eight weeks training, and later on, three further periods of four weeks. I asked him what he thought of the idea of my going to Germany to escape military service altogether. He was shocked by this unusual suggestion and energetically advised me against it.

For Adolf, even the idea of my serving in the Reserve was too great a concession to the Hapsburg Empire, and he went on and on, trying to persuade me to fall in with his plan right up to the moment I had finished my packing.

In Linz, I told my father what my friend had suggested, for I was more than a little intrigued by the idea. I could not get up any enthusiasm for military service, and even the eight weeks in the Reserve seemed to me dreadful.

My father was even more horrified than the Director had been. "In Heaven's name, what are you thinking of?" he exclaimed, shaking his head. If I went over the border secretly or, to call a spade a spade, deserted, I would be liable to prosecution, he declared. On top of that, I could never come home again and my parents, who had already sacrificed so much for me, would lose me altogether.

These words of my father's, together with my mother's tears, sufficed to bring me to my senses.

My father that very day went to see a government official, with whom he was friendly, about the possibility of getting me put down for the Reserve, and he immediately drafted an application, which he advised me to hand in, should I be passed fit for service.

I wrote Adolf that I had decided to follow the Conservatory Director's advice and was attending for the medical examination in a few days. After that I would be coming to Vienna with my father.

Perhaps Adolf, too, had meanwhile thought better of it, and had realised that the way he had devised for himself was not suitable for me, because in his reply he did not even mention it. Or, of course, perhaps he did not like to put down this plan, which after all was, fairly risky, in black and white. On the other hand, he was obviously very pleased that my father intended coming back with me when I returned to Vienna. (Actually the trip never took place.) I had also written Adolf that I was bringing my viola with me, in case I had the chance of an orchestra engagement, so that I could make a little extra money. During my studies in Vienna, I had contracted conjunctivitis, and was treated in Linz by an oculist, and I warned Adolf that he should not be surprised if I arrived at the Westbahnhof wearing spectacles.

Fortunately I still have the letter he wrote in reply, addressed to the "stud. mus. Gustav Kubizek":

Dear Gustl, While thanking you for your letter, I must tell you immediately how pleased I am that your dear father is really coming with

Chapter 20 — Unmilitary Interlude

you to Vienna. Providing that you and he have no objection, I will meet you at the station on Thursday at 11 o'clock. You write that you are having such lovely weather, which almost upsets me as, if it were not raining here, we too should be having lovely weather. I am very pleased that you are bringing a viola. On Tuesday I shall buy myself 2 crowns' worth of cotton wool and 20 kreuzers' worth of paste, for my ears naturally. That — on top of this — you are going blind affects me very deeply; you will play more wrong notes than ever. Then you will become blind and I gradually mad. Oh, dear! But meanwhile I wish you and your esteemed parents at least a happy Easter and send them my hearty greetings as well as to you.

Your friend, ADOLF HITLER

The letter is dated April 20, so Adolf had written it on his birthday. In view of his circumstances at that time, it is not surprising that he does not mention it. Perhaps he had not even realised that it was his birthday.

Everything in the letter that concerns my father is perfectly polite. He even asks if it is in order to come and meet us. But as soon as he refers to the weather, his sarcasm breaks through, "If it were not raining, we, too, should be having lovely weather." And then, when he comes to my viola, he gives full play to his grim humour. He even jokes about the trouble with my eyes until he pulls himself up with the "Oh dear!" and then closes the letter in a very formal manner. That Adolf still had not come to terms with spelling is particularly clear in the original German of this letter.

His former German teacher, Professor Huemer, would not even have given him a "Fair" for it, and the punctuation is even worse.

On the appointed day I went for my medical examination. I was passed as fit and presented the application for acceptance in the Reserve.

When I returned to Vienna — without the dreaded spectacles — Adolf greeted me very warmly, because, in spite of everything, he was glad that I would continue to live with him. Of course, he made great fun of the "Reservist." He could not possibly imagine how they would make a soldier out of me, he said. For that matter, neither could I. But it was something, that I could go on with my studies. At home, Adolf sketched my head and drew a cocked hat with a plume on top of it.

"There you are, Gustl," he joked, "you look like a veteran even before you're a recruit." After the long, dull winter, spring was making its appearance. Since I had seen once again, on my visit to Linz, the familiar meadows, woods and hills, our gloomy back room in the Stumpergasse seemed to me gloomier than ever. Looking back on our countless walks throughout the length and breadth of the countryside around Linz, I tried to persuade Adolf to make some excursions into the country around Vienna. I had more time to spare now as my pupils, having successfully passed their examinations, had returned home, but not without giving me a nice little present, which came as a pleasant surprise; so that there was once again a little money in the kitty (so far as I was concerned, at any rate). When, in the gardens along the Ring, the blossoms came out and the mild spring sunshine enticed us, I could not stand the stifling walls of the city any longer.

Adolf, too, was longing to get out into the open.

I knew how fond he was of the open country, the woods and, in the distance, the blue range of mountains. He found a solution to this problem, in his own way, long before I did when it became too close and stuffy for him at Frau Zakreys' and the stink of kerosene became unbearable, he went off to the Schönbrunn Park. But this was not enough for me. I wanted to see more of the country around Vienna. So did Adolf, but first, he explained, he had no money for such "extra expenses." That could be got over, as I invited him to be my guest on such excusions and, to make sure of it, I bought provisions for both of us the day before. Secondly — and this was much more difficult — if we really wanted to make a full day's excusions, he had to get up early. He would rather do anything than this, as it was a most difficult thing for him.

To try to shake him awake was a risky undertaking — he was likely to become utterly impossible.

"Why do you wake me so early?" he would shout at me. When I told him that the day was well advanced, he would never believe me. I would lean right out of the window and twist my head upwards so that I could see the small strip of sky. "Not a cloud in sight; the sun is shining brightly," I would announce, but even as I turned round, Adolf was fast asleep again.

If I succeeded in getting him out of bed and on the move, I had to consider the first few hours lost, because after having been awaked so "early," he would be silent and sullen for a long time, replying to questions only with reluctant grunts, Only when we got far away in the bright green countryside did he finally come out of his sulks. Then, to be sure, he was happy and contented and even thanked me for having persisted in my efforts to get him up.

Our first objective was the Hermannskogel in the Vienna woods and we were very lucky with the weather. On the summit, we vowed to go out far more frequently.

The next Sunday we went to the Vienna woods again. We felt ready for anything, although we certainly did not look very enterprising in our city

Chapter 20 — Unmilitary Interlude

clothes and light shoes. We made a very long trip that day, according to our standards, from the start of the Tullner Feld, and by Ried and Purkersdorf, back to the city. Adolf was enchanted by that part of the countryside and said it reminded him of a certain part of the Mühlviertel, of which he was very fond. Undoubtedly, he too suffered inwardly from homesickness for the land of his childhood and adolescence, although not a single soul remained there who still cared about him.

I took a day off from the Conservatory for the trip to the Wachau. We had to get to the station very early to catch a train to Melk, and it was not till he saw the marvellous monastery that Adolf became reconciled to this early rising. But then how he enjoyed it-I could hardly tear him away.

He would not stick to the conducted tour, but sought everywhere for secret passages and hidden steps which would take him to the foundations; he wanted to examine how these had been built into the rocks. Indeed, one could almost believe that the mighty pile had grown out of the stone.

After that, we spent a long time in the beautiful library.

Then we went, on the steamer, through the glory of Maybedecked Wachau. Adolf was a changed person, even if only through being on the Danube, his beloved river, again. For Vienna was not so closely built about the Danube as was, for instance, Linz, where one could stand on the bridge and await the approach of a distinguished, blond maiden from Urfahr. He missed the Danube almost as much as he still missed Stefanie. And now the castles, the villages, the hillside vineyards passed us gently by. For it did not seem as though we were moving forward; but rather as though we were standing still with this wonderful landscape floating by us in a peaceful rhythm. What a romantic world. It acts on us like magic. Adolf stands in the bows, engrossed in the landscape. Till long past Krems, sailing along through the broad monotonous woods that line the river on either bank, he does not utter a word. Who knows where his thoughts may be? As though this magic trip needed a counterbalance, our next trip was down the Danube to Fischamend. I was disappointed. Was this really the same river that had so delighted us, our dear, familiar Danube? Wharves, warehouses, oil refineries, and in between them miserable fishermen's huts, slums, and even real gypsy encampments. Where on earth had we to go? This was the "other" Danube which no longer belonged to the picture of our homeland, but was part of the strange, eastern world. We went home, Adolf very thoughtful and I disillusioned.

But most vivid in my memory is a mountain excursion we made in early summer. The journey to Semmering was far enough to allow Adolf to recover from his early rising. Immediately after Wiener Neustadt the country became mountainous. The railway had to reach the heights of the Semmering in wide curves. To attain a height of 980 metres, many turns, tunnels and viaducts were necessary. Adolf was thrilled by the bold design of the track; one surprise came on top of another. He would have liked to get out and walk this stretch of the track, so that he could inspect it all. I was already prepared to listen to a fundamental lecture on the building of mountain railways at the next opportunity, for certainly he had already thought out a bolder design, even higher viaducts and longer tunnels.

Semmering! We got out. A beautiful day. How pure the air was here after all the dust and smoke, how blue the sky! The meadows gleamed green, with the dark woods rising from them, and above, their peaks still snow-covered, towered the mountains.

The train back to Vienna did not leave till evening; we had plenty of time, the whole day was ours. Adolf quickly made up his mind what our target should be. Which was the highest of these mountains? We were told, I believe, the Rax. So, let us climb the Rax.

Neither Adolf nor I had the faintest idea of mountaineering. The highest "mountains" we had conquered in our lives were the gentle hills of Mühlviertel. The Alps, themselves, we had till now only seen at a distance. But we were now in the midst of them and very impressed by the thought that this mountain was over two thousand metres high. As always with Adolf, his will had to make up for whatever else was lacking. We had no food with us, because we had originally intended just to walk down from the Semmering heights to Gloggnitz. We did not even have a rucksack and our clothes were those that we wore for our strolls through the city. Our shoes were much too light, with thin soles and without nails. We had trousers and jacket, but not a scrap of warm clothing. But the sun was shining, and we were young — so forward! The adventure we had on our way down overshadowed our upward climb so completely that I can no longer tell which route we took. I only remember now that we climbed for several hours before we reached the plain at the summit of the mountain. We now seemed to be on a peak, though it might not have been the Rax. I had never climbed a mountain peak; I had a strange, unfettered feeling, as though I no longer belonged to the earth, but was already close to heaven.

Adolf, deeply affected, stood on the plateau and said not a word.

We could see far and wide across the land. Here and there in the colourful pattern of meadow and forest a church tower or a village would spring up. How puny and unimportant did the works of man look! It was a wonderful moment, perhaps the most beautiful that I have ever experienced with my friend.

Chapter 20 — Unmilitary Interlude

Tiredness was forgotten in our enthusiasm. Somewhere in our pockets we found a bit of dry bread and we made do with that. In the pleasure of the day, we had hardly noticed the weather.

Had not the sun just been shining? Now, suddenly, dark clouds made their appearance and a mist fell; this happened as rapidly as though it were the change of a stage set.

The wind sprang up and whipped the mist before us in long, fluttering shrouds. Far off a storm was rumbling; hollow and uncanny, the thunder rolled around the mountains.

We began to freeze in our pitiful "Ringstrasse suitings." Our thin trousers fluttered round our legs as we hurried down to the valley. But the path was stony, and our shoes not up to the demands the mountain made on them. Moreover, for al! our haste, the storm gained on us. Already the first drops were spattering down in the woods; and then the rain really set in. And what rain! Actual streams of water poured down on us from the clouds that seemed to hang just above the treetops. We ran and ran, as hard as we could. It was hopeless to try to protect ourselves. Soon there was not a single dry spot on us and our shoes, too, were full of water.

And no house, no hut, no kind of shelter wherever we turned. Adolf was not at all put out by the thunder and lightning, the storm and the rain. To my surprise he was in a splendid mood and, although soaked to the skin, became more and more genial as the rain grew heavier.

We skipped along the stony path and suddenly, just off it, I spotted a little hut. There was no sense in continuing to run in the rain, besides, it was getting dark, so I suggested to Adolf that we should stay in this little cabin overnight. He immediately agreed — for him the adventure could not go on long enough.

I searched the little wooden hut. In the lower half lay a pile of hay, dry, and sufficient for us both to sleep in. Adolf took off his shoes, jacket and trousers and began to wring out his clothes. "Are you terribly hungry, too?" he asked. He felt somewhat better when I told him that I was. A sorrow shared is a sorrow halved; apparently that applied to hunger too.

Meanwhile, in the upper part of the hut, I had found some large squares of canvas, which were used by the peasants to carry the hay down the steep mountain sides. I felt very sorry for Adolf, standing there in the doorway in his soaking underclothes, chattering with cold as he wrung out the sleeves of his jacket. Sensitive as he was to any kind of chill, how easily he could catch pneumonia. So I took one of the big squares, stretched it out on the hay and told Adolf to take off his wet shirt and pants and to wrap himself in the cloth. This he did.

He laid himself naked on the cloth and I took hold of the ends and wrapped it firmly round him.

Then I fetched a second square and put that over him. This done, I wrung out all our clothes and hung them up, wrapped myself, too, in a canvas and lay down. So that we should not get icy cold in the night, I threw a bale of hay over the bundle that was Adolf, and another one over myself.

We did not know the time as neither of us had a watch. But for us it was enough to know that outside it was pitchdark with the rain rattling unceasingly on to the roof of the hut. Somewhere in the distance a dog barked; so we were not too far away from human habitation, a thought that comforted me. When I mentioned it to Adolf, however, it left him quite indifferent. In the present circumstances people were quite superfluous for him. He was enjoying the whole adventure hugely and its romantic ending especially appealed to him. Now we were getting warm, and it would have been almost cosy in the little hut, if we had not been racked with hunger.

I thought once more of my parents, then I fell asleep.

When I awoke in the morning, daylight was already showing through the gaps in the boards. I got up. Our clothes were almost dry.

I still remember what a job it was to get Adolf to wake up. When he was finally roused, he worked his feet free of their wrappings and, with the canvas wrapped round him, walked to the door to look at the weather. His slim, straight figure, with the white cloth thrown toga-wise across the shoulders, looked like that of an Indian ascetic.

This was our last great excursion together.

Just as my journey to the medical board had unpleasantly interrupted our stay in Vienna, so were these walks and adventures beautiful and extremely welcome interruptions in our gloomy sunless existence in the Stumpergasse.

Chapter 21 — Adolf's Attitude to Women

When we used to walk up and down the foyer during the intervals at the Opera, I was struck by how much attention the girls and women paid to us. Understandably enough, at first I used to wonder which of us was the object of this undisguised interest, and secretly thought that it must be me. Closer observation, however, soon taught me that the obvious preference was not for me, but for my friend. Adolf appealed so much to the passing ladies, in spite of his modest clothing and his cold, reserved manner in public, that occasionally one or the other of them would turn round to look at him, which, according to the strict etiquette prevailing at the Opera, was considered highly improper.

I was all the more surprised at this as Adolf did nothing to provoke this behavior; on the contrary, he hardly noticed the ladies' encouraging glances, or, at most, would make an annoyed comment about them to me. But these observations were enough to prove to me that my friend undoubtedly found favour with the opposite sex, although, to my amazement, he never took advantage of this. Did he not understand these unequivocal invitations, or did he not want to understand them?

I gathered it was the latter, as Adolf was too sharp and critical an observer not to see what was going on around him, especially if it concerned himself. Then why did he not seize these opportunities? That comfortless, boring life in the back room in the Mariahilf suburb, which he himself called a "dog's life," how much more beautiful it would have been made by a friendship with an attractive, intelligent girl! Was not Vienna known as the city of beautiful women? That this was true, we needed no convincing. What was it, then, that held him back from doing what was normal for other young men? That he had never considered this possibility was proved by the very fact that, at his suggestion, we shared a room together. He did not ask me at the time whether that suited me or not. As was his habit, he took it for granted that I should be willing to do what he considered to be the right thing. As far as girls were concerned, he was doubtless quite pleased about my shyness, if only for the reason that it left me with more free time to spare for him.

One small episode has stayed in my memory. One evening at the Opera, as we went back to our places in the Promenade, a liveried attendant came up to us and, plucking Adolf by the sleeve, handed him a note. Adolf, in no way surprised but as though this were an everyday happening, took the note, thanked him and hastily read it. Now, I thought, I was on the track of a great secret, or at least the beginning of a romantic one. But all Adolf said, contemptuously, was, "Another one," and passed the note over to me. Then, with a semi-mocking glance, he asked me whether perhaps I would like to keep the suggested appointment. "It's your affair, not mine," I replied, a bit sharply, "and anyhow I wouldn't like the lady to be disappointed." Each time when it had to do with members of the fair sex, it was "his affair, not mine," no matter to what class the woman in question might belong. Even in the street my friend was shown preference. When, at night, we came home from the Opera or the Burg Theatre, now and again one of the streetwalkers would approach us, in spite of our poor appearance, and ask us to come home with her. But here again it was only Adolf who got the invitation.

I remember quite well that in those days I used to ask myself what the girls found so attractive about Adolf. He was certainly a well-set-up young man, with regular features, but not at all what is understood by a "handsome" man. I had seen handsome men often enough on the stage to know what women meant by that. Perhaps it was the extraordinarily bright eyes that attracted them. Or was it the strangely stern expression of the ascetic countenance? Or perhaps it was just his obvious indifference to the opposite sex that invited them to test his resistance. Whatever it was, women seemed to sense something exceptional about my friend — as opposed to men, such as, for instance, his teachers and professors.

The presentiment of decay that existed in those years in the Hapsburg Empire had produced in Vienna a shallow, easy-going atmosphere, whose empty moral sense was covered by the famous Viennese charm. The slogan then so much in vogue, "Sell my clothes, I'm going to Heaven," drew even the solid bourgeois classes into the superficiality of the morbid "higher circles." That sultry eroticism which held sway in Arthur Schnitzler's plays set the tone of society. The then famous saying, "Austria is going to the bad through her women," certainly seemed to be true as far as Viennese society was concerned. In the midst of this brittle milieu, whose persistent, erotic undertone insinuated itself everywhere, my friend lived in his self-imposed asceticism, regarding girls and women with lively and critical sympathy, while completely excluding anything personal, and handled matters which other young men of his age turned into their own experiences, as problems for discussion. And this he would do in his evening talks, as coldly and factually as though he himself were quite remote from such things.

As in all the other chapters of this book, so in this one dealing with Adolf's attitude to women during our friendship, I am concerned with

Chapter 21 — Adolf's Attitude to Women

keeping entirely to my own personal experience. From the autumn of 1904 to the summer of 1908, that is, for almost four years, I lived side by side with Adolf. In these decisive years when he grew from a boy of fifteen to a young man, Adolf confided to me things that he had told to no one, not even his mother. As far back as the days in Linz, our friendship was so intimate that I should have noticed if he had actually made the acquaintance of a girl. He would have had less time for me, his interests would have taken a different direction, and there would have been many similar signs. Yet, apart from his dream-love for Stefanie, no such thing happened. I cannot give any information about May and June 1906, nor the Autumn of 1907, the periods when Adolf was alone in Vienna. But I can only imagine that any really serious love affair would have continued into the period when we were living together. I think I can say, with certainty, Adolf never met a girl, either in Linz or in Vienna, who actually gave herself to him.

My own personal experience from living with him, based on small, apparently insignificant, details, was confirmed by the profound and penetrating discussions which Adolf used to have with me on all questions concerning the relations between the sexes. I knew from previous experience that between what Adolf preached and what he practised there was indeed no difference. His social and moral conduct was not governed by his own desires and feelings, but by his knowledge and judgment. In this respect, he displayed the utmost self-control. He could not bear the shallow superficiality of certain circles in Vienna, and I cannot remember a single occasion when he let himself go in his attitude to the other sex. At the same time, I must categorically assert that Adolf, in physical as well as sexual respects, was absolutely normal.

What was extraordinary in him was not to be found in the erotic or sexual spheres, but in quite other realms of his being.

When he used to describe to me in vivid terms the necessity of early marriage, which alone was capable of ensuring the future of the people; when he used to set forth for my benefit measures for increasing the number of children per family, measures which later were actually put into practice; when he expounded to me the connection between healthy housing and a healthy family life and described how, in his Ideal State, the problems of love, sexual relations, of marriage, of family, of children would be solved, I would think of Stefanie; for, after all, what Adolf was laying down here in such a convincing manner was really only the dreamed-of, ideal life with her, transported to a political and social plane. He had wanted Stefanie for his wife, for him she was the ideal of German womanhood personified. From her he hoped for children, for her he had planned that beautiful country house, which had become for him a model of the abode for the ideal family life.

But all this was illusion, wishful thinking. He had not seen Stefanie for several months, and spoke less and less of her. Even when I left for Linz for my call-up, he did not ask me to find out about Stefanie. Did she still mean anything to him? Had the enforced separation convinced Adolf that the most practical course was to forget Stefanie altogether? Just as I had persuaded myself that this was so, there would be certain to come another tempestuous outburst to prove to me that he still clung to Stefanie with every fibre of his being.

In spite of this, it was clear to me that Stefanie was losing her reality for Adolf more and more, and becoming purely an ideal. He could no longer rush to the Landstrasse to convince himself of the existence of the beloved. He received no further news about her. His feelings for Stefanie were plainly losing real foundation. Was this, then, the end of a love that had begun with such great hopes? Yes and no! It was the end in so far as Adolf was no longer the sentimental youth who, with the usual extravagance of the adolescent, compensated for the slightness of his hopes by a boundless conceit in himself. And yet, on the other hand, I could not understand how Adolf, now a young man with very concrete ideas and aims, could, nevertheless, still cling so firmly to this hopeless love; to such an extent, indeed, that it was sufficient to render him immune to the temptations of the big city.

I knew the very strict ideas of my friend about the relations between men and women, and had often wondered how Adolf came to be possessed of this strict moral attitude. His conceptions of love and marriage were definitely not those of his father, and while his mother loved him dearly, she certainly had not influenced him much in this respect; nor was such influence needed, as she could see that Adolf was quite correct in his behaviour towards girls. Adolf's background was that of an Austrian civil servant's family and a bourgeois household. Consequently, my only explanation of his strict views-which I shared with him to a certain degree, without being dogmatic about them, was his passion for social and political problems. His ideas of morality were based not upon experience, but on abstract, logical conclusions.

In addition, he still looked upon Stefanie, although she had become unattainable for him, as the ideal model of German womanhood, unrivalled by anything he saw in Vienna. When a woman made a strong impression on him, I often noticed how he immediately began to talk about Stefanie and to draw comparisons which were always in her favour.

Chapter 21 — Adolf's Attitude to Women

Incredible as it may sound, the "distant beloved," who did not even know the name of the young man whose love she was supposed to return, exercised such a strong influence over Adolf that not only did he find his own ideas of morality confirmed in his relations with her, but he regulated his life in accordance with them as seriously and consistently as a monk who has consecrated his life to God. In Vienna, this sink of iniquity, where even prostitution was made the object of the artist's glorification — this was an exception indeed! Actually, Adolf had written to Stefanie once during that period. It can no longer be established whether this letter was sent before or during our time together in Vienna.

The letter itself is lost, and I came to hear about it in a curious manner, I told a friend of mine, an archivist, who is working on a biography of Adolf Hitler and of whose scientific soundness I am assured, about Adolf's love for Stefanie. The scholar ascertained the address of the old lady, the widow of a colonel, living in Vienna, called on her and laid before her his peculiar request-that she should tell him about her youthful acquaintance with a young, pale student from the Humboldtstrasse, who later moved to the Blütengasse in Urfahr.

He used to stand and wait for her at the Schmiedtoreck every evening, he added, accompanied by his friend. Upon this, the old lady began telling him about balls, excursions, carriage trips and so on which she had enjoyed with young men, mostly officers, but with the best will in the world she could not recollect this strange young man; even when, to her astonishment, she learnt his name. But suddenly a memory awoke within her. Didn't she once receive a letter, written in a confused manner, which spoke of a solemn vow, begged her to keep faith and only to expect further news of the writer when he had finished his training as an artist and had an assured position? The letter was not signed. From its style, it can almost certainly be concluded that it was Adolf who sent it. And that was all the old lady could tell him.

When the thought of his beloved became too much for him, he no longer spoke directly of Stefanie, but threw himself headlong, with a great display of feeling, into dissertations about early marriages to be promoted by the State, about the possibility of helping working girls to get their trousseaus by means of a loan, and assisting young families with many children to acquire a house and garden, I remember that here, on one particular point, we had the most violent arguments. Adolf suggested the establishment of State furniture factories, in order that young married couples should be able to furnish their homes cheaply. I was strongly against this idea of mass-produced furniture. After all, on this subject I was qualified to speak. Furniture must be of good, high-quality craftsmanship, not machine made. We made our calculations and economised in other ways, so that the newly married couple could have fine, good-quality furniture in their home, soft featherbeds, cloth-covered chairs and couches in good taste, so that one could see there still existed master upholsterers who knew their job.

Much that Adolf used to tell me in those long nightly talks is concentrated into one particular phrase in my memory, and in this case, that which connotes these passionate discussions is the strange cliché, "The Flame of Life." Whenever the questions of love, marriage or sex relations were raised, this magic formula would crop up. To keep the Flame of Life pure and unsullied would be the most important task of that Ideal State with which my friend occupied himself in his lonely hours. With my inherent preference for precision, I was not quite sure what Adolf meant by this Flame of Life, and occasionally the phrase would change its meaning. But I think, in the end, I did understand him aright. The Flame of Life was the symbol of sacred love which is awakened between man and woman who have kept themselves pure in body and soul and are worthy of a union which would produce healthy children for the nation.

Such phrases, impressively delivered and repeated again and again — and Adolf had a large stock of these expressions — had quite a queer effect on me. When I heard them solemnly proclaimed for the first time they seemed to me rather pathetic, and I smiled inwardly at these bombastic formulas which were in such contrast to our insignificant existence, But despite that, the words stayed in my memory. Just as a thistle clings to one's sleeve with a hundred barbs, so did this phrase cling. I could not get rid of it. Then, if I found myself in a situation which had only the remotest connection with this theme — I would meet a girl as I went along the Mariahilferstrasse, let us say, alone in the evening; a pretty young lady she seemed to me, a little flighty perhaps, for she turned round very openly to look at me. At least, this time I was sure it was I in whom she was interested!

As a matter of fact, she must have been very flighty, because she waved to me invitingly! But then, suddenly, the words "Flame of Life" would appear before me — one single, thoughtless hour and this holy flame is extinguished forever! — and even though I was annoyed by these moralisings, nevertheless, in such moments, they worked. One phrase was linked to another. It began with the "Storm of the Revolution," and went on through countless political and social slogans to the "Holy Reich of all the Germans." Perhaps Adolf found a certain number of these phrases in books, but others I knew he coined himself.

Gradually, these single statements evolved into one compact system. As everything that happened was of interest to Adolf, each new phenomenon of the times was examined to see how it would fit into his political philosophy.

Sometimes my memory indulges in strange juxtapositions; so that immediately following the holy, unapproachable Flame of Life would come the Sink of Iniquity, although in my friend's world of ideas this expression represented the lowest grade. Of course, in the Ideal State there was no longer any Sink of Iniquity. With these words Adolf described the prostitution which was then rife in Vienna. As a typical phenomenon of those years of general moral decadence, we would come across it in the most varied forms, both in the elegant streets of the centre, and in the slums of the suburbs. All this filled Adolf with boundless rage. But for this spreading prostitution he blamed not only those actually practising it, but those responsible for the prevailing social and economic conditions. A "Monument to the Shame of our Times," he called this prostitution. Ever and again he tackled the problem and searched for a solution whereby in the future any kind of "commercial love" would be rendered impossible.

There was one evening that I have never forgotten. We had been to a performance of Wedekind's Frühlingserwachen and, as an exception, had stayed for the last act. Then we made our way across the Ring homewards and turned down into the Siebensterngasse. Then Adolf took my arm and said, unexpectedly, "Come, Gustl. We must see the Sink of Iniquity once." I do not know what had given him the idea, but he had already turned into the small, ill-lit Spittelberggasse.

So there we were. We walked along past the low, one-story houses. The windows, which were on street level, were lighted so that we could see directly into the rooms. The girls sat there, some behind the windowpane, some at the open window; a few of them were still remarkably young, others prematurely aged and faded. In their scanty and slovenly attire they sat there, making up their faces or combing their hair or looking at themselves in the mirror, without, however, for one moment losing sight of the men strolling by. Here and there a man would stop, lean towards the window to look at the girl of his choice; a hasty, whispered interchange would take place. Then, as a sign that the deal was concluded, the light would be turned out. I still remember how this custom in particular struck me, as one could tell by the darkening of the windows how trade was going. Among the men, it was the accepted convention not to stand before the unlighted windows.

We, for our part, did not even stand in front of the lighted windows, but made our way along to the Burggasse at the other end of the street. Arrived there, however, Adolf made an about-turn and we walked once more along the Sink of Iniquity. I was of the opinion that the one experience would have sufficed, but Adolf was already dragging me along to the lighted windows.

Perhaps these girls, too, had noticed the "something special" about Adolf, perhaps they had realised that here they had to deal with men of moral restraint, such as came sometimes from the religious countryside to the unholy city; at any rate, they thought it necessary to redouble their efforts. I recall how one of these girls seized just the moment when we were passing her window to take off her chemise, presumably to change it, while another busied herself with her stockings, showing her naked legs. I was genuinely glad when this exciting running of the gantlet was over and we finally reached the Westbahnstrasse, but I said nothing, while Adolf grew angry at the prostitutes' tricks of seduction.

At home, Adolf started on a lecture on his newly acquired impressions, with a cold objectivity as though it were a question of his attitude towards the fight against tuberculosis, or towards cremation. I was amazed that he could speak about it without any inner emotion. Now he had learnt the customs of the market for commercial love, he declared, and thus the purpose of his visit was fulfilled. The origin lay in the fact that man felt the necessity for sexual satisfaction, while the girls in question thought only of their earnings; earnings with which, possibly, they kept one man whom they really loved, always assuming that these girls were capable of love. In practice, the Flame of Life in these poor creatures was long since extinct.

There is another incident I should like to recount. One evening, at the corner of Mariahilferstrasse-Neubaugasse, a well-dressed, prosperous-looking man spoke to us and asked us about ourselves. When we told him that we were students ("My friend studies music," explained Adolf, "and I architecture"), he invited us to supper at the Hotel Kummer. He allowed us to order anything we pleased and for once Adolf could eat as many tarts and pastries as he could manage. Meanwhile, he told us that he was a manufacturer from Vöcklabruck and did not like anything to do with women, as they were only gold diggers. I was especially interested in what he said about the chamber music which appealed to him. We thanked him, he came out of the restaurant with us, and we went home.

There Adolf asked me if I liked the man. "Very much," I replied. "A very cultured man, with pronounced artistic leanings." "And what else?" continued Adolf with an enigmatic expression on his face.

"What else should there be?" I asked, surprised.

"As apparently you don't understand, Gustl, what it's all about, look at this little card!" "Which card?" For, in fact, this man had slipped Adolf a card without my noticing it, on which he had scribbled an invitation to visit him at the Hotel Kummer.

"He's a homosexual," explained Adolf in a matter-of-fact manner.

I was startled. I had never even heard the word, much less had I any conception of what it actually meant. So Adolf explained this phenomenon to me. Naturally this, too, had long been one of his problems and, as an abnormal practice, he wished to see it fought against relentlessly, and he himself scrupulously avoided all personal contact with such men. The visiting card of the famous manufacturer from Vöcklabruck disappeared into our stove.

It seemed to me quite natural that Adolf should turn with disgust and repugnance from these and other sexual aberrations of the big city, that he refrained from masturbation which was commonly indulged in by youths, and that in all matters of sex he obeyed those strict rules that he laid down for himself and for the future state. But then why did he not try to escape from his loneliness, to make friends and find stimulus in serious, intelligent and progressive company? Why did he always remain the lone wolf, who avoided any contact with people, although he was passionately interested in all human affairs? How easy it would have been for him, with his obvious talents, to win himself a place in those social circles in Vienna which held themselves aloof from the general decadence, from which he would not only have gained new insight and enlightenment, but which would have wrought a change in his lonely life. There were many more thoroughly decent people in Vienna than the other kind, though they were less in evidence. So he had no reason to avoid people on moral grounds. As a matter of fact, it was not arrogance that held him back. It was rather his poverty, and the consequent sensitiveness, that caused him to live on his own.

Moreover, he thought he was lowering himself if he went to a social gathering, or any kind of distraction. He had too high an opinion of himself for a superficial flirtation or for a merely physical relation with a girl. For that matter, he would never have allowed me to indulge in such affairs.

Any step in this direction would have meant the inevitable end of our friendship, as, apart from the distaste with which Adolf viewed such connections, he would never have tolerated my having any interest in other people. As always, our friendship had to be utterly exclusive of all other interests.

One day, although I knew how opposed Adolf was to all social activities, I nevertheless attempted to arrange something for him. The opportunity which occurred seemed to me too good to be missed.

Sometimes music lovers came to the office of the Conservatory looking for students to take part in a musical evening at their houses. This meant not only much-needed extra money — we usually received a fee of five crowns, as well as supper — but also brought a little social glamour into my humble student's life. As a good viola player, I was much sought after, and it was through this that I came to know the family of a wealthy manufacturer in the Heiligenstädterstrasse, Dr. Jahoda. They were people with a deep appreciation of art, of very cultivated tastes, a really intellectual group of the kind that flourished only in Vienna, who traditionally enriched the artistic life of the city. When, at table, the opportunity arose, I mentioned my friend, and was invited to bring him with me the next time. This was what I had been aiming at, and now I was content.

And Adolf did indeed go with me, and he enjoyed himself very much. He was particularly impressed with the library, which for Adolf was a real yardstick for judging these people. What pleased him less, however, was that throughout the whole evening he had to remain a silent listener, although he himself had chosen this role. On the way home, he said he would have got on quite well with these people, but as he was not a musician he had not been able to join in the conversation. Nevertheless, he also came with me to musical evenings in one or two other houses, where it was only his inadequate dress that upset him.

In the midst of this corrupt city, my friend surrounded himself with a wall of unshakable principles which enabled him to build up an inner freedom, in spite of all the dangers around. him. He was afraid of infection, as he often said. Now I understand that he meant, not only venereal infection, but a much more general infection, namely, the danger of being caught up in the prevailing conditions and finally being dragged down into the vortex of corruption. It is not surprising that no one understood him, that they took him for an eccentric, and that those few who came in contact with him called him presumptuous and arrogant.

But he went his way, untouched by what went on around him, but also untouched by a really great, consuming love. He remained a man alone and guarded — an odd contradiction — in strict monklike asceticism, the holy Flame of Life.

Chapter 22 — Political Awakening

The picture of my friend, as I have drawn it so far, would be incomplete without a reference to his immense interest in politics. If I deal with it only at the end of this book and, in spite of all my efforts, inadequately, it is not because of my lack of understanding, but because my interest lay more in art and was hardly concerned with politics at all.

Even more so than in Linz, I felt myself a budding artist at the Vienna Conservatory, and had no wish to be mixed up in politics. My friend's development was just in the opposite direction.

Though in Linz his interest in art had far surpassed that of politics, in Vienna, the centre of the political life of the Hapsburg Empire, politics prevailed to the extent of absorbing all other interests.

I began to understand how almost every problem which he encountered led him ultimately into the political sphere, however little real connection it might have with politics. His original way of looking at the phenomena which surrounded him through the eyes of an artist and aesthete increasingly turned into a habit of regarding them from a politician's standpoint.

Human beings interested him so much that he began to adjust his professional plans to political considerations. For, if he really wanted to build all that was ready in his mind and even partly laid down in elaborate schemes — a new Linz embellished by impressive edifices such as a bridge over the Danube, a town hall, and so forth, and a Vienna whose slums were to be replaced by vast residential districts, a revolutionary storm had first to put an end to the existing political conditions which had become unbearable, and to open up the possibility for creative work on an ambitious scale.

Politics came to assume an increasingly important position in his scale of values. The most difficult problems became easy when they were transferred to the political plane.

With the same consistency with which he explored all phenomena which occupied him until he had reached rock bottom, he discovered amid the noisy, political life of the metropolis the focal point of all political events: Parliament.

"Come with me, Gustl," he said one day. I asked him where he wanted to go — I had to attend my lectures at the University and to practise for my examination in piano-playing. But my objections did not impress him at all. He said none of that was as important as what he intended to do; he had already procured a ticket for me.

I wondered what this could be — an organ concert, perhaps, or a conducted tour through the picture gallery of the Hof Museum? But my lectures and my exam? It would be very bad for me if I failed.

"Oh, come on, hurry!" he cried angrily. I was familiar with that look on his face, which would not tolerate any contradiction. Besides, it must be something very special, for it was unusual for Adolf to be up and about as early as half past eight in the morning.

So I yielded, and went with him to the Ring. At nine o'clock sharp we turned into the Stadiongasse, and stopped in front of a small side entrance where a few nondescript people, idlers apparently, had collected. At long last, I saw daylight.

"To Parliament?" I asked apprehensively. "What am I supposed to do there?" I remembered that Adolf had occasionally mentioned his visits to Parliament — I personally considered it sheer waste of time. But before I could say another word, he pressed the ticket into my hand, the door opened, and we were directed to the Strangers' Gallery.

Looking down from the gallery, one had a very good view of the imposing semicircle which the great assembly chamber formed. Its classic beauty would have provided a fitting background for any artistic performance — a concert, a choir singing hymns, or even with some adjustments, an opera.

Adolf tried to explain to me what was really happening. "The man who sits up there, looking rather helpless, and who rings a bell every now and then, is the President. The worthies on the raised seats are the Ministers; in front of them are the shorthand writers, the only people who do any work in this house. That is why I rather like them, though I can assure you that these hardworking men are of no importance whatsoever.

On the opposite benches there should be seated all the deputies of the realms and provinces represented in the Austrian Parliament. But most of them are strolling round the lobbies." My friend went on to describe the procedure. One member has tabled a motion and is now speaking in support of it. Almost all the other deputies, not being interested in the motion, have left the room. But soon the chairman would call for a debate and things would become lively. Adolf was really well versed in parliamentary procedure; he even had an order paper in front of him. Everything happened exactly as he had foretold.

As soon as, to put it into musical terms, the solo performance of the deputy had ended, the orchestra struck up. The deputies flowed back

Chapter 22 — Political Awakening

into the Chamber and all started shouting together, interrupting each other remorselessly in the process. The President rang his bell. The deputies responded by lifting the lids of their desks and banging them down again. Some whistled, and words of abuse, shouted in German, Czech, Italian, Polish and God knows what other language filled the air.

I looked at Adolf. Was not this the appropriate moment to leave? But what had happened to my friend? He had jumped to his feet, his hands clenched, his face burning with excitement. This being so, I preferred to remain quietly in my seat, although I had no idea what the tumult was about.

Parliament attracted my friend more and more, while I tried to wriggle out of it. Once, when Adolf had forced me to go with him — I would have risked the end of our friendship if I had refused — a Czech member was "filibustering." Adolf explained to me that this was a speech which was only made to fill in time and prevent another member from speaking. It did not matter what the Czech said, he could even go on repeating his words, but on no account must he stop. It really seemed to me as though this man was speaking all the time "da capo al fine." Of course, I did not understand a word of Czech, nor did Adolf, and I was really upset about wasting my time.

"You don't mind if I go now?" I said to Adolf.

He replied angrily, "What, now, in the middle of the sitting?" "But I don't understand a word the man is saying." "You don't have to understand it. This is `filibustering.' I've already explained it to you." "So I can go, then?" "No!" be cried furiously, and pulled me back on to the seat by my coattails.

So I just sat there and let the valiant Czech, who was already nearly exhausted, talk on. I have never been so puzzled by Adolf as I was at that moment. He was so extraordinarily intelligent and certainly had all his senses about him, and I just could not comprehend how he was able to sit there, tense, listening to every word of a speech which, after all, he did not understand. But perhaps, I thought, the fault is mine and I presumably do not realise wherein lies the essence of politics.

In those days I often asked myself why Adolf compelled me to go with him to Parliament. I could not solve this riddle until one day I realised that Adolf needed a partner with whom he could discuss his own impressions. On such days he would wait impatiently for my return in the evening. Hardly had I opened the door, when he would start, "Where have you been all this time?" and before I had had time to gut myself a bite of supper, would come, "When are you going to bed?" This question had a particular significance. As our room was so small, Adolf could only walk up and down if I either crouched on the stool behind the piano or went to bed, and so he wanted to clear the decks for what he had to say.

No sooner had I crept into bed, than he began to stride up and down, holding forth. If only by the excited tone of his voice, I could tell how much his thoughts were pressing upon him. He simply had to have an outlet in order to bear the enormous tension.

So there I lay in bed, while Adolf, as usual, strode up and down ranting at me as passionately as though I were a political power who could decide the existence or non-existence of the German people, instead of only a poor little music student.

Another of these nocturnal talks remains in my memory. Hysterically he described the sufferings of this people, the fate that threatened it, and its future full of danger. He was near tears.

But after these bitter words, he came back to more optimistic thoughts. Once more he was building the "Reich of all the Germans," which put the "Guest Nations," as he called the other races of the Empire, where they belonged.

Sometimes, when his diatribes became too lengthy, I fell asleep. As soon as he noticed it, he shook me awake and shouted at me to know whether I was no longer interested in his words; if so, I should go on sleeping, like all those who had no national conscience. So I made an effort and forced myself to keep my eyes open.

Later, Adolf developed more friendly methods on these occasions. Instead of losing himself in Utopias, he raised questions which he thought would be of more interest to me, As for instance, one day when he inveighed against the Savings Groups which had been formed in many of the small inns of the working-class districts. Each member paid in a weekly sum and received his savings at Christmas. The treasurer was usually the innkeeper. Adolf criticised these groups, because the money the worker spent on such "Savings Evenings" was greater than the amount laid by, so that in reality the publican was the only one to benefit. Another time he described to me in vivid colours what he imagined the student hostels would be like in his Ideal State. Bright, sunny bedrooms, common rooms for study, music and drawing, simple but nourishing food, free tickets for concerts, opera and exhibitions, and free transport to their colleges.

One night he spoke of the aeroplane of the Wright brothers. He quoted from a newspaper that these famous aviators had built a small, comparatively lightweight gun into their aircraft and had made experiments in the effect that shooting from the air would be likely to have. Adolf, who was a pronounced pacifist, was outraged. As soon as a new invention is

Chapter 22 — Political Awakening

made, he said, it is immediately put to the service of war. Who wants war? he asked. Certainly not the "little man" — far from it. Wars are arranged by crowned and uncrowned rulers, who in turn are guided and driven by their armament industry. While these gentlemen earned gigantic sums and remained far from the firing line, the "little man" has to risk his life without knowing to what purpose.

Altogether the "little man," the "poor, betrayed masses," played a dominating role in his thoughts.

One day we saw workers demonstrating on the Ring. We were hemmed in among the onlookers near the House of Parliament and got a good view of the exciting scene. Is this the mood, I asked myself anxiously, that Adolf calls the "Storm of the Revolution"? Some men walked ahead of the procession carrying a big banner on which was written the one word "Hunger!" There could not have been any more stirring appeal to my friend, because he had so often suffered himself from bitter hunger.

There he stood, next to me, and absorbed the picture eagerly. However strongly he might have felt with these people, he remained aloof and viewed the whole event, in all its detail, objectively and coolly as though his only interest were to study the technique of such a demonstration. In spite of his solidarity with the "little man" he would never have dreamed of taking an active part in this manifestation, which was, in fact, protesting against increase in the price of beer.

More and more people were arriving. The whole Ring seemed to be crammed with excited humanity. Red flags were carried. But the seriousness of the situation was shown by the ragged appearance and the hunger-lined faces of the demonstrators; far more than by flags and slogans.

The head of the procession had reached the House of Parliament and was trying to storm it.

Suddenly the mounted police who had accompanied it, drew their swords and began to lay about them. The reply was a hail of stones. For a moment the situation balanced on a razor's edge, but in the end police reinforcements managed to disperse the demonstrators.

The spectacle had shaken Adolf to the core. But not until we had arrived home did he voice his feelings. Yes, he was on the side of the hungry, the underprivileged. But he was also against the men who organised such demonstrations. Who are the wire-pullers who stand behind these doubly betrayed masses and guide them according to their will? None of them appeared on the scene. Why? Because it suited them better to conduct their affairs in obscurity — they did not want to risk their lives. Who are the leaders of the wretched masses? Not men who had themselves experienced the misery of the "little man," but ambitious politicians, lusting for power, who wanted to exploit the people's poverty for their own benefit. An outburst of rage against these political vultures brought my friend's embittered harangue to an end. That was his demonstration.

One question tormented him after such occurrences, although he never gave expression to it: Where did he, himself, belong? To judge by his own circumstances and the social environment in which he lived, there was no doubt that he belonged to those who followed the Hunger banner.

He lived in a miserable, bug-ridden back room; many times his lunch consisted of nothing but a piece of dry bread. Some of the demonstrators were perhaps better off than he. Why, therefore, did he not march with these men? What held him back? Perhaps he felt that he belonged to a different social class. He was the son of an Austrian State official, whose rank was equivalent to a Captain's. He remembered his father as a muchrespected customs official, to whom people raised their hats, and whose word carried much weight among his friends. His father had absolutely nothing to do with these people in the street.

Greater even than his fear of being infected by the moral and political decadence of the ruling classes, was his fear of becoming a proletarian. Undoubtedly he lived like one, but he did not want to become one. Perhaps what drove him to his intensive studies was his instinctive feeling that only a thorough education could save him from descending to the level of the masses.

In the last resort, the decisive point for Adolf was that he did not feel attracted to any of the existing parties or movements. To be sure he often told me that he was a convinced follower of Schönerer, but he said so only in the privacy of our room. He, the hungry, penniless student, would have cut a very poor figure in the ranks of Georg Ritten von Schönerer. The Schönerer movement would have needed much stronger socialist tendencies to capture Adolf fully. What had Schönerer to offer to the hungry masses demonstrating in the Ring? On the other hand, however, the Social Democrats had no comprehension of German nationalism in Austria. Among the leading political personalities of those days, Adolf had most admiration for Vienna's Burgomaster, Karl Lueger. But what put him off his party was the connection with the church, which was constantly interfering in political questions. Thus, in those days, Adolf found no spiritual home for his political ideals.

In spite of his unwillingness to join a party, or organisation — with one exception which I shall mention later — one had only to walk along the street with him to see how intensely interested he was in the fate of others.

Chapter 22 — Political Awakening

The city of Vienna offered him excellent object lessons in this respect.

For instance, when home-going workers passed us by, Adolf would grip my arm and say, "Did you hear, Gustl? Czechs!" Another time, we encountered some brickmakers speaking loudly in Italian, with florid gestures. "There you have your German Vienna," he cried, indignantly.

This, too, was one of his oft-repeated phrases: "German Vienna," but Adolf pronounced it with a bitter undertone. Was this Vienna, into which streamed from all sides Czechs, Magyars, Croats, Poles, Italians, Slovaks, Ruthenians, and above all Galician Jews, still indeed a German city? In the state of affairs in Vienna my friend saw a symbol of the struggle of the Germans in the Hapsburg Empire. He hated the babel in the streets of Vienna, this "incest incarnate" as he called it later. He hated this State, which ruined Germanism, and the pillars that supported this State: the reigning house, the Church, the nobility, the capitalists and the Jews.

This Hapsburg State, he felt, must fall, and the sooner the better, for every moment of its continued existence cost the Germans honour, property and their very life. He saw in the fanatical internecine strife of its races the decisive symptoms of its coming downfall. He visited Parliament to feel, so to speak, the pulse of the patient, whose early demise was expected by all. He looked forward to that hour full of impatience, for only the collapse of the Hapsburg Empire could open the road to those schemes of which he dreamed in his lonely hours.

His accumulated hatred of all forces which threatened the Germans was mainly concentrated upon the Jews, who played a leading role in Vienna. I soon came to notice this, and a small, seemingly trivial occurrence stands out in my memory.

I had come to the conclusion that my friend could no longer go on in his poverty-stricken circumstances. The easiest way of helping him, I thought, would be to make use of some of his literary work. A fellow student of mine at the Conservatory worked as a journalist on the Wiener Tagblatt, and I mentioned Adolf to him. The young man was full of sympathy with Adolf's precarious situation and suggested that my friend should bring some of his work to him in his office, where the matter could be discussed. During the night Adolf wrote a short story, of which I remember nothing but the title, It was "The Next Morning," an ominous one, for the next morning when we went to see my fellow student, there was a terrific row. As soon as Adolf had seen the man, he turned about, even before he had entered the room, and going down the stairs shouted at me, "You idiot! Didn't you see that he is a Jew?" Actually, I had not. But in future I took care not to burn my fingers.

Things got worse. One day, when I was very busy with preparations for my exam, Adolf stormed into our room, full of excitement. He had just come from the police, he said; there had been an incident in the Mariahilferstrasse, connected with a Jew, of course. A Handelee had been standing in front of the Gerngross store. The word "Handelee" was used to designate eastern Jews who, dressed in caftan and boots, sold shoe laces, buttons, braces and other small articles in the streets. The Handelee was the lowest stage in the career of those quickly assimilated Jews, who often occupied leading positions in Austria's economic life. The Handelees were forbidden to beg. But this man had whiningly approached passers-by, his hand outstretched, and had collected some money. A policeman asked him to produce his papers. He began to wring his hands and said he was a poor, sick man who had only this little trading to live on, but he had not been begging. The policeman took him to the police station, and asked bystanders to act as witnesses. In spite of his dislike of publicity, Adolf had presented himself as a witness, and he saw with his own eyes that the Handelee had three thousand crowns in his caftan, conclusive evidence, according to Adolf, of the exploitation of Vienna by immigrant eastern Jews.

I well remember, at that time, how eagerly Adolf studied the Jewish problem, talking to me of it again and again, although I was not interested. At the Conservatory there were Jews among both teachers and students, and I had never had any trouble with them and, in deed, had made some friends among them. Was not Adolf himself enthusiastic about Gustav Mahler, and was he not fond of the works of Mendelssohn-Bartholdy? One should not judge the Jewish question only on the strength of Handelees. I cautiously tried to deflect Adolf from his point of view. His reaction was very strange.

"Come, Gustl," he said, and once again, to save the fare, I had to walk with him to the Brigittenau.

I was astounded when Adolf led me to the Synagogue. We entered. "Keep your hat on," Adolf whispered. And indeed, all the men had their heads covered. Adolf had discovered that at this time a wedding was taking place in the Synagogue. The ceremony impressed me deeply. The congregation started with an alternate chant, which I liked. Then the Rabbi gave a sermon in Hebrew and finally laid the phylacteries of the foreheads of the bridal pair.

I concluded from our strange visit that Adolf really wanted to study thoroughly the Jewish problem and thereby convince himself that the religious practices of the Jews still survived. This, I hoped, might soften his biased view. But I was mistaken, for one day Adolf came home and announced decidedly, "Today, I joined the Anti-Semite Union and have put down your name as well." Although I had got used to his domineering over me in political matters, this was the culminating point. It was all the more surprising, as Adolf usually avoided joining any society or organisation. I kept silent, but I resolved to handle my affairs myself in future.

Looking back on those days in Vienna and on our long, nocturnal conversations, I can assert that Adolf then adopted that philosophy of life which was to guide him henceforward. He gathered it from his immediate impressions and experiences in the streets and extended and deepened it by his reading. What I heard was its first version, often still unbalanced and immature, but propounded with all the more passion.

But at that time I did not take all these things very seriously, because my friend played no part in public life, never had anybody but me, and accordingly all his plans and political projects were floating in mid-air. That later he would bring them to fruition, I would never have dared to think.

Chapter 23 — The Lost Friendship

The competitive examinations at the Conservatory were over, and I had come out of them very well. Now I had only to conduct the end-of-term concert in the Johannessaal which, in view of the stagefright of the performers-and the conductor-was not an easy task. But everything went well.

Much more exciting for me was the second evening when the singer, Rossi, sang three songs I had composed, and two movements from my sextet for strings were performed for the first time.

Both compositions met with great success. Adolf was in the artists' room when Professor Max Jentsch, my composition teacher, congratulated me. The Head of the Conductors' School, Gustav Gutheil, also added his congratulations and, to crown all, the Director of the Conservatory came into the artists' room and shook me warmly by the hand. This was a little too much for me, who only a year ago had been working in the dusty upholsterer's workshop. Adolf glowed with enthusiasm and seemed genuinely proud of his friend. But I could well imagine what he was thinking in his heart of hearts. Certainly, he had never realised with such bitterness the futility of his time in Vienna as when he saw me in the midst of my resounding triumphs with my feet firmly planted on the road which led to my ultimate goal.

Only a few more days and the term would end. I was looking forward with great pleasure to going home, as, in spite of my successful studies, the dire feeling of homesickness had never left me throughout the time I had been in Vienna.

Adolf had no home and did not know where he would go, We discussed how we should pass the coming months. Frau Zakreys joined us in our room and hesitantly asked us what our plans were.

"Whatever happens we shall stay together," I declared immediately; I did not mean only that I should stay with Adolf — that seemed to me a matter of course — but also that we should both go on lodging with Frau Zakreys, with whom we got on so well. Moreover, my plans were quite decided. Immediately after the end of term I would go to Linz and stay with my parents till the autumn, when I would undergo my eight weeks' training with the Army Reserve. At the latest, I wanted to be back in Vienna by the second half of November. I promised to send my share of the rent regularly to Frau Zakreys so that she could keep the room for us.

Chapter 23 — The Lost Friendship

Frau Zakreys, too, wanted to go to visit relatives in Moravia during the next few days, and she was worried about leaving the flat empty. But Adolf soon reassured the old dear. He would stay there and wait until she came back. Then he could still go for a few days to his mother's family in the Waldviertel.

Frau Zakreys was very pleased with this solution, and assured us that we had been most satisfactory lodgers: two such nice young gentlemen, who paid their rent punctually and never brought girls home, you wouldn't find anywhere else in Vienna.

When I was alone with Adolf, I told him that I would try to get an engagement as a viola player with the Vienna Symphony Orchestra during the next school year. Then I would be so much better off that I would be able to help him substantially as well. Adolf, who in those days was very irritable, made no response to my suggestion. Neither did he tell me a word of his future plans, but in view of my own success, I did not take offence at this. Moreover, to my great astonishment, I was not instructed to keep him informed about Stefanie. Nevertheless, I made up my mind to write him all that I could find out about her. Adolf promised to write often and keep me informed of everything of interest to me that went on in Vienna.

The parting was hard for both of us; its date, the beginning of July 1908, is of particular significance. Although it had not always been easy, in spite of my compliant nature, to get on with Adolf, yet our friendship had always triumphed over personal difficulties. We had known each other now for nearly four years and had got used to each other's ways. The rich treasure of artistic experiences enjoyed together in Linz, as well as the joy of lovely excursions, had been increased and deepened by our time together in Vienna. In Vienna, Adolf was like a bit of home for me; he had shared the most beautiful impressions of my boyhood, and knew me better than anybody else. It was him I had to thank for the fact that I was at the Conservatory.

This feeling of gratitude, strengthened by a friendship springing from shared experiences, bound me firmly to him. I was more than willing, in the future, to put up with any of the peculiarities caused by his impulsive temperament. With growing maturity and discernment, my appreciation of Adolf as my friend increased, as is proved by the fact that in spite of our cramped quarters and the divergence of our interests, we had got on much better together in Vienna than in Linz. I was prepared, for his sake, to go not only to Parliament, and to a Synagogue, but even to the Spittelberggasse, and God knows where, and was already looking forward to spending my next year with him. Naturally, I meant far less to Adolf than he did to me. That I had come with him to Vienna from his home town only served to remind him, perhaps unwillingly, of his own difficult family background and the apparent hopelessness of his boyhood, though, to be sure, my presence also reminded him of Stefanie. Above all, he had learnt to appreciate me as an eager audience. He could not wish for a better public as, because of his overwhelming gift of persuasion, I agreed with him even when in my heart I held a completely different opinion. For him, and with what he had in mind, however, my views were quite unimportant. He needed me just to talk to, for, after all, he could not sit on the bench in the Schönbrunn and make long speeches to himself. When he was full of an idea and had to unburden himself, then he needed me as a soloist needs an instrument to give expression to his feelings. This, if I may use the expression, "instrumental character" of our friendship rendered me of more value to him than my own modest nature merited.

So we said goodbye. Adolf assured me, for the hundredth time, how little he wanted to be left alone. I could imagine, he said, how dull it would be for him alone in the room we had shared.

Had I not already written the date of my arrival to my parents, perhaps, in spite of my attacks of grievous homesickness, I might have stayed in Vienna another couple of weeks.

He accompanied me to the West Bahnhof; I stowed away my luggage and joined him on the platform. Adolf hated sentimentality of any kind. The more anything touched him, the cooler he became. So now, he just took both my hands — two hands was most unusual for him — and pressed them firmly. Then he turned and made for the exit, perhaps a little overhastily, without once turning round. I was feeling wretched. I got onto the train and was glad that it started right away and prevented me from changing my mind.

My parents were delighted to have their son home again. In the evening, I had to tell them all about the end-of-term concert; my mother's eyes, shining with happiness, were my greatest reward. When, the next morning, I appeared in the workshop in my blue apron with my shirt sleeves rolled up and set to work, my father, too, was satisfied. Without more ado, he asked me to carry out an important order commissioned by the government.

In my free time I missed Adolf sadly. I would have liked to write him about Stefanie, although he had not asked me to do so, but I never managed to see her. Probably she had gone on holiday with her mother.

As there were still some things to be settled in Vienna, I wrote to Adolf and asked him to deal with them. There were my dues to be paid to Riedl, the treasurer of the Musician's Union, and I also wished him to

Chapter 23 — The Lost Friendship

collect my Member's book and send on to me all the Union's publications.

Adolf attended to all this most conscientiously, and on a picture postcard dated July 15, 1908, depicting the so-called "Graben," he confirms this, The card reads:

> Dear Gustl, I called on Riedl three times and never found him in and it was not until Thursday evening that I could pay him. My heartiest thanks for your letter and particularly your postcard. It looks very prosaic, I mean the fountain. I've been working very hard since you left, sometimes till two or three in the morning. I'll write you when I'm leaving. I'm not very keen on it if my sister is coming, too. It is not warm here now, and it even rains occasionally. I am sending you your newspapers and also the little book. Kindest regards to you and your esteemed parents. ADOLF HITLER

The fountain which Adolf describes as very "prosaic" had been erected in the public park. The sculpture that was supposed to adorn it was by the sculptor Hanak and was called "The Joy of Beauty," a description which Adolf, in view of the dullness of the work, considered ironical.

The remark concerning his sister is interesting; he means Angela Raubal. Adolf was not at all pleased with the idea that his sister should also go to the Waldviertel, as, after his violent quarrel with her husband, he did not wish to meet her again.

A few days later another card arrived from Adolf dated July 19, 1908, showing a picture of the airship Zeppelin. It read:

> Dear Friend, My best thanks for your kindness. You don't need to send me butter and cheese now. But I thank you most gratefully for the kind thought. Tonight I am going to see Lohengrin. Kindest regards to you and your esteemed parents. ADOLF HITLER

Around the edge is written, "Frau Zakreys thanks you for the money and send regards to you and parents." I had told my mother how hard up my friend was and that he sometimes went hungry. That was enough for my dear mother.

Without saying a word to me she had sent Adolf, during that summer of 1908, a number of food parcels. The reason he asked her not to send any more was because of his forthcoming trip to the Waldviertel. But more important than all this was the fact that he could see Lohengrin. I was with him in this.

I wondered what he would be doing alone in our room, and I often thought of him. Perhaps he took advantage of the fact that he now had the room to himself to start, once again, on his big building plans. He had long ago decided to rebuild the Vienna Hofburg. On our strolls through the centre of the city he was always coming back to this project, the ideas for which were already formulated and needed only to be put on paper. It annoyed him that the old Hofburg and the court stables were built of brick. Bricks, according to him, were not a solid enough material for monumental buildings. So these buildings must come down and be rebuilt in a similar style in stone. In addition, Adolf wanted to match the wonderful semicircle of columns of the new Burg with a corresponding one on the opposite side, and thus magnificently enclose the Heldenplatz.

The Burgtor should remain. Across the Ring, two mighty triumphal arches — the question which "triumphs" they should commemorate Adolf very wisely left unanswered — should bring the wonderful square and the Hof Museum into one design. The old court stables should be demolished and be replaced by a monumental building equal to the Hofberg and linked by two other triumphal arches to the whole complex. Thus, according to my friend, Vienna would have a square worthy of a metropolis.

But I was mistaken. Adolf was not concerned about Vienna, but about Linz. Perhaps this was for him the best way to still that bitter feeling which the loss of his parental home and the estrangement from his home town had roused in him. Linz, where he had suffered such cruel blows from Fate, should now learn how much be loved her.

A letter arrived, a rarity for Adolf for, if only to save the postage, he used only to write postcards.

Although he has no idea what he can "dish up" for me, he feels the urge to chat with me about his hermit's life. The letter is dated July 21, 1908, and reads:

Dear Friend, Perhaps you have wondered why I haven't written for so long. The answer is simple. I didn't know what I could dish up for you and what would be of particular interest to you. First, I am still in Vienna and will stay here. I am alone here because Frau Zakreys is at her brother's.

Nevertheless, I'm getting on quite well in my hermit's life. There's only one thing I miss. Until now, Frau Zakreys always banged on my door early in the morning and I got up and started work, whereas now I have to depend on myself. Has anything happened in Linz? One doesn't hear any more of the Society for Rebuilding the Theatre. When the bank is finished, please send me a picture postcard. And now I have two favours to ask

Chapter 23 — The Lost Friendship

of you. First, would you be so good as to buy for me the Guide to the Danube City of Linz, not the Wöhrl, but the actual Linz one published by Krakowitzer. On the cover there is a picture of a Linz girl, and the background shows Linz from the Danube, with the bridge and castle. It costs 60 hellers which I enclose in postage stamps.

Please send it to me immediately, either postage paid, or collect. 1 will repay you the expense.

But be sure that the timetable of the steamship company, as well as the map of the town, are both there. I need a few figures which I have forgotten and which I can't find in the Wöhrl. And secondly, I would ask you, when you go on the boat again, to get me a copy of the guide you had this year. This "pay-what-you-wish" cost I will refund to you. So, you will do this for me, won't you? There is no other news, except that this morning I caught an army of bugs which were soon swimming in my blood, and now my teeth are chattering with the "heat." I think there have been very few summers with such cold days as this. It's the same with you, isn't it? Now with kindest regards to you and your esteemed parents, and once more repeating my requests, I remain your friend. ADOLF HITLER

Adolf was so keenly interested in his new plans for rebuilding Linz that he spared from his scanty means sixty hellers for me to buy the Krakowitzer edition of the Town Guide. The "bank" he refers to is the building of the Bank for Upper Austria and Salzburg. Adolf was very worried lest this building should detract from the compact appearance of the Linz main square. I could understand that he awaited impatiently for definite news of the Theatre Building Society because the theatre, together with the Danube bridge, were his favourite building projects.

How conscientious Adolf was, in spite of his desperate poverty, is shown not only by the enclosure to pay for the Guide, but by the remark that he would repay me the small sum I might spend for the "pay-what-you-wish" Guide that was obtainable on board the steamers.

And, oh, the bugs! That spiteful trick of fate's. I myself was practically immune, while Adolf was terribly afflicted by them. When I used to sleep through his nightly bug hunt, how often the next morning would he show me, carefully spiked on a pin, the result of his night's activity. At that time many houses in Vienna suffered from bugs. Well, another army of them had paid the extreme penalty.

For some time I did not hear from him. But then there came a lovely letter, dated August 17, 1908, probably the most revealing letter that he ever sent me. It reads:

Good Friend, First I must ask you to forgive me for not having written for so long. This had its own good — or rather bad — reasons; I didn't know what I could find to tell you. That I am writing you now only shows how long I had to search before I could collect together a little news. First, our land-lady, Zakreys, thanks you for the money. And secondly, 1 want to thank you heartily for your letter.

Probably Frau Zakreys finds writing letters difficult (her German is so bad) but she has asked me to thank you and your esteemed parents for the money. I have just got over a sharp attack of bronchial catarrh. It seems that your Musician's Union is facing a crisis. Who actually published the newspaper that I sent you last time? I had already paid the money long since. Do you know anything more about it? We're having nice fine weather now; it's pouring rain. And this year, with the baking heat we've had, that's really a blessing from heaven. But I shall only be able to enjoy it for a little while now. Probably Saturday or Sunday I shall have to leave. Shall let you know exactly. Am writing quite a lot lately, mostly afternoons and evenings, Have you read the latest decision of the Council with regard to the new theatre? It seems to me they intend to patch up the old junk heap once more. It can't go on like this any longer, because they won't get the permission from the authorities. In any case, the whole claptrap of these highly respected and allpowerful people shows that they understand about as much about building a theatre as a hippopotamus does of playing the violin. If my architect's manual didn't look so shabby, I would like to pack it up and send it to them with the following address: Theatre - Rebuilding - Society - Committee - for - the - Execution - of - the - Project - for - the - Rebuilding - of - the - Theatre. To the local, highly well-born, most strict and archlaudable committee for the eventual construction and required decoration! ...

And with this I close. With kindest regards to you and your esteemed parents, I remain, your friend, ADOLF HITLER

This is absolutely typical of Adolf. Even the unusual opening, "Good Friend," shows that he is in an emotional state. Then follows the long-winded introduction corresponding to that characteristic "take-off" of his which he always used for his nocturnal orations in order to get going.

The joke about "pleasant rainy weather," which already appears in another guise in his letter of April 20 of the same year, is warmed up to loosen the hesitant pen. To begin with, our good old landlady, with her melodious accent, is pulled to pieces. Then Adolf has a go at the Musician's

Chapter 23 — The Lost Friendship

Union. But these are only preliminary skirmishes, just to sharpen up the sword, for now he slashes out with all his own special vehemence against the Linz Theatre Society, which is not putting up a new building, but which proposes to renovate the "old junk heap." Bitterly he denounces these retrograde philistines who are mucking up his favourite project, one that has occupied him for years. Reading this letter I could, so to speak, see Adolf pacing up and down between the door and the piano, going bald-headed for these bureaucratic city councillors. He did actually go on the journey that he mentions in this letter, as on August 20, that is, three days later, he sent me a picture postcard of Weitra Castle from the Waldviertel. He does not seem to have liked it at his relatives', as very soon there comes a card from Vienna, congratulating me on my Saint's Day.

So everything went according to plan. Frau Zakreys went to Moravia, Adolf to the Waldviertel.

While life in the Stumpergasse was once again running on its accustomed lines, I — greatly to my distress — had to report at the barracks of the Austro-Hungarian Infantry Regiment No. 2. What I had to do in those, eight weeks — or to be more precise, what was done with me in this period of training — I prefer to leave unrecorded. These eight weeks represent, so to speak, a complete void in my life. But even they came to an end and finally, on November 20, I was able to inform Adolf of my arrival in Vienna.

I had, as I wrote him, taken the early train to save time, and arrived at the West Bahnhof at three o'clock in the afternoon. He would be waiting, I thought, at the usual spot, the platform barrier.

Then he could help me to carry the heavy case which also contained something for him from my mother. Had I missed him? I went back again, but he was certainly not at the barrier. I went into the waiting room. In vain I looked around me; Adolf was not there. Perhaps he was ill. He had indeed written me in his last letter that he was still being plagued by his old trouble, bronchial catarrh. I put my case in the left-luggage office and, very worried, hastened to the Stumpergasse.

Frau Zakreys was delighted to see me, but told me immediately that the room was taken. "But Adolf, my friend?" I asked her astonished.

Frau Zakreys stared at me with wide open eyes from her lined, withered face. "But don't you know that Herr Hitler has moved out?"

"No, I didn't know. Where has he moved to?" I asked.

"Herr Hitler didn't tell me that."

"But he must have left a message for me-a letter perhaps, or a note. How else shall I get hold of him?"

The landlady shook her head. "No, Herr Hitler didn't leave anything."

"Not even a greeting?"

"He didn't say anything."

I asked Frau Zakreys if the rent had been paid. Yes, Adolf had duly paid his share. Frau Zakreys gave me back the money that was due to me, as I had already paid my rent until November. She was very sorry to lose us both, but nothing could be done about it, and she gave me a makeshift bed for the night.

The next morning I went to look for another room, found a pleasant, light little room in the Glasauerhof, and hired an upright piano.

Nevertheless, I missed Adolf very much, although I was convinced that someday he would turn up again at my lodgings. To make it easier for him I left my new address with Frau Zakreys. Now Adolf had three ways of getting into touch with me—through Frau Zakreys, through the Office of the Conservatory or through my parents. He would certainly adopt one of these ways if he wanted to see me again.

That I could have found him through the Central Registration Office at Police Headquarters naturally did not occur to me. But days went by. A week, another week — Adolf still did not come. What had happened to him? Had something come between us which made him leave me? In my thoughts I went over again the last weeks we had spent together. Of course there had been differences of opinion and rows, but with Adolf this was quite normal. It had always been the same with him.

However much I pondered, I could not discover the slightest reason for his silence. After all, he himself had said many times that when I came back to Vienna in the autumn, we should live together again. He had never so much as hinted at our parting, even in moments of anger. In these four years, our friendship had become so close that it was taken for granted, and so was our resolve to stay together in the future.

When I thought back over the last weeks we had spent together I could only establish, on the contrary, that our relationship had been better than ever before, closer and more full of meaning.

Yes, those last few weeks in Vienna, when we had so many marvellous experiences at the Opera, at the Burg Theatre, and on the adventurous trip to the Rax, had indeed been the climax of our friendship.

What could have made Adolf leave me without a word or a sign? The more I racked my brain about it, the more I realised how much Adolf had meant to me. I felt deserted and alone, and with the constant memory of our friendship in my mind, I just could not decide to turn elsewhere for

Chapter 23 — The Lost Friendship

companionship. Although I appreciated that my studies would gain by it, yet my whole life now seemed to me so ordinary, almost boring. It certainly was some consolation to hear beautiful performances at concerts and at the Opera. But it was depressing to have no one to share them with. At every concert and every opera I went to, I hoped to see Adolf.

Perhaps he would be standing at the exit at the end of the performance, waiting for me, and I should hear again his familiar, impatient voice saying, "Oh, come on, Gustl!" But all my hopes of seeing Adolf again proved vain, and meanwhile something became clear: he did not want to come back to me. It was not by chance that he had left, neither was it the outcome of a passing mood or a series of mishaps. Had he wanted to find me, he certainly could have done so. It distressed me that he should want to break off this friendship, that had meant so much to me, without a sign of thanks, a token of future meetings. So, the next time I was in Linz, I went to see Frau Raubal in the Bürgergasse, to get his address from her.

She was alone, and received me with perceptible coolness. I asked her where Adolf was now living in Vienna. She did not know, she answered crossly, Adolf had never written to her again. So here, once more, I met with failure. And when Frau Raubal began to reproach me, saying that it was partly through my artistic ambitions that Adolf, now twenty years of age, still had no profession and no position, I told her plainly what I thought and defended Adolf vigorously, for, after all, Angela was only repeating her husband's opinion. And my opinion of the latter was no better than Adolf's. As the conversation was growing more and more unpleasant, I rose and took my leave abruptly.

The year came to an end, without my having heard or seen anything of Adolf. It was from a Linz archivist's research into Adolf Hitler's life that I was to learn, forty years later, that my friend had moved out of the Stumpergasse because the rent was too much for him and had found much cheaper accommodations at a so-called Men's Hostel in the Meldemannstrasse.

Adolf had disappeared into the shadowy depths of the metropolis. Then began for him those years of bitter misery of which he himself says little, and concerning which there is no reliable witness; for one thing is certain, that in this most difficult phase of his life, he no longer had a friend. I can now understand his behaviour at that time. He did not wish to have a friend, because he was ashamed of his own poverty. He wanted to go his way alone, and bear alone whatever destiny brought him. It was the road into the wilderness. I personally experienced, after that parting, that one is never so lonely as in the midst of the crowds of people in a big city.

Thus, our fine adolescent friendship came to an end that was anything but beautiful. But, with the passing of time, I became reconciled. Indeed, I came to feel that this sudden termination of our friendship by Adolf was of much more significance than if it had finished through our growing indifference towards each other, or if I had ceased to mean anything to him. Certainly such an end would have been harder for me to bear than that forced farewell, which was really not a farewell at all.

Epilogue

After a course of four years intensive study at the Vienna Conservatory, I was engaged as assistant conductor by the Municipal Theatre in Marburg on the Drau and opened my career there with Lortzing's *Der Waffenschmied*. I was very happy about this first, independent job.

Although the town was smaller than Linz, it was very interested in art. I produced several good light operas, of which, in particular, Flotow's *Martha* had a great success. At the end of the season I moved, with my orchestra, to Bad Pystian to conduct the music there for the summer season. My engagement in Marburg continued for the following season and I was already completely at home in that bright little town. The support which I encountered on all sides increased my youthful self-assurance and spurred on my enthusiasm.

One night, after a first performance of Eva, the director called me to his box and introduced me to the Head of the Klagenfurt Municipal Theatre, who was looking for an opera conductor. He was, apparently, so impressed by my performance that he engaged me on the spot for the next season. So in the early summer of 1914, at the close of the season in Marburg, on my way home to Linz I broke my journey in Klagenfurt and made some enquiries about my future sphere of activities. A good orchestra, forty strong, a nice house, a modern stage, and all this in the capital city of Carinthia, renowned for its love of music. Here I could give *Lohengrin*, perhaps even the *Meistersinger*. What more could I ask? Truly the heavenly violins were, almost literally, already playing for me.

Then, so near to their fulfillment, my youthful dreams disappeared in the fire of the Russian batteries when, a few months later, as a reservist of the Austro-Hungarian Infantry Regiment No. 2, I experienced my baptism of fire on the Galician front. This was not the music I had dreamed of. Although I was so unsuited to soldiering, I tried, like all my comrades, to do my duty. This endeavour brought me, after the frightful winter of 1915 in the Carpathians, to the wretched field hospital of Eperjes in Hungary.

The sick and severely wounded were taken to Budapest, a terrible journey of seven days; at all the larger stations the dead were unloaded. I had given up hope and had already calculated at which station they would dump me. By a miracle I survived all the horrors and miseries of this journey — but my strength was gone forever. When, after months of sickness, I was so much improved as to be able to visit my parents again, there too I found everything changed. My father, worn out by work and betrayed in his fond hope of handing over to his only son the firm he had so painstakingly built up had given up the business in 1916 and had bought a small farm at Fraham, near Eferding. There he sought to regain his health, but in vain, and, while I was at the front for a second time in September 1918, he died in all the misery and despair that filled those days. How I wish I could have made his old age happier! The end of the war came while I was with a transport formation in Vienna and here, on November 8, 1918, I was demobilised. What should I do now? All the provincial theatres were closed, so I travelled to Vienna to look for some kind of job. To be sure, both the state theatres were still open, but it was hopeless to try to get a position in one.

The orchestra in which for many years, while studying, I had earned my keep as a cellist had been disbanded. Nothing remained but a few dance bands in the big cafes. No, that was no good for me. For some while I conducted a six piece band in one of the new cinemas, a band that was supposed to "provide the musical illustration" for the silent films, but I got no satisfaction out of this. I tried to get a job as a cellist or at least to get some occasional engagements of this kind, but with no success. Nor was there any demand for private lessons.

I was at the end of my tether when a letter came from my mother. She wrote me that in the town of Eferding they were advertising for a Secretary to the Council. With all her mother's guile she knew how to make this far from attractive job seem more palatable to me. She had told the Mayor of my musical ability and added that, in addition, they would like the future Council Secretary to reorganise the Music Society that had broken up during the war and to undertake its direction.

I went home and looked into the proposition; the salary was small and the artistic possibilities seemed very limited. But meanwhile I had given up hope of becoming a professional conductor and, mainly to please my mother, I sent in my application. Then I returned to Vienna still hoping to get into an orchestra. There, in January 1920, I received a notification from the Mayor advising me that the job of Secretary to the Council had been awarded to me out of a list of thirty-eight applicants. Thus I became a civil servant.

Gradually I became familiar with the work and some years later I passed the Upper Austrian State examination for municipal employees. It was a humble job but it left me free to give myself up to my music. I built up a respectable orchestra and soon the musical life of the little town began to develop very well indeed. What with the quiet chamber music of a string quartet, the open-air performances of the brass band and the gala performances of the choral society there was much satisfying and successful work for me.

Throughout all this period I never succeeded in getting any news of the friend of my earlier years who had deserted me in such a strange fashion and I had finally given up trying. Besides, I had no idea how to try to find out about him. His brother-in-law Raubal was long since dead. Angela, his sister, was no longer living in Linz. Anything might have happened to my friend. That he was a better soldier than I had been, I was convinced; perhaps he, like so many of our generation, had been killed.

Now and again I would hear talk of a German politician who was called Adolf Hitler. But I thought it must refer to some other man who happened to have the same name. After all, the name of Hitler was not so uncommon. I imagined that if ever again I heard of my erstwhile friend it would be to learn that he had become an important architect, or at least an artist, not just some insignificant politician, least of all in Munich.

Then one evening, as I was crossing our quiet market square, for no particular reason I stopped to look into the bookshop. There in the show window lay the *Münchner Illustrierte*. On the front page was the picture of a man in about the middle thirties with small, pale features — I recognised him the very first moment. That was Adolf; he had hardly changed at all. I reckoned how long it was since the days when we had lived together in the Stumpergasse — fifteen years! The face seemed to have become sterner, more mature, more manly, but hardly any older.

The caption read, "The well-known National Socialist orator, Adolf Hitler." So my friend was in fact one and the same as that politician of whom there was so much talk. I was very sorry that he, like myself, had not been able to achieve an artistic career. I knew only too well what it meant to bury all one's hopes and dreams. And now he had to earn his living by making speeches at meetings.

A hard job, although he was indeed a good and convincing speaker — I had had proof of that often enough. I could also understand his interest in politics, but politics was a thankless task as well as being dangerous. I was glad that, if only through my professional position, I was obliged to hold myself aloof from political events as, now being Town Clerk, I had to work in the interests of all the townsfolk alike, without any distinction. But my friend went full steam ahead into politics and I was not at all surprised that his stormy activities of which I read in the papers landed him in jail at Landsberg. But he turned up again and the press gave him more space than ever. His political ideas, which gradually found supporters in Austria too, did not surprise me in the least because, fundamentally, they were the same as those he used to expound to me, admittedly still confused and exaggerated, in Vienna. When I read his speeches I could actually see him in front of me, striding up and down in the gloomy back room in the Stumpergasse between the door and the piano, holding forth unceasingly.

In those days I was his only listener; now his audience was counted in thousands. One heard his name everywhere and soon they were asking, "Where does he come from, this Hitler?" Well, I was certainly in a better position than many others to tell them. Did I not still have letters and drawings of his? I had forgotten all about them, but now I climbed up to the loft and there it still stood, the old wooden chest that had remained in my parents' house at Fraham until the time my mother sold the little farm and moved in with me, bringing It with her. I found the key and unlocked the chest. And, in fact, there lay a large blue envelope bearing the name "Adolf Hitler," written in my hand. I could not recollect this envelope. In the frightful happenings of the war and the misery that followed I had completely forgotten about it, just as my friend, too, would have faded slowly from my mind if he had not appeared again as a politician.

I opened the envelope; there were my friend's postcards, letters and drawings, though certainly only a part of those I had received from him. But nevertheless, some well worthy of interest; I reread his cards and letters. What should I do with them? Should I send him back the whole correspondence. But why? He had other things to do now than to warm up old boyhood memories. Perhaps he had long since forgotten the lanky, music-mad carpenter's apprentice whom he had met in the Linz Theatre. Should I write to him? That, too, seemed to me pointless, as even in those days he had scorned me for my feeble interest in politics and now he would be more than ever disappointed in me.

So I contented myself with reading what the newspapers said about him. His supporters could now be counted by the million. Without stepping onto Austrian soil he managed, with his radical conceptions and ideas, to bring excitement and unrest to our shrunken little Austria, and this was even more reason for me to keep quiet. It might seem incomprehensible that, after Adolf had made himself a name as a politician, I did not immediately try to get in touch with him. But yet, looking back, I must say this: our boyhood friendship had sprung from our common interest in art; politics had no attraction for me and so I no longer felt drawn towards Adolf who, in turn, could not be expected to have any interest in me.

Then on January 30, 1933, I heard the news that Adolf Hitler had become Reichs Chancellor.

Epilogue

Immediately I thought back to that night on the Freinberg when Adolf had described to me how he, like Rienzi, would rise to be the Tribune of the people. What the sixteen-year-old had seen then in a visionary's trance had really come to pass. So I sat down and wrote a few lines to "The Reichs Chancellor Adolf Hitler in Berlin." I didn't expect any reply. A chancellor had more important things to do than to answer the letter of one August Kubizek from Eferding with whom he had been friendly a quarter of a century earlier.

But it seemed to me, politics apart, the right thing to do as a former friend to congratulate him on the position he had reached.

But one day to my great astonishment I received the following letter:

> To the Town Clerk
> Mr. AUGUST KUBIZEK
> Eferding, Upper Austria
> ADOLF HITLER
> Munich, August 4, 1933
> The Brown House
>
> My dear Kubizek, I have only just been shown your letter of February 2. In view of the hundreds of thousands of letters I have received since January this is not to be wondered at. So much the greater was my pleasure to receive news of you after so many years and to have your address. I should be very glad — once the period of my hardest struggles is past — to revive once more with you those memories of the best years of my life. Perhaps you could come to visit me. With all good wishes to you and your mother, I remain, in memory of our old friendship.
>
> Yours, ADOLF HITLER

So he had not forgotten me. That in spite of all the strain of his work he remembered me made me very happy. He called the years we had spent together the "best years" of his life.

So he had already forgotten the misery that went with them and only the exuberance of his youth remained a fond memory. But the end of the letter caused me some embarrassment. "Perhaps you could come to visit me," he wrote. That was easier said than done. I couldn't just simply go up to his house on the Obersalzberg and say "Here I am." Besides, this reunion would only have been a nuisance to him. What could I have told him? My own life, compared with his, was unimportant and uninteresting; to tell him about Eferding would only bore him. And for the rest I had nothing to relate. So I let the matter rest and persuaded myself that this friendly invitation was just a formal courtesy, like the stereotyped greetings at the end of his letters; twenty-five years ago to my parents, now only for my mother.

Of course it is very nice when a friend is so consistent in his behaviour, but I thought it was nonsense to be equally consistent in the continuance of our friendship, as fate had only too obviously cast us into paths so widely divergent.

On March 12, 1938, however, on the very spot where his father had once served as a customs official, Adolf Hitler crossed the frontier. The German Army marched into Austria. On the evening of March 12 Adolf Hitler addressed the assembled populace from the balcony of the Linz Town Hall, which was still as modest and as shabby as it had been in our youth. I should have liked to have gone to hear him speak, but I was so busy with the billeting of the German troops that I could not leave Eferding.

But when Hitler came again to Linz, on April 8, and stayed at the Hotel Weinzinger after a political demonstration at the Kraus locomotive works, I did make an attempt to see him. The Square in front of the hotel was crammed with people, but I made my way through to the cordon of S.A. men and told them that I would like to speak to the Chancellor. At first they gave me a queer look, probably thinking I was mad. Only after I had shown them one of Hitler's letters did they prick up their ears. They called over an officer and when he too had seen the letter he let me through immediately and conducted me to the entrance hall of the hotel.

But in there it was like a beehive; generals were standing around in groups waiting and discussing events. Ministers of State whom I recognised from the illustrated papers, high-up Party leaders and other uniformed personalities came and went. A.D.C.s, recognisable by their gleaming shoulder tabs, strode busily about. And all this exciting activity centred around the man to whom I, too, wished to speak. I became quite giddy and realised that it had been foolish of me to come. I had to accept the fact that my erstwhile friend had become Reichs Chancellor and this highest position in the State had created between us an unbridgeable gulf. The years when I had been the only one to whom he gave his friendship and when he had confided to me the most intimate affairs of his heart, were definitely over.

Therefore the best thing I could do was to disappear quietly and not be a nuisance to these high-ranking gentlemen who undoubtedly were there on most important missions.

One of the senior A.D.C.s, Albert Bormann to whom I had confided my request, soon approached me and told me that the Reichs

Epilogue

Chancellor was not very well and would not be receiving anybody else that day; would I come again tomorrow at lunchtime. Bormann then invited me to sit down for a moment as there were things he wished to ask me.

Had the Chancellor in his youth always gone to bed so late? he inquired plaintively; he never went to bed before midnight and slept far into the morning, whereas his entourage who were obliged to stay up late with him in the evening had to be up and about early the next day. Bormann went on to complain about Hitler's outbursts of temper which nobody could cope with and about his queer diet, which consisted of meatless dishes, puddings and fruit juices. Had the Chancellor always eaten thus? I said yes, only adding that in his youth he had still been fond of meat. With this I took my leave.

This Albert Bormann was a brother of the well-known Martin Bormann.

The next day again I went to Linz. Everybody was out in the streets, which were packed with people, and the closer I got to the Hotel Weinzinger the thicker became the throng. Finally I managed to fight my way through to the hotel and once more took up my obscure position in the foyer. The excitement and agitation was even greater than the previous day. For this was the eve of the plebiscite in Austria.

It can be imagined that all big decisions had to be taken by Hitler himself. At any rate I could not have chosen a more unfortunate moment for our reunion than this. I recalled that at the beginning of July, 1908, we had said goodbye in the hall of the Westbahnhof; today was April 9, 1938. So almost exactly thirty years had passed between our abrupt separation and today's meeting — always supposing this did take place. Thirty years — a whole lifetime! And what world-shaking events these thirty years had brought.

I had no illusions about what would happen if Hitler did see me. A brief handshake, perhaps a familiar clap on the shoulder, a few friendly, hasty words in passing — I would have to be satisfied with this modest portion. For my part, I had prepared a few suitable words but I was somewhat worried about the form of address. I couldn't possibly call the Reichs Chancellor "Adolf." I knew what a stickler for form he was. It would be best to keep to the formal mode of address. But then, I didn't even know if I would get as far as making the little speech.

The memory of what really did happen is naturally influenced by my deep emotional feelings at the time. As Hitler suddenly came out of one of the hotel rooms, he recognised me immediately and with the joyful cry, "Gustl!" he left his entourage standing there and came and took me by the arm. I still remember how he took my outstretched right hand in both of his and held it firmly and how his eyes, which were still as bright and as piercing as ever, gazed into mine. He was obviously moved, just as I was. I could hear it in his voice.

The worthy gentlemen in the hall looked at each other. Nobody knew this curious civilian whom the Führer and Chancellor greeted with such warmth. Then I pulled myself together and delivered myself of the speech I had prepared. He listened attentively, smiling slightly. When I had finished he nodded at me, as if to say, You've learnt it well, Gustl, or perhaps even, And now my boyhood friend talks to me just like all the others. But to me, any familiarity on my part seemed out of place.

After a little pause he said, "Come with me," using the formal mode of address "Sie." Perhaps through my prepared speech I had forfeited that familiar "Du" which he had used in his letter of 1933. But, to tell the truth, I was relieved to hear him use "Sie." The Chancellor preceded me to the lift. We went up to the second floor where he had his rooms; the A.D.C. opened the door. We entered; the A.D.C. left. We were alone. Once more Hitler took my hand, gazed at me for a long time and said, "You are just the same as you always were, Kubizek. I should have recognised you immediately anywhere. You have not changed at all, just got older."

Then he led me to the table and invited me to take a seat. He assured me how glad he was to see me once again after so long. He had been particularly pleased with my congratulations, as nobody knew better than I what a hard fight he had had. The present moment was not suitable for a heart-to-heart talk, but he hoped to have an opportunity for it in the future. He would let me know; it was not advisable to write to him direct as such letters often never even reached him, and all had to be carefully gone through to save his time.

"I no longer have a private life as in those days, and can't do just what I want like other people." With these words he rose and went over to the window which looked out onto the Danube. The old iron bridge which, even in his boyhood, used to annoy him still stood there. As was to be expected, he started immediately: "That ugly thing," he exclaimed, "still there! But not for much longer, you can be sure of that, Kubizek."

And then he turned to me again and smiled. "Just the same I'd like to stroll across the old bridge with you once again. But that's no longer possible. Wherever I go I'm surrounded. But believe me, Kubizek, I've got a lot of plans for Linz." Nobody knew that better than I. As I expected, he propounded once again all the plans which had occupied him in his youth as though not thirty years, but at the most three years had passed since then.

Shortly before he received me, he had driven through the streets of the town to find out what alterations there had been. Now he went through each single plan. The new Danube bridge, which was to be called the Nibelungs Bridge, was to be a masterpiece. He described to me in detail the shape of the two bridgeheads. Then he went on to talk —I knew in advance in which order he would discuss things — of the theatre which, above everything, was going to be equipped with a modern stage. When the new Opera House, to be built on the site of the ugly station, was ready, that theatre would only be used for plays and operettas. In addition to this Linz needed a modern concert hall if it were to be worthy to be known as the "City of Bruckner." "I want Linz to have a leading place in culture and I will see that everything is done to this end." I thought that now the interview was finished. But then Hitler began to speak of setting up a grand symphony orchestra in Linz and, with this, the conversation suddenly took a more personal turn.

"Now tell me, Kubizek, what have you become?" I told him that since 1920 I had been a municipal employee and at that moment had the job of Town Clerk.

"Town Clerk," he asked, "what's that?"

I was a bit embarrassed. How could I describe to him briefly what this job really involved? While I was still searching for suitable words he broke in. "So you've become a civil servant, a pen pusher! That's not the right thing for you. What has happened to your music?" I answered truthfully that the war we had lost had completely ruined my career. I had to get a different job, or starve.

He nodded grimly and said, "Yes, the war we lost." Then, looking at me he said, "You won't end your days as a pen-pusher, Kubizek." Moreover, he would like once to have a look at this Eferding place I had mentioned.

I asked him if he really meant it.

"Of course I will come to see you, Kubizek," he remarked, "but my visit will be for you alone. Then we will go strolling along the Danube. I can't manage it here — they don't leave me alone." He wanted to know if I was still so keen on music.

And now I was off on my hobby-horse and I told him at length of the musical activities in our little town. Considering the weighty and world-shaking problems that he had to deal with, I was afraid that my recital would bore him; but I was mistaken. If, to save time, I mentioned something only cursorily, he interrupted me immediately.

"What, Kubizek, you even give symphonies in this little Eferding! But that's marvellous. Which symphonies have you played?" I recounted,

Schubert's Unfinished, Beethoven's Third, Mozart's Jupiter Symphony, Beethoven's Fifth.

He wanted to know how many strong my orchestra was and how it was composed, was amazed at the details I gave him and congratulated me on my success.

"This is where I must help you, Kubizek," he exclaimed. "Make me out a report and tell me what you need. And how are you getting on, personally; you are not hard up?" I replied that while my job brought in only a modest income it was enough for my needs and consequently I had no personal requests.

Astonished, he glanced up; it was obviously new to him that one should have no personal wishes.

"Have you any children, Kubizek?"

"Yes, three sons."

"Three sons," he shouted, impressed. He repeated it several times with a most earnest expression. "So you've got three sons, Kubizek. I have no family. I am alone. But I should like to look after your sons."

I had to tell him all about my boys — he wanted to know every detail. He was pleased that they were all three musically gifted and that two of them were also clever draughtsmen.

"I shall make myself responsible for the training of your three sons, Kubizek," he said to me.

"I don't want gifted young people to have such a hard time of it as we had. You know best what we had to go through in Vienna. But the worst time came for me later on, after we bad parted. Young talent must no longer be allowed to perish through sheer poverty. Wherever I can help personally, I do, and all the more when it's a question of your children, Kubizek!"

I hasten to add here that the Chancellor did indeed arrange for the musical studies of my three sons at the Bruckner Conservatory in Linz to be paid through his office, and on his orders the drawings of my son Rudolf were examined by a Professor of the Academy in Munich.

I had reckoned on a hasty handshake, and here we were sitting together for a good hour.

The Chancellor rose. I thought the interview was now at an end and I rose too. But he only called in his A.D.C. and gave him instructions concerning my sons; the A.D.C. took the opportunity of reminding him of his youthful letters which were still in my possession.

And now I had to spread the letters, postcards and drawings out on the table. He was greatly surprised to see the number of mementoes I had and asked how these papers had come to be preserved. I told him

Epilogue

of the black-painted trunk in the attic with the pocket in the lid and the envelope bearing the words, "Adolf Hitler." He paid particular attention to the water colour of the Pöstlingberg. He explained to me that there were certain clever painters who could copy his water colours so exactly that they couldn't be distinguished from the original. These people carried on a flourishing business and could always find fools ready to be taken in; the safest thing was never to let the original out of my hands.

As there had already been attempts to get this material from me, I asked the Chancellor his opinion. "These documents are your own personal property, Kubizek," he answered, "No one can claim them."

This led him to speak of Rabitsch's book. Rabitsch had attended the Linz Technical School a couple of years after Hitler and, certainly with the best of intentions, had written a book about Hitler's school years. But Hitler was very angry about it because Rabitsch had never known him personally.

"You see, Kubizek, from the very beginning I was not in favour of this book being written; only those who really know me should write about me. If anybody is indicated for it, it is you, Kubizek," and turning to his A.D.C. he added, "Make a note of that immediately."

Then he once more gripped my hand, "See, Kubizek, it's really necessary that we should meet more often. As soon as it's possible I will send for you."

The meeting was over; in a state of numbness I left the hotel. Unrest entered into my quiet, retired life during the following days and I was to discover that it was not all honey to have been the boyhood friend of such a famous man. Although I had told hardly anybody about it and was determined to be even more discreet in the future, I was soon to experience the drawbacks of having been a friend of Hitler's.

Already in the previous March I had had a taste of what was in store for me. Hardly had Austria become part of the German Reich, than one day a motorcar drew up at my house in Eferding. The three men in uniform who got out of it had come direct from Berlin. They had instructions from the Führer to collect from me all the documents relative to his youth and to take them to the Chancellery so that they could be kept in safety.

Luckily I did not allow myself to be taken in. As was now clear to me Hitler, at the time that attempt at confiscation had been made, had no idea that I was in possession of these papers. It was the independent move of some Party Office which had learned of my existence.

In any case I refused to hand over the papers to the three S.S. men, which seemed to them hardly believable. Evidently they had expected to find the people in Austria more pliable than I was. Their brusque manner did not make the desired impression — and to make matters worse this obstinate civilian wasn't even a member of the Party! Extraordinary what queer fish the Führer had chosen for friends in his youth, they must have thought, as they went off with empty hands.

It was lucky that I had stood firm against this first attack. Those that followed were easier to parry as I could quote Hitler's own words, that these documents were my own personal property.

In the following months the various Party Offices tried to outdo each other. As I now learned, often, when among his intimates the conversation turned on his youth, Hitler would refer them to me. "Ask Gustl" was the stereotyped reply they would get for anything that concerned his youthful experiences. But now this "Gustl," who had previously been more or less out of reach, had with the Anschluss suddenly become a German citizen and well within the grasp of all the political departments.

Reichs Minister Goebbels sent a very likable young man to me. His name was Karl Cerff, but his rank and position I have forgotten. Cerff explained to me that they were preparing the publication of a great biography of the Führer, of which I was to be in charge of the period 1904-1908. At the appropriate time I would be called to Berlin so that I could carry out this work with the help of acknowledged specialists. Meanwhile they would like me to make a start with detailed notes of my memoirs. I explained to the young man that I could not possibly find the time then as, since the Anschluss, we municipal employees were overwhelmed with work. He realised that I didn't wish to bind myself and was very amused at my way of putting it. But he exhorted me not to underrate my "unique responsibility to History," as he expressed it. If I so wished, he could easily get me leave of absence. This I refused definitely. So he departed, promising to come at a "better moment." But as the future only brought "worse moments," I never saw Karl Cerff again. In any case, he had tried to carry out his ticklish job with tact and charm.

Much more insistent and unpleasant were the instructions that reached me from Martin Bormann, who seemed to feel himself solely responsible for me and my affairs and kept an anxious watch that no one else should come in contact with me. His letters and orders read as though he had taken a lease on the life of Adolf Hitler and nobody must say or write one word about it without its being examined and agreed on by him.

When he failed in his attempts to get these documents from me to deposit them with the Party Central Office "where they belonged," as he wrote, he sent me strict orders that these papers should never be given up without his permission and that no outsider should be permitted a glimpse

Epilogue

of them. For this I certainly didn't need Martin Bormann's admonition — this had always been my intention. But when he instructed me to write out immediately the memoirs of my youthful friendship with Adolf Hitler and submit the draft to him, then I replied that I should have first to talk this over with Hitler himself. This method was a decided success. In future when I was being pressed by any of these bullying gentlemen, I had only to say, "Excuse me, but I must first discuss your suggestions with the Chancellor personally ... what was the name again?" This changed their attitude completely and I was then handled with the utmost delicacy and care.

In contrast to this, I recollect my meeting with Rudolf Hess with pleasure. He had come to Linz and invited me to call on him; he sent a car for me which took me to the Bergbahn Hotel on the Pöstlingberg. Reichs Minister Hess greeted me warmly. "So this is Kubizek!" he exclaimed, beaming. "The Führer has told me so much about you." I sensed immediately that this friendliness was really genuine and heartfelt.

Also, through this visit I was able to confirm an impression I had that the closer to the Chancellor a person stood, the more he had been told about me. Rudolf Hess and Frau Winifred Wagner were the most fully informed about Hitler's youth and, consequently, about me. The Minister invited me to lunch which was served on the beautiful terrace of the hotel. After the meal I had to recount to him all my memories in great detail. He frequently commented and again and again asked me questions. I had the feeling that, in a real, human way, Rudolf Hess was much closer to Hitler than many others and I was glad about this. The other gentlemen, too, who were at the table joined in and we had an animated and unrestrained conversation, markedly different from those dealings with the officials of the Party Central Office. I was particularly glad that from this wonderful spot high above the city I could point out to the Minister the position of all the places of which we spoke as they lay before us.

Rudolf Hess made a good impression on me with his simple, straightforward manner which differed so much from the behaviour of other, far less important political personalities. I was only sorry that he appeared so ill.

Meanwhile, in my own country, too, they seemed to have become aware of me. To be sure I was still not a Party member, which seemed strange to many, as in their opinion, the boyhood friend of Hitler's should actually have been Party member No. 2. But even in those days, politically I had always been a dubious supporter of my friend, not exactly because I actively disagreed with his politics, but politics did not interest me; or rather, I did not understand them.

Naturally, too, I was soon flooded with requests for help and support from people who, for one reason or another, were in trouble and wanted me to intercede for them. I was willing to help, although I had no illusion about my actual influence over political decisions and it was soon made clear to me that being "a boyhood friend of Adolf Hitler's" was not sufficient title to warrant an active interference in these affairs. It was pointed out to me, politely but firmly, that this or that particular matter was quite outside my sphere.

As I expected, the visit to Eferding that Hitler had planned did not take place. Then, suddenly, my state of resignation, induced more by common sense than by sentiment, was broken into by the unexpected arrival of a registered letter from the Reichs Chancellery. My heart was thudding as I opened the envelope. There in its full glory, printed on the finest handmade paper stood what was to become the greatest joy of my whole life. By the command of the Reichs Chancellor I was invited to be present at this year's Richard Wagner Festival in Bayreuth. I was to report to Herr Kannenberg in Haus Wahnfried on July 25, 1939.

It had always been my greatest desire to make the pilgrimage to Bayreuth to experience a performance of the great Master there. But I was not well off and with my humble position could never even contemplate such a journey. And now suddenly I was going! I arrived in good time for the performance; the Festival in 1939 opened with the *Flying Dutchman*.

An orchestra 132 strong — I was bewitched.

The next day they gave *Tristan and Isolde*, an unforgettable performance. Thursday, July 27, *Parsifal* was presented. I had already prepared myself for this at home, had studied the piano score and read all the relative literature. The soft strains of the Abendmahl motif were heard, the world around me changed and I lived through the most happy hours of my earthly existence.

With *Götterdämmerung* on Wednesday, August 2, my stay in Bayreuth came to an end. I prepared for my journey home and went once more to Herr Kannenberg to thank him for his care of me. "Must you really leave?" he asked me with a meaning smile. "It would be a good idea if you could stay another day." I understood his hint immediately and stayed in Bayreuth till August 3.

At two o'clock in the afternoon an S.S. officer came to fetch me; it was not far to Haus Wahnfried.

In the hall Obergruppenführer Julius Schaub was waiting for me and he led me to a large salon where many people, whom I recognised from the former Linz visit or from the illustrated papers, were present. There stood Frau Winifred Wagner in lively conversation with Reichs Minister Hess. Obergruppenführer Brückner was chatting with Herr von Neurath and several generals.

Indeed there was a preponderance of military personalities present and it struck me that the general situation was very strained, in particular with regard to Poland, and there was even talk of a resort to arms. I felt very out of place in this tense atmosphere and the same sinking feeling, like stagefright, that I had experienced in the Hotel Weinzinger in Linz came back to me. Probably the Reichs Chancellor wanted to exchange a few friendly words with me before he went back to the capital. With my heart beating wildly I prepared a few words of thanks. On the far side of the hall were large double folding doors.

Suddenly the A.D.C. standing by these doors signals to Obergruppenführer Schaub, whereupon he leads me forward. The A.D.C. opens both doors and steps aside. Obergruppenführer Schaub steps in with me and announces, "Mein Führer, here is Herr Kubizek." Saying which, he steps back and closes the doors behind him. I am alone with the Reichs Chancellor.

His bright eyes shine with the pleasure of seeing me again and he comes towards me with a beaming face. Nothing in his behaviour betrays the immense responsibility which rests on his shoulders; he seems to me just like any ordinary visitor to the Festival. He, too, shares that happy atmosphere which pervades Bayreuth. Now he takes my right hand in both of his and wishes me welcome. This heartfelt greeting on this holy spot moves me so much that I can hardly speak.

My expressions of gratitude must have sounded very awkward and I was much relieved when his friendly "Well, let's sit down" released me from my confusion. I had to tell him all about my journey to Bayreuth, my visits to the various places associated with Wagner and, of course in the greatest detail, what I thought of the Festival performances. In doing this I recovered my self-control and now we were talking in just the same way as we had done in our youth about all that enchanted us. And this brought him round to the Wagner performances we had seen in Linz and Vienna and he exposed to me his plan to make the work of Richard Wagner available to the greatest possible number of the German people. Ah, how well I knew these plans from long ago!

In his talks of nearly thirty-five years ago their fundamentals were already determined. But now it was no longer mere fantasy. Six thousand people, he told me, who had previously never been able to afford it were this year, as a result of excellent organisation, among the guests at the Bayreuth

Festival. I replied that I myself was among the number. He laughed and said-I remember his words exactly — "Now I have you as my witness in Bayreuth, Kubizek, for you were the only one present when as a poor, unknown person I first gave utterance to these ideas. In those days you used to ask me how these plans could be realised. And now you can see what has come of it." He went on to describe to me all that had been done up till then and what was still going to be done for Bayreuth, almost as though he had to render account to me.

But now I had a very concrete problem. In my pocket was a large bundle of postcards, bearing his picture. In Eferding and Linz there were a great number of worthy people whom I could make happy with a photograph with Hitler's autograph. For some time I hesitated to bring out the cards as my desire seemed then very commonplace. On the other hand Hitler was just sitting there at his desk; if I missed this opportunity, perhaps I should never get such a one again. I thought of the people at home and plucked up courage.

He took the cards and, as he looked for his glasses, I handed him my fountain pen. Then he signed and I helped him by drying the signatures with the blotting pad. In the middle of signing the cards he looked up, and seeing me standing by with the uplifted blotter, said smilingly, "One can see that you're a pen-pusher, Kubizek. But I just don't understand how you can stick to that job. In your place I'd have cut loose long ago. And, incidentally, why didn't you come and see me much earlier?"

I was very embarrassed and searched for a suitable excuse. "Seeing that you wrote me on the fourth of August, 1933, that you would like to revive our common memories but only when the period of sternest struggle was over," I said, "I wanted to wait until then. Besides, until 1938, as an Austrian subject I would have needed a passport to come to Germany. And I certainly should not have got that if I had revealed the true purpose of my visit."

He laughed heartily and answered, "Yes, politically you were always a child." I too laughed now because I had expected him to use a different word. The "fool" of the Stumpergasse had meanwhile become a "child."

Then the Reichs Chancellor packed the cards together and got up. I thanked him and put them carefully in my coat pocket. Now, I thought, the interview was at an end. Then he said solemnly, "Come!" He opened the french windows and preceded me into the garden down the stone steps. Well-tended paths brought us to a high, wrought-iron gate. He opened it. There were flowers and shrubs in full bloom, and the mighty trees, forming a roof above us, threw the place into semidarkness.

A few more paces and we stood in front of Richard Wagner's tomb. Hitler took my hand and I could feel how moved he was.

It was quite still; nothing disturbed the solemn peace.

Hitler broke the silence, "I am happy that we have met once more on this spot which always was the most venerable place for us both." I pondered on the inscrutable ways of destiny.

Whoever had known us both in those days in Vienna must have been certain that my future was, to all intents and purposes, predictable. After finishing at the Conservatory I would start my career as an opera conductor, a career to which my early successes pointed. It must have seemed equally certain that Adolf, with his purposeless studies and his disdain for all professional training, would turn out a failure.

Now fate had given its verdict. Here at Richard Wagner's tomb stood, hand in hand, the two poor unknown students from the dark back room of the Stumpergasse. And what were they now? The "dead cert" was a little insignificant clerk in a small Austrian town who also dabbled in music, and the other whose future had been so much in doubt had risen to be the Chancellor of the Reich. And what did the future have in store for us? Only one thing could be safely predicted: while the one would remain in his obscurity, whatever might happen the other would go down in history.

Afterwards the Reichs Chancellor showed me round Haus Wahnfried. Wieland Wagner, Frau Winifred's son and the Master's grandson, was waiting for us at the garden entrance. He unlocked the various rooms for us and the Chancellor showed me all the relics. We started our tour with the old building, whose rooms were already familiar to me from pictures. In the music room there was the grand piano at which the Master had worked; it was left open, a gesture which moved me deeply. I saw also the magnificent library. Then Wieland left us and the Chancellor introduced me to Frau Wagner, who was obviously pleased to meet me. When our conversation turned on the youthful enthusiasm with which we had dedicated ourselves to the works of the Master, I recalled again that memorable Rienzi performance in Linz. And now Hitler evoked for Frau Wagner the unique experience of that night, concluding with the words that have remained engraved in my memory, "In that hour it began."

Before we parted, Hitler gave me a few more words of advice. On my way home, he said, I should stop in Munich and hear the Reichs Symphony Orchestra, which had been so much on our minds when we were young, and I should also visit the great German Art Exhibition. He thought it would not be a good thing for us to meet in his home on the Obersalzberg, so he had given orders that I should always be able to come to Bayreuth when he was there. "I should like you to be always here with me," he said, and shook me by the hand. He stood at the garden gate and waved to me as I went. Soon I heard the cheers of the crowds greeting him in the RichardWagner-Strasse — the Chancellor was leaving Bayreuth to fly to Berlin.

When, on July 8, 1940, I received the tickets for the first cycle of the Richard Wagner Festival which the Chancellor's office had sent me, I was faced with a dilemma. War had brought changes to our service and duties at home, too; would it not be irresponsible of me to leave my urgent tasks to go to Bayreuth? True the Chancellor had expressed the desire to have me there with him. But there was a war on, and nobody was more occupied with it than Hitler himself. Would he even be able to come? Unlike the previous year, apart from the *Flying Dutchman*, only *The Ring* was performed. Frau Wagner informed me that she had spoken to the Führer on the telephone and confirmed that he would be flying straight from his Headquarters to the performance of *Götterdämmerung* but had to return immediately afterwards.

"He asked me whether you were here, Herr Kubizek," she added. "He wants to talk to you during the interval." On Tuesday, July 23, at three o'clock in the afternoon, the trumpets — provided for the occasion by the Wehrmacht — sounded the Siegfried motif, announcing the beginning of the opera. I took my seat and shortly after, Hitler entered his box. The Awakening Motif, the solemn, fateful tones swelled out. I forgot my surroundings and gave myself up to the magic of the wonderful work.

During the first interval Wolfgang Wagner came hurriedly to tell me that the Führer wanted to see me. We went to the drawing room where there were about twenty people standing around in groups engaged in lively conversation. I could not spot Hitler immediately as he was no longer in civilian clothes but in uniform. But his personal A.D.C. had already told him of my presence and he came towards me with both hands outstretched. He wore a simple grey-green tunic and his face was fresh and sunburnt. His delight at seeing me seemed to be even deeper, more heartfelt.

Perhaps the war had made him even more serious. And I represented for him one who had known his youth, a friend who had been at his side during one period of his life.

Hitler took me aside and we stood alone while the other guests continued their conversations at a distance. "This year this is the only performance which I can see," he said. "But it can't be helped, there's a war on." And then with an undertone of anger in his voice: "This war is holding up our work of reconstruction for many years. It is a shame. After all I have not become the Chancellor of the Greater German Reich to make war."

I was astonished to hear the Chancellor speak in this way after the great military victories in Poland and France. Perhaps he was influenced by the fact that my presence reminded him of his age; for we had been young together, and as he noticed in me the unmistakable signs of the advancing years, he must have realised that the years must also have left their mark on him, although in all the time of our acquaintance I had never seen him looking so strong and healthy.

"This war is robbing me of my best years. You know my plans, Kubizek, you know how much I still want to build. That's what I want to see in my lifetime, you understand? You know best how many projects I have made ever since I was young. And only a few of them have I been able to realise so far. I still have so infinitely much to do. Who else is there to do it? And here I have to stand by and watch the war robbing me of my best years. It is a shame. Time doesn't stand still.

"We are growing older, Kubizek. Not many more years — and it will be too late to do what remains to be done."

And with that strangely excited voice so familiar to me from our early years, vibrating with impatience, he began to detail for me his great plans for the future, the development of the Autobahnen, of canals, the modernisation of the railways and much else. I was hardly able to follow. But once again, as in the previous year, I felt that he wanted to justify himself before me, the witness of his youthful ideas.

I tried to turn the conversation to the experiences we had shared in our youth. He immediately picked up a remark of mine and said, "Poor students, that's what we were. And, Heaven knows, we starved. Off we used to go with only a crust of bread in our pocket. But all this has changed now. It was only last year that young people went to Madeira in our ships." And so Hitler came to speak of his cultural plans. The crowds in front of the Festival Theatre were wanting to see him. But he had worked himself up to such a state that it was not possible to interrupt him, perhaps because he felt, just as in our conversations in the gloomy room of Frau Zakreys, that I followed him with full enthusiasm whenever he spoke of art and its problems.

"I am still tied up by the war. But, I hope it won't last much longer and then I'll be able to build again and to carry out what remains to be done. When that moment comes I shall call you, Kubizek, and then you must stay with me always," he concluded.

Outside the trumpets sounded to remind us that the performance was about to continue. I thanked the Chancellor for this demonstration of his friendship and wished him luck and success for the future.

The *Götterdämmerung* came to an end; it was a performance that moved me to the core. I walked slowly down the drive leading from the theatre and noticed that the street was roped off. I stopped at the corner of Adolf-Hitler-Strasse to see the Chancellor once more. A few minutes later a motor column approached along the street. Hitler stood erect in his car; on either side, close to the ropes, moved the cars of his entourage.

I shall never forget what happened during the next few moments. General Music Director Elmendorf with Frau Lange and Sister Susi, and an old lady, a painter, whose name I don't remember — she was living in the Haus Wahnfried — stood with me and congratulated me. I didn't really know why. But now the motor column had reached us and was passing at a slow pace. I was standing near the cordon and I saluted. At this moment the Chancellor recognised me and made a sign to the driver. The column halted and his car approached me. Hitler smiled at me, leaned out of his car and, taking my hand, shook it heartily, saying, "Auf Wiedersehen." And as the car moved off, Hitler turned round and waved farewell. Then the column proceeded to the airfield.

Pandemonium broke out around me. The bystanders wanted to know who that strange civilian was to whom Hitler had paid so much attention in public. I myself was hardly able to utter a word.

The shouting and pushing grew frightening. Up to this moment my meetings with the Chancellor had always been in private or, at the most, in the presence of a limited number of people, which had preserved the personal and intimate character of our friendship. But now it had become, so to speak, a matter of public interest, and only now did I fully understand how much this friendship of my youth really meant. Everybody wanted to shake hands with me.

My friends tried to give some explanations to the crowd-in vain! They were unable to make themselves heard. I was being pushed and knocked about-everybody wanted to see me. Heaven knows what the people thought I was. Perhaps a foreign diplomat who had come to offer peace — this at least would have made the pushing worthwhile. At long last I could breathe more freely. "Ladies and gentlemen," I shouted, "let me go — I'm only a boyhood friend of his!" On that twenty-third of July, 1940, I saw Hitler for the last time. The war went on, grew more widespread and bitter. There was no end in sight.

I was fully occupied by my work in the municipal administration. The war heaped ever more burdens on the population with the result that my tasks increased. I was hardly able to cope with the work. Personal worries were added; my sons were called up.

Epilogue

In 1942 I joined the National Socialist Party. Not that I had changed my basic ideas about politics. But my superiors were of the opinion that, now the struggle had become one of life and death, everyone must avow his principles. Of course, I was a follower of Adolf Hitler, but not in any political sense — rather in a much wider and deeper way, namely as a friend of his early years. I could easily have refused to join the Party with the usual formula, "I would like to talk this over with Hitler personally." But we were in the midst of a war and I did not wish to claim any special position for myself. The Mayor of my town wanted to know: "Did the Führer never ask you about your Party membership?" Of course not — I was his friend, and that was all. Had he not shown clearly enough that he valued me as a friend and as a human being although I was — as he had now come to term it — politically "a child"? So I told the Mayor that Hitler had never asked me why I had not joined his party.

Yet I remember an episode in which Hitler seemed to be hinting at this matter. When, on the occasion of my visit in 1939, Hitler introduced me to Frau Winifred Wagner, he pointed smilingly at me, unadorned as I was with any Party badge or decoration and, knowing that I represented the Linz branch of the Richard Wagner Union of German Women, he remarked, "And this is Herr Kubizek. He is a member of your Union of German Women. Isn't that charming!"

What he probably meant was — the only organisation to which my friend belongs is — a women's organisation. This shows you just what kind of fellow he is! The shadows of the war were darkening. To the general distress and preoccupations were added disappointments and bitter experiences of a personal kind. It was especially the case of Dr. Bloch which made me think. This kind "poor man's doctor," as he was called in the town, lived in Linz, a very old man, and wrote to me through an intermediary, Professor Huemer who had been Hitler's form master; he asked me to intercede for him with the Chancellor so that he, who was a Jew, would not be molested.

He had been, he pointed out, the doctor of Adolf Hitler's mother. To me this request seemed only fair. Far back in the Vienna days I had had frequent arguments with my friend about the Jewish problem because I did not share his radical views in this matter. I remembered that he had once been very rude to me when I, quite innocently, had brought him in touch with a Jewish journalist. I was convinced that Hitler would be reasonable as far as Dr. Bloch was concerned. I had never met the old gentleman personally, but I wrote at once to the Reichs Chancellery and enclosed the letter which I had received from Dr. Bloch.

After some weeks I got a reply from Bormann who strictly forbade me to intercede in future for any third person; as for Bloch, he had to inform me that the case would be dealt with in the same way as any other of its kind; these were the Führer's express orders. Thus, I did not even know if the case had really been brought to Hitler's attention. As far as I was able to find out, Dr. Bloch was left in peace; but this alone did not allay my misgivings. For what struck me most was that I had no access to Hitler as long as I was unable to meet him in person; and this was out of the question for the duration of the war.

The end came; the war was lost. Even though I, a fundamentally unpolitical individual, had always kept aloof from the political events of the period which ended forever in 1945, nevertheless no power on earth could compel me to deny my friendship with Adolf Hitler.

My first and most pressing worry in this respect was the safety of the Hitler papers I possessed, Come what may, they must be saved for posterity. Years before I had carefully put the letters, postcards and drawings in cellophane covers to protect them from wear as I showed them around. Now I locked them up in a solid leather case. Then I removed several bricks in the deep, vaulted cellar of my house in Eferding, thrust the case into the cavity and filled in the hole again so carefully that not the slightest trace of this work remained. It was only just in time as the very next day I was arrested and held for sixteen months in the notorious detention camp of Glasenbach. Naturally, an intensive search was made during my absence for the Hitler papers, but with no success.

In the beginning I was often questioned, first in Eferding, then in Gmunden. These interrogations all ran on the same lines; something like:

"You are a friend of Adolf Hitler's?"

"Yes."

"Since when?"

"Since 1904."

"What do you mean by that? At that time he was nobody."

"Nevertheless, I was his friend."

"How could you be his friend when he was still a nobody?"

An American officer of the Central Intelligence Corps asked: "So you are a friend of Adolf Hitler's. What did you get out of it?"

"Nothing."

"But you admit that you were his friend. Did he give you money?"

"No."

"Or food?"

"Neither."

Epilogue

"A car, a house?"
"Not that either."
"Did he introduce you to beautiful women?"
"Nor that."
"Did he receive you again, later on?"
"Yes."
"Did you see him often?"
"Occasionally."
"How did you manage to see him?"
"I just went to him."
"So you were with him. Really? Quite close?"
"Yes, quite close."
"Alone?"
"Alone."
"Without any guard?"
"Without any guard."
"So you could have killed him?"
"Yes, I could have."
"And why didn't you kill him?"
"Because he was my friend."

Part II: My Patient, Hitler: A Memoir of Hitler's Jewish Physician By Dr. Eduard Bloch

Introduction

"My Patient, Hitler," by Dr. Eduard Bloch "as told to J. D. Ratcliff," originally appeared in two parts in the March 15 and March 22, 1941, issues of *Collier's Weekly*, one of the most influential and widely-read periodicals in the United States.

Dr. Bloch was the Jewish physician who attended to the young Hitler and his mother in Linz, Austria. He was born in 1872 and after serving as a medical officer in the Austrian army, opened a private practice in Liunz in 1901.

He first treated Adolf when the latter was 15 years old, in 1904. Three years later he diagnosed—and attempted to treat—Adolf's mother, Klara, for cancer. Despite his best efforts, Klara died. Bloch's kindness earned Adolf's eternal gratitude (*"Ich werde Ihnen ewig dankbar sein"*). The doctor was later referred to by the Chancellor of Germany as a "Edeljude" (noble Jew) of who, Hitler said, "if all Jews were like that, there would be no Jewish question."

When Austria was annexed to Germany, Dr. Bloch was given special protection, and finally emigrated to the US in 1940. He died in June 1945 in New York City, where he is buried.

My Patient Hitler: A Memoir of Hitler's Jewish Physician

Part 1.

We were three days out of Lisbon bound west for New York. The storm on Saturday had been bad, but on Sunday the sea had subsided. A little before eleven o'clock that night our ship, the small Spanish liner Marques de Comillas, got orders to stop. British control officers aboard a trawler wanted to examine the passengers. Everyone was told to line up in the main lounge.

Four British officers, wearing life jackets, entered. Without comment they worked their way down the line, scrutinizing passports. There was a feeling of tenseness. Many of those aboard the ship were fleeing; they thought they had made good their escape from Europe once anchor was hoisted in Lisbon.

Now? No one knew. Perhaps some of us would be taken off the ship. Finally it was my turn. The officer in charge took my passport, glanced at it and looked up, smiling. "You were Hitler's physician, weren't you?" he asked. This was correct. It would also have been correct for him to add that I am a Jew.

I knew Adolf Hitler as a boy and as a young man. I treated him many times and was intimately familiar with the modest surroundings in which he grew to manhood. I attended, in her final illness, the person nearer and dearer to him than all others — his mother. Most biographers — both sympathetic and unsympathetic — have avoided the youth of Adolf Hitler. The unsympathetic ones have done this of necessity. They could lay their hands on only the most meager facts.

The official party biographies have skipped over this period because of the dictator's wishes. Why this abnormal sensitivity about his youth? I do not know. There are no scandalous chapters which Hitler might wish to hide, unless one goes back over a hundred years to the birth of his father. Some biographers say that Alois Hitler was an illegitimate child. I cannot speak for the accuracy of this statement.

What of those early years in Linz, Austria, where Hitler spent his formative years? What kind of boy was he? What kind of a life did he lead? It is of these things that we shall speak here.

When Adolf Hitler Was Thirteen

First, I might introduce myself. I was born in Frauenburg, a tiny village in southern Bohemia which, in the course of my lifetime, had been under three flags: Austrian, Czechoslovakian and German. I am sixty-nine years old. I studied medicine in Prague, then joined the Austrian army as a military doctor. In 1899 I was ordered to Linz, capital of Upper Austria, and the third largest city in the country. When I completed my army service in 1901 I decided to remain in Linz and practice medicine.

As a city, Linz has always been as quiet and reserved as Vienna was gay and noisy. In the period of which we are about the speak – when— Adolf Hitler was a boy of 13 — Linz was a city of 80,000 people. My consultation rooms and home were in the same house, an ancient baroque structure on Landstrasse, the main thoroughfare of the city.

The Hitler family moved to Linz in 1903, because, I believe, of the good schools there. The family background is well known. Alois Schicklgruber Hitler was the son of a poor peasant girl. When he was old enough to work he got a job as a cobbler's apprentice, worked his way into the government service and became a customs inspector at Braunau, a tiny frontier town between Bavaria and Austria. Braunau is fifty miles from Linz. At fifty-six Alois Hitler became eligible for a pension and retired. Proud of his own success, he was anxious for his son to enter government service. Young Adolf violently opposed the idea. He would be an artist. Father and son fought over this while the mother, Klara Hitler, tried to maintain peace.

As long as he lived Alois Hitler persevered in trying to shape his son's destiny to his own desires. His son would have the education which had been denied him; an education which would secure him a good government job. So Father Alois prepared to leave the hamlet of Braunau for the city of Linz. Because of his government service, he would not be required to pay the full tuition for his son at the *Realschule*. With all this in mind he bought a small farm in Leonding, a Linz suburb.

The family was rather large. In later life Adolf has so overshadowed the others that they are, for the better part, forgotten. There was half-brother Alois, whom I never met. He left home at an early age, got a job as a waiter in London, and later opened his own restaurant in Berlin. He was never friendly with his younger brother.

Then there was Paula, the oldest of the girls. She [actually Angela] later married Herr Rubal [Raubal], an official in the tax bureau in Linz. Later still, after her husband's death [?] and her brother's rise to power, she went to Berchtesgaden to become house-keeper at Hitler's villa. Sister Klara for a while managed a restaurant for Jewish students at the University of

Vienna; and sister Angela, youngest of the girls, [later] married a Professor Hamitsch [Hammitzsch] at Dresden, where she still lives.

A Job for Frau Hitler

The family had barely settled in their new home outside of Linz when Alois, the father, died suddenly from an apoplectic stroke [in Jan. 1903]. At the time Frau Hitler was in her early forties. She was a simple, modest, kindly woman. She was tall, had brownish hair, which she kept neatly plaited, and a long, oval face with beautifully expressive gray-blue eyes. She was desperately worried about the responsibilities thrust upon her by her husband's death. Alois, twenty-three years her senior, had always managed the family. Now the job was hers.

It was readily apparent that son Adolf was too young [not yet 14] and altogether too fragile to become a farmer. So her best move seemed to be to sell the place and rent a small apartment. This she did, soon after her husband's death. With the proceeds of this sale and the small pension which came to her because of her husband's government position, she managed to hold the family together.

In a small town in Austria poverty doesn't force upon one the indignities that it does in a large city. There are no slums and no serious overcrowding. I do not know the exact income of the Hitler family, but being familiar with the scale of government pensions I should estimate it at $25 a month. This small sum allowed them to live quietly and decently — unnoticed little people in an out-of-the-way town.

Their apartment consisted of three small rooms in the two-story house at No. 9 Bluetenstrasse, which is across the Danube from the main portion of Linz. Its windows gave an excellent view of the mountains.

My predominant impression of the simple furnished apartment was its cleanliness. It glistened; not a speck of dust on the chairs or tables, not a stray fleck of mud on the scrubbed floor, not a smudge on the panes in the windows. Frau Hitler was a superb housekeeper.

The Hitler's had only a few friends. One stood out above the others; the widow of the postmaster who lived in the same house.

The limited budget allowed not even the smallest extravagance. We had the usual provincial opera in Linz: not good, and not bad. Those who would hear the best went to Vienna. Seats in the gallery of our theater, the *Schauspielhaus*, sold for the equivalent of 10 to 15 cents in American money. Yet occupying one of these seats to hear an indifferent troupe sing Lohengrin was such a memorable occasion that Hitler records it in *Mein Kampf*. For the most part the boy's recreations were limited to those things which were free: walks in the mountains, a swim in the Danube, a free band concert. He read extensively, and was particularly fascinated by stories about American Indians. He devoured the books of James Fenimore Cooper, and the German writer Karl May — who never visited America and never saw an Indian.

The family diet was, of necessity, simple and rugged. Food was cheap and plentiful in Linz; and the Hitler family ate much the same diet as other people in their circumstance. Meat would be served perhaps twice a week. Most of the meals they sat down to consisted of cabbage or potato soup, bread, dumplings and a pitcher of pear and apple cider.

For clothing, they wore the rough woolen cloth we call *Loden*. Adolf, of course, dressed in the uniform of all small boys: leather shorts, embroidered suspenders, a small green hat with a feather in its band.

A Remarkable Mother Love

What kind of boy was Adolf Hitler? Many biographers have put him down as harsh-voiced, defiant, untidy; as a young ruffian who personified all that is unattractive. This simply is not true. As a youth he was quiet, well-mannered and neatly dressed.

He records that at the age of fifteen he regarded himself as a political revolutionary. Possibly. But let us look at Adolf Hitler as he impressed people about him, not as he impressed himself.

He was tall, sallow, old for his age. He was neither robust nor sickly. Perhaps "frail looking" would best describe him. His eyes — inherited from his mother — were large, melancholy and thoughtful. To a very large extent this boy lived within himself. What dreams he dreamed I do not know. Outwardly, his love for his mother was his most striking feature. While he was not a "mother's boy" in the usual sense, I have never witnessed a closer attachment. Some insist that this love verged on the pathological. As a former intimate of the family, I do not believe this is true.

Klara Hitler adored her son, the youngest of the family. She allowed him his own way wherever possible. His father had insisted that he become an official. He rebelled and won his mother to his side. He soon tired of school, so his mother allowed him to drop his studies.

All friends of the family know how Frau Hitler encouraged his boyish efforts to become an artist; at what cost to herself one may guess. Despite their poverty, she permitted him to reject a job which was offered in the post office, so that he could continue his painting. She admired his water colors and his sketches of the countryside. Whether this was honest admiration or whether it was merely an effort to encourage his talent I do not know. She did her best to raise her boy well. She saw that he was neat, clean and as well fed as her purse would permit. Whenever he came to my consultation room this strange boy would sit among the other patients, awaiting his turn. There was never anything seriously wrong. Possibly his tonsils would be inflamed. He would stand obedient and unflinching while I depressed his tongue and swabbed the trouble spots. Or, possibly, he would be suffering with a cold. I would treat him and send him on his way. Like any well-bred boy of fourteen or fifteen he would bow and thank me courteously. I, of course, know of the stomach trouble that beset him later in life, largely as a result of bad diet while working as a common laborer in Vienna. I cannot understand the many references to his lung trouble as a youth. I was the only doctor treating him during the period in which he is supposed to have suffered from this. My records show nothing of the sort. To be sure, he didn't have the rosy cheeks and the robust good health of most of the other youngsters; but at the same time he was not sickly.

At the *Realschule* young Adolfs work was anything but brilliant. As authority for this, I have the word of his former teacher, Dr. Karl Huemer, an old acquaintance of mine. I was Frau Huemer's physician. In *Mein Kampf*, Hitler records that he was an indifferent student in most subjects, but that he loved history. This agrees with the recollections of Professor Huemer.

Desiring additional training in painting, Hitler decided he would go to Vienna to study at the Academy. This was a momentous decision for a member of a poor family. His mother worried about how he would get along. I understand that she even suggested pinching the family budget a little tighter to enable her to send him a tiny allowance. Credit to the boy, he refused. He even went further: he signed his minute inheritance over to his sisters. He was eighteen at the time.

I am not sure of the exact details of what happened on that trip to Vienna. Some contend that he was not admitted to the Academy because of his unsatisfactory art work. Others accept Hitler's statement that his rejection was due to his failure to graduate from the *Realschule* — the equivalent of an American high school. In any case he was home again within a few weeks. It was later in this year — 1908 [actually, 1907] — that it became my duty to give Hitler what was perhaps the saddest news of his life.

One day Frau Hitler came to visit me during my morning office hours. She complained of a pain in her chest. She spoke in a quiet, hushed voice; almost a whisper. The pain, she said, had been great; enough to keep her awake nights on end. She had been busy with her household so had neglected to seek medical aid. Besides, she thought the pain would pass away. When a physician hears such a story he almost automatically thinks of cancer. An examination showed that Frau Hitler had an extensive tumor of the breast. I did not tell her of my diagnosis.

The Family Decides

I summoned the children to my office next day and stated the case frankly. Their mother, I told them, was a gravely ill woman. A malignant tumor is serious enough today, but it was even more serious thirty years ago. Surgical techniques were not so advanced and knowledge of cancer not so extensive.

Without surgery, I explained, there was absolutely no hope of recovery. Even with surgery there was but the slightest chance that she would live. In family council they must decide what was to be done.

Adolf Hitler's reaction to this news was touching. His long, sallow face was contorted. Tears flowed from his eyes. Did his mother, he asked, have no chance? Only then did I realize the magnitude of the attachment that existed between mother and son. I explained that she did have a chance; but a small one. Even this shred of hope gave him some comfort.

The children carried my message to their mother. She accepted the verdict as I was sure she would — with fortitude. Deeply religious, she assumed that her fate was God's will. It would never have occurred to her to complain. She would submit to the operation as soon as I could make preparations.

I explained the case to Dr. Karl Urban, the chief of the surgical staff at the Hospital of the Sisters of Mercy in Linz. Urban was one of the best-known surgeons in Upper Austria. He was — and is — a generous man, a credit to his profession. He willingly agreed to undertake the operation on any basis I suggested. After examination he concurred in my belief that Frau Hitler had very little chance of surviving, but that surgery offered the only hope.

It is interesting to note what happened to this generous man nearly three decades later — after *Anschluss* [union] with Germany. Because of his political connections he was forced to abandon his position at the hospital. His son, who pioneered in brain surgery, was likewise forced from several offices.

Frau Hitler arrived at the hospital one evening in the early summer of 1908 [1907]. I do not have the exact date, for my records of the case were placed in the archives of the Nazi party in Munich. In any case, Frau Hitler spent the night in the hospital and was operated on the following morning. At the request of this gentle, harried soul I remained beside the operating table while Dr. Urban and his assistant performed the surgery. Two hours later I drove in my carriage across the Danube to the little house at No. 9 Bluetenstrasse, in the section of the city known as Urfahr. There the children awaited me. The girls received the word I brought with calm and reserve. The face of the boy was streaked with tears, and his eyes were tired and red. He listened until I had finished speaking. He had but one question. In a choked voice he asked: "Does my mother suffer?"

Hitler's Worst Moment

As weeks and months passed after the operation Frau Hitler's strength began visibly to fail. At most she could be out of bed for an hour or two a day. During this period Adolf spent most of his time around the house, to which his mother had returned.

He slept in the tiny bedroom adjoining that of his mother so that he could be summoned at any time during the night. During the day he hovered about the large bed in which she lay. In illness such as that suffered by Frau Hitler, there is usually a great amount of pain. She bore her burden well; unflinching and uncomplaining. But it seemed to torture her son. An anguished grimace would come over him when he saw pain contract her face. There was little that could be done. An injection of morphine from time to time would give temporary relief; but nothing lasting. Yet Adolf seemed enormously grateful even for these short periods of release.

I shall never forget Klara Hitler during those days. She was forty-eight [forty-seven] at the time; tall, slender and rather handsome, yet wasted by disease. She was soft-spoken, patient; more concerned about what would happen to her family than she was about her approaching death. She made no secret of these worries; or about the fact that most of her thoughts were for her son. "Adolf is still so young," she said repeatedly.

On the day of December 20, 1908 [1907], I made two calls. The end was approaching and I wanted this good woman to be as comfortable as I could make her. I didn't know whether she would live another week, or another month; or whether death would come in a matter of hours.

So, the word that Angela Hitler brought me the following morning came as no surprise. Her mother had died quietly in the night. The children had decided not to disturb me, knowing that their mother was beyond all medical aid. But, she asked, could I come now? Someone in an official position would have to sign the death certificate. I put on my coat and drove with her to the grief-stricken cottage.

The postmaster's widow, their closest friend, was with the children, having more or less taken charge of things. Adolf, his face showing the weariness of a sleepless night, sat beside his mother. In order to preserve a last impression, he had sketched her as she lay on her deathbed.

I sat with the family for a while, trying to ease their grief. I explained that in this case death had been a savior. They understood. In the practice of my profession it is natural that I should have witnessed many scenes such as this one, yet none of them left me with quite the same impression. In all my career I have never seen anyone so prostrate with grief as Adolf Hitler.

I did not attend Klara Hitler's funeral, which was held on Christmas Eve. The body was taken from Urfahr to Leonding, only a few miles distant. Klara Hitler was buried beside her husband in the Catholic cemetery, behind the small, yellow stucco church. After the others - the girls, and the postmaster's widow — had left, Adolf remained behind; unable to tear himself away from the freshly filled grave. And so this gaunt, pale young man stood alone in the cold. Alone with his thoughts on Christmas Eve while the rest of the world was gay and happy.

A few days after the funeral the family came to my office. They wished to thank me for the help I had given them. There was Paula, fair and stocky; Angela, slender, pretty but rather anemic; Klara and Adolf. The girls spoke what was in their hearts while Adolf remained silent. I recall this particular scene as vividly as I might recall something that took place last week.

Adolf wore a dark suit and a loosely knotted cravat. Then, as now, a shock of hair tumbled over his forehead. His eyes were on the floor while his sisters were talking. Then came his turn. He stepped forward and took my hand. Looking into my eyes, he said "I shall be grateful to you forever." That was all. Then he bowed. I wonder if today he recalls this scene. I am quite sure that he does, for in a sparing sense Adolf had kept to his promise of gratitude. Favors were granted me which I feel sure were accorded no other Jew in all Germany or Austria.

Part II

Almost immediately after his mother's funeral Hitler left for Vienna, to attempt once more a career as an artist. His growth to manhood had been a painful experience for this was a boy who lived within himself. But ever more trying days were coming. Poor as the family was, he had at least been assured food and shelter while living at home. This couldn't be said of the days in Vienna. Hitler was entirely engrossed with the business of keeping body and soul together.

We all know something of his life there — how he worked as a hod carrier on building-construction jobs until workmen threatened to push him off a scaffold. And we know that he shoveled snow and took any other job he could find. During this period, for three years in fact, Hitler lived in a men's hostel, the equivalent of a flophouse in any large American city. It was here that he began to dream of a world remade to his pattern. While living in the hostel, surrounded by the human dregs of the large city, Hitler says, "I became dissatisfied with myself for the first time in my life." The dissatisfaction with himself was followed by dissatisfaction with everything about him — and the desire to alter things to his own liking.

The vitriol of hate began to creep through his body. The grim realities of the life he lived encouraged him to hate the government, labor unions, the very men he lived with. But he had not yet begun to hate the Jews. During this period he took time out to send me a penny postcard. On the back was a message: "From Vienna I send you my greetings. Yours, always faithfully, Adolf Hitler." It was a small thing, yet I appreciated it. I had spent a great deal of time treating the Hitler family, and it was nice to know that this effort on my part had not been forgotten.

Official Nazi publications also record that I received one of Hitler's paintings — a small landscape. If I did I am not aware of it. But it is quite possible that he sent me one and that I have forgotten the matter. In Austria patients frequently send paintings or other gifts to their physicians as a mark of gratitude. Even now I have half a dozen of these oils and water colors which I have saved; but none painted by Hitler among them.

I did, however, preserve one piece of Hitler's art work. This came during the period in Vienna when he was painting post cards, posters, etc., making enough money to support himself. This was the one time in his life that Hitler was able to make successful use of his talent.

He would paint these cards and dry them in front of a hot fire, which would give them a rather pleasing antique quality. Then other inmates of the hostel would peddle them. Today in Germany the few remaining samples of this work are more highly prized and sought after than the works of Picasso, Gauguin and Cézanne!

Hitler sent me one of these cards. It showed a hooded Capuchin monk hoisting a glass of bubbling champagne. Under the picture was a caption: *"Prosit Neujahr* - A toast to the New Year." On the reverse side he had written a message: "The Hitler family sends you the best wishes for a Happy New Year. In everlasting thankfulness, Adolf Hitler."

Why I put these cards aside to be saved, I do not know. Possibly it was because of the impression made upon me by that unhappy boy. Even today I cannot help thinking of him in terms of his grief and not in terms of what he has done to the world.

Those postal cards had a curious history. They indicated the extent to which Hitler has captured the imagination of some people. A rich Viennese industrialist — I do not know his name because he dealt through an intermediary — later made me an astonishing offer. He wanted to buy those two cards and was willing to pay 20,000 marks for them! I rejected the offer on the ground that I could not ethically make such a sale.

There is still another story in those two cards. Seventeen days after the collapse of the Schuschnigg government and the occupation of Austria by German troops [March 1938], an agent of the Gestapo called at my home. At the time I was making a professional call, but my wife received him.

'Retained for Safekeeping'

"I am informed," he said, "that you have some souvenirs of the Fuehrer. I should like to see them." Acting sensibly, my wife made no protest. She didn't wish to have her home torn apart as so many Jewish homes had been. She found the two cards and handed them over. The agent scribbled a receipt which read: "Certificate for the safekeeping of two post cards (one of them painted by the hand of Adolf Hitler) confiscated in the house of Dr. Eduard Bloch." It was signed by the agent, named Groemer, who was previously unknown to us. He said I was to come to headquarters the following morning.

Almost as soon as the Nazis entered the city the Gestapo took over the small hotel in Gesellenhausstrasse formally patronized by traveling clergymen. I went to this place and was received almost immediately. I was greeted courteously by Dr. Rasch, head of the local bureau. I asked him why these bits of property had been taken.

Those were busy days for the Gestapo. There were many things to be looked after in a town of 120,000 people. It developed that Dr. Rasch was not familiar with my case. He asked if I were under suspicion for any political activity unfavorable to the Nazis. I replied that I was not; that I was a professional man with no political connections.

Apparently as an afterthought, he asked if I were a non-Aryan. I answered without compromise: "I am a 100 percent Jew." The change that came over him was instantaneous. Previously he had been businesslike but courteous. Now he became distant.

The cards, he said, would be retained for safekeeping. Then he dismissed me, neither rising nor shaking hands as he had when I entered. So far as I know the cards are still in the hands of the Gestapo. I never saw them again.

When he left for Vienna, Adolf Hitler was destined to disappear from our lives for a great many years. He had no friends in Linz to whom he might return to visit and few with whom he might exchange correspondence. So, it was much later that we learned of his wretched poverty on those days, and of his subsequent moving to Munich in 1912 [actually, in May 1913].

No news came back of the way in which he fell on his knees and thanked God when war was declared in 1914; and no news of his war service as a corporal with the 16th Bavarian Reserve Infantry. We heard nothing of his being wounded and gassed. Not until the beginning of his political career in 1920 were we again to get news of this quiet, polite boy who grew up among us.

Could This Be Adolf?

Occasionally the local newspapers would run items about the group of political supporters that Hitler was gathering about himself in Munich; stories of their hatred of the Jews, of the Versailles Peace, of nearly everything else. But no particular importance was attached to these activities. Not until twenty people died in the beer-hall putsch of November 8, 1923, did Hitler achieve local notoriety. Was it possible, I asked myself, that the man behind these things was the quiet boy I had known — the son of the gentle Klara Hitler?

Eventually even the mention of Hitler's name in the Austrian press was prohibited; still we continued to get word-of-mouth news of our former townsman: stories of the persecutions he had launched; of German rearmament; of war to come. This smuggled news reached responsive ears. A local Nazi party sprang up.

In theory such a party could not exist; it had been outlawed by the government. In practice authorities gave it their blessings. Denied uniforms, local Nazis adopted methods of identifying themselves to everyone. They wore white stockings. On their coats they wore a small wild flower, very much like the American daisy, and at Christmas time they burned blue candles in their homes.

We all knew these things, but nothing was done. From time to time local authorities would find a Nazi flag on Klara Hitler's grave in Leonding, and would remove it without ceremony. Still, the gathering storm in Germany seemed remote. It was quite a while before I got any firsthand word from Adolf Hitler. Then, in 1937, a number of local Nazis attended the party conference at Nuremberg. After the conference Hitler invited several of these people to come with him to his mountain villa at Berchtesgaden. The Fuehrer asked for news of Linz. How was the town? Were people there supporting him? He asked for news of me.

Was I still alive, still practicing? Then he made a statement irritating to local Nazis. "Dr. Bloch," said Hitler, "is an *Edeljude* - a noble Jew. If all Jews were like him, there would be no Jewish question." It was strange, and in a way flattering, that Adolf Hitler could see good in at least one member of my race.

It is curious now to look back on the feeling of security that we had by virtue of living on the right side of an imaginary line, the international boundary. Surely Germany would not chance invading Austria. France was friendly. Occupation of Austria would be inimical to the interests of Italy. Oh, but we were blind, in those days! Then we were caught up in a breathless rush of events. It was with hope that we read of [Austrian chancellor] Schuschnigg's trip to Berchtesgaden; his plebiscite; his inclusion of Seyss-Inquart in his cabinet. Possibly we would ride through this crisis untouched. But hope was doomed to death within a very few hours. As soon as Seyss-Inquart was taken into the cabinet, buttons sprouted in every lapel: "One People, One Realm, One Leader."

While Austria Died

On Friday, March 11, 1938, the Vienna radio was broadcasting a program of light music. It was 7:45 at night. Suddenly the announcer broke in. The chancellor would speak. Schuschnigg came on the air and said that to prevent bloodshed he was capitulating to the wishes of Hitler. The frontiers would be opened, he ended his address with the words: *"Gott schütze Oesterreich"* — May God protect Austria. Hitler was coming home to Linz.

In the sleepless days that followed we clung to our radios. Troops were pouring over the border at Passau, Kufstein, Mittenwalde and elsewhere. Hitler himself was crossing the Inn River at Braunau, his birthplace. Breathlessly, the announcer told us the story of the march. The Fuehrer himself would pause in Linz. The town went mad with joy. The reader should have no doubts about the popularity of *Anschluss* with Germany. The people favored it. They greeted the onrushing tide of German troops with flowers, cheers and songs. Church bells rang. Austrian troops and police fraternized with the invaders and there was general rejoicing.

The public square in Linz, a block from my home, was a turmoil. All afternoon it rang with the Horst Wessel song and *Deutschland über Alles*. Planes droned overhead, and advance units of the German army were given deafening cheers. Finally the radio announced that Hitler was in Linz. Advance instructions had been given to the townspeople. All windows along the procession route were to be closed. Each should be lighted. I stood at the window of my home facing Landstrasse. Hitler would pass before me.

The Hero Returns

Soon the procession arrived — the great, black Mercedes car, a six-wheeled affair, flanked by motorcycles. The frail boy I had treated so often, and whom I had not seen for thirty years — stood in the car. I had accorded him only kindness; what was he now to do to the people I loved? I peered over the heads of the crowd at Adolf Hitler. It was a moment of tense excitement. For years Hitler had been denied the right to visit the country of his birth. Now that country belonged to him. The elation that he felt was written on his features. He smiled, waved, gave the Nazi salute to the people that crowded the street. Then, for a moment he glanced up at my window. I doubt that he saw me but he must have had a moment of reflection. Here was the home of the *Edeljude* who had diagnosed his mother's fatal cancer; here was the consultation room of the man who had treated his sisters; here was the place he had gone as a boy to have his minor ailments attended.

It was a brief moment. Then the procession was gone. It moved slowly into the town square — once Franz Josef Platz, soon to be renamed Adolf Hitler Platz. He spoke from the balcony of the town hall. I listened on the radio. Historic words: Germany and Austria were now one.

Hitler established himself in the Weinzinger Hotel, particularly requesting an apartment with a view of the Poestling Mountain. This scene had been visible from the windows of the modest apartment where he spent his boyhood.

The following day he called in a few old acquaintances: Oberhummer, a local party functionary; Kubitschek [August Kubizek], the musician; Liedel, the watchmaker; Dr. Huemer, his former history teacher. It was understandable that he couldn't ask me, a Jew, to such a meeting, yet he did inquire after me. For a while I thought of asking for an audience, then decided this would be unwise.

Hitler arrived Saturday evening. Sunday he visited his mother's grave, and reviewed local Nazis as they marched before him. Not equipped with uniforms, they wore knickerbockers, ski pants or leather shorts. On Monday Hitler departed for Vienna.

Soon we were brought to a sharp realization of how different things were to be. There were 700 Jews in Linz. Shops, homes and offices of all these people were marked with the yellow-paper banners now visible throughout Germany, *JUDE* - Jew.

The first suggestion that I was to receive special favors came one day when the local Gestapo telephoned. I was to remove the yellow signs from my office and home. Then a second thing happened: My landlord, an Aryan, went to Gestapo headquarters to ask if I were to be allowed to remain in my apartment. "We wouldn't dare touch that matter," he was told. "It will be handled by Berlin." Hitler, apparently, had remembered. Then something happened that made me doubt.

For no reason whatsoever my son-in-law, a young physician, was jailed. No one was allowed to see him, and we received no news of him.

My daughter went to the Gestapo. "Would the Leader like to know that the son-in-law of his old physician had been sent to prison?," she asked. She was treated rudely and brusquely for her temerity. Hadn't the signs been removed from her father's house? Wasn't that enough? Yet her visit must have had some effect. Within three weeks her husband was released.

My practice, which I believe was one of the largest in Linz, had begun to dwindle as long as a year before the arrival of Hitler. In this I might have seen a portent of things to come. Faithful older patients were quite frank in their explanations. The hatred preached by the Nazis was taking hold with the younger people. They would no longer patronize a Jew.

By decree, my active practice was limited to Jewish patients. This was another way of saying that I was to cease work altogether. For plans were in the making for ridding the town of all Jews. On November 10, 1938, the ruling was issued that all Jews were to leave Linz within forty-eight hours. They were to go to Vienna. The shock that attended this edict may be imagined. People who had lived all their lives in Linz were to sell their property, pack and depart in the space of two days.

I called at the Gestapo. Was I to leave? I was informed that an exception had been made in my case. I could remain. My daughter and her husband? Since they had already signified their intention of emigrating to America, they also could stay. But they would have to vacate their house. If there was room in my apartment they would be permitted to move there.

No More Favors

After thirty-seven years of active work my practice was at an end. I was permitted to treat only Jews. After the evacuation order there were but seven members of this race left in Linz. All were over eighty years of age.

It is understandable that my daughter and her husband would wish to take their life savings with them when they departed for America. So would I when my turn came to depart. Getting any local ruling on such a matter was out of the question. I knew that I couldn't see Adolf Hitler. Yet I felt that if I could get a message to him he would perhaps give us some help.

If Hitler himself was inaccessible perhaps one of his sisters would aid us. Klara was the nearest; she lived in Vienna. Her husband had died and she lived alone in a modest apartment in a quiet residential district. Plans were made for my daughter, Gertrude, to make the trip to Vienna to see her. She went to the apartment, knocked, but got no answer. Yet she was sure that there was someone at home.

She sought the aid of a neighbor. Frau Wolf — Klara Hitler — received no one, the neighbor said, except a few intimate friends. But this kind woman agreed to carry a message and report Frau Wolf's reply. My daughter waited. Soon the answer came back. Frau Wolf sent greetings and would do whatever she could. By good fortune Hitler was in Vienna that night for one of his frequent but unheralded visits to the opera. Frau Wolf saw him and, I feel sure, gave him the message. But no exception was made in our case. When our turn came we were forced to go penniless, like so many thousands of others.

How has Hitler treated an old friend — one who cared for his family with patience, consideration and charity? Let's sum up the favors:

I don't believe that another Jew in all Austria was allowed to keep his passport. No J was stamped on my ration card, once food became scarce. This was most helpful because Jews today [1940-1941] are allowed to shop only during restricted hours which are often inconvenient. Without the J on my card I could buy at any time. I was even given a ration card for clothes — something generally denied Jews.

If my relations with the Gestapo were not precisely cordial, I at least didn't suffer at their hands as did so many others. I was told on good authority, and I can well believe it, that the bureau in Linz had received special instructions from the chancellery in Berlin that I was to be accorded any reasonable favor.

It is possible, but unlikely, that my war record was particularly responsible for these small considerations. During the war I had charge of a 1,000- bed military hospital, and my wife supervised welfare work among the sick. I was twice decorated for this service.

Hitler Rebuilds His Home City

Hitler still regards Linz as his true home, and the changes he has wrought are astonishing. The once quiet, sleepy town had been transformed by its "godfather" — an honorary title particularly dear to Hitler. Whole blocks of old houses have been pulled down to make way for modern apartment houses; thereby causing an acute but temporary housing shortage. A new theater has gone up and a new bridge has been built over the Danube. The bridge, according to local legend, was designed by Hitler himself and plans were already completed at the time of *Anschluss*. The vast Hermann Goering Iron Works, built in the past two years, is just starting operations. To carry on this program of reconstruction whole trainloads of laborers have been imported: Czechs, Poles, Belgians.

Hitler has visited the city twice since the *Anschluss*, once at the time of the election which was to approve union with Germany; a second time secretly to see how reconstruction of the town was progressing. Each time had has stayed at the Weinzinger Hotel. On the second visit the proprietor of the hotel was informed that Hitler's presence in town was not to be announced; that he would make his inspection tour in the morning. Delighted at having such an important personage in his house, the proprietor could not resist boasting. He telephoned several friends to give them the news. For this breach of discipline he paid heavily. His hotel was confiscated.

Many times I have been approached by Hitler biographers for notes on his youth. In most instances I have refused to speak. But I did talk to one of these men. He was a pleasant middle-aged gentleman from Vienna, who came from the government department headed by Rudolf Hess, of the Nazi inner circle. He was writing an official biography. I gave him such details as I could recall, and my medical records which he subsequently sent to Nazi party headquarters in Munich. He stayed in Linz and Braunau for several weeks; then the project terminated abruptly. I was told he had been sent to the silence of the concentration camp. Why, I do not know.

When it finally became my turn to leave Linz for America I knew that it would be impossible for me to take my savings with me. But the Gestapo had one more favor for me. I was to be allowed to take sixteen marks from the country instead of the customary ten!

The Nazi organization of physicians gave me a letter, of what value I do not know, which states that I was "worthy of recommendation." It went on to say that, because of my "character, medical knowledge and readiness to help the sick," I had won "the appreciation and esteem of my fellow men." A party official suggested that I was expected to show some gratitude for all these favors. Perhaps a letter to the Fuehrer? Before I left Linz on a cold, foggy November morning, I wrote it. I wonder if it was ever received. It read:

Your Excellency:

Before passing the border I want to express my thanks for the protection which I have received. In material poverty I am now leaving the town where I have lived for forty-one years; but I leave conscious of having lived in the most exact fulfillment of my duty. At sixty-nine I will start my life anew in a strange country where my daughter is working hard to support her family.

Yours faithfully,
Eduard Bloch

Printed in Great Britain
by Amazon